Solomon Higgins, William Brisbane, Joseph Castle

Illustrations of the Divine Government in Remarkable Providences

Seventh Edition

Solomon Higgins, William Brisbane, Joseph Castle

Illustrations of the Divine Government in Remarkable Providences
Seventh Edition

ISBN/EAN: 9783337779412

Printed in Europe, USA, Canada, Australia, Japan

Cover: Foto ©Lupo / pixelio.de

More available books at **www.hansebooks.com**

ILLUSTRATIONS

OF THE

DIVINE GOVERNMENT

IN

REMARKABLE PROVIDENCES.

COLLECTED AND ARRANGED BY

S. HIGGINS AND W. H. BRISBANE.

WITH AN

INTRODUCTORY ESSAY ON PROVIDENCE.

BY

REV. JOSEPH CASTLE, D. D.

Seventh Edition.

PHILADELPHIA:
PERKINPINE & HIGGINS,
No. 56 NORTH FOURTH STREET.
1865.

TABLE OF CONTENTS.

                                                  PAGE

INTRODUCTORY ESSAY   v

PART I.

ILLUSTRATIONS OF DIVINE PROVIDENCE IN THE PRESERVATION OF HUMAN LIFE 15

SECTION I.—PRESERVATION OF HUMAN LIFE BY INTELLIGENT
    AGENTS 17
  II.—PRESERVATION OF HUMAN LIFE BY UNINTELLIGENT
    AGENTS 35
  III.—PRESERVATION OF HUMAN LIFE BY MENTAL IMPRESSIONS, DREAMS, &c. 48

PART II.

ILLUSTRATIONS OF DIVINE PROVIDENCE IN THE RELIEF OF SUFFERING AND DELIVERANCE FROM DANGER   71

SECTION I.—RELIEF AFFORDED THROUGH INTELLIGENT AGENTS . 73
  II.—RELIEF AFFORDED THROUGH UNINTELLIGENT AGENTS . 106
  III.—RELIEF AFFORDED THROUGH MENTAL IMPRESSIONS, DREAMS, &c. 120

PART III.

ILLUSTRATIONS OF DIVINE PROVIDENCE IN THE PUNISHMENT OF SIN AND THE DEFEAT OF WICKED PLANS 147

SECTION I.—PUNISHMENT AND DEFEAT OF WICKEDNESS THROUGH INTELLIGENT AGENTS 149
II.—PUNISHMENT AND DEFEAT OF WICKEDNESS THROUGH UNINTELLIGENT AGENTS 156
III.—PUNISHMENT AND DEFEAT OF WICKEDNESS THROUGH MENTAL IMPRESSIONS, DREAMS, &c. . . . 165
IV.—PUNISHMENT AND DEFEAT OF WICKEDNESS THROUGH MEANS UNKNOWN 182

PART IV.

ILLUSTRATIONS OF DIVINE PROVIDENCE IN THE CONVERSION OF MEN 195

SECTION I.—CONVERSIONS EFFECTED THROUGH HUMAN AGENCY . 197
II.—CONVERSIONS EFFECTED BY MEANS OF THE BIBLE OR UNINTELLIGENT AGENTS 225
III.—CONVERSIONS EFFECTED THROUGH MENTAL IMPRESSIONS, DREAMS, &c. 236

PART V.

ILLUSTRATIONS OF DIVINE PROVIDENCE IN RELATION TO THE SABBATH 277

PART VI.

ILLUSTRATIONS OF FAITH IN DIVINE PROVIDENCE . 303

PART VII.

MISCELLANEOUS ILLUSTRATIONS OF DIVINE PROVIDENCE 369

INTRODUCTORY ESSAY.

That we are, and that we have sorrows, and need comforts, and must die, are stern realities. What we are, whence we came, and where we are to go, after life's fitful fever, are questions of deep, absorbing interest, in comparison with which every other question, relating to earth and time, is light as air. Either we came from nothing, and to nothing we must return, or there is an infinitely wise and almighty first Cause, the Author of all things, who made us, and made us for some great end, worthy of Himself, and of the nature he has given us. Which shall we choose? Reason rejects the former, for it contradicts all reason, and makes Reason a name without a meaning; the latter satisfies many of the demands of reason, while it leaves unexplored, depths reason at present cannot fathom, and heights to which it may not soar. The finite cannot comprehend perfectly the infinite. We can merely touch upon some of the segments of a circle, the circumference of which is boundless. "Canst thou by searching find out God? Canst thou find out the Almighty unto perfection? It is high as heaven, what canst thou do? Deeper than hell, what canst thou know? The measure thereof is longer than the earth, and broader than the sea." Shall we, therefore, reject it, though reasonable, because we cannot wholly comprehend it, and embrace the unreasonable which reason repudiates? This would be the extreme of folly.

The belief in the existence of one true God is vital to every great and sublime verity of religion, whether natural or revealed. It is the only foundation which can sustain conscience, faith, hope, charity, and all which tends to adorn and exalt humanity. We can conceive of no other source from which the voice of authority can be uttered, making known man's whole duty, interest, and destiny. He who rejects it, rejects the noblest part of his nature, and the grandest revealings of his privileges, and sinks himself to a common brotherhood with brutes. There may be men in the pride of a perverted intellect, while surrounded by the fascinations of an infamous falsehood, and cheered on by kindred spirits, who have the hardihood to profess faith in unbelief: but whether any man can be so lost to all that constitutes the nobility of his nature, as in the sanctuary of his retirement to persuade himself into the belief that there is no God, may be seriously doubted. Nature revolts against it, and Reason cries shame! But if such there be, who can thus outrage nature and all that is godlike in man, we will merely say in the language of Scripture, "the devils believe and tremble," and it is the "*fool*" who hath said in his heart, "*there is no God.*" "That which may be known of God is manifest in them; for God hath showed it unto them; for the invisible things of him from the creation of the world are clearly seen, being understood by the things which are made, even his eternal power and Godhead; so that they are without excuse."

From the slightest view of nature the truth comes with

thrilling interest, we are not monstrous abortions, or fatherless children in a godless world, for there is an infinite Creator, wise as he is powerful, and good as he is great, the father of the spirits of all flesh. Whether we look upon the sun, moon, and stars, the work of his fingers; the green fields and rolling floods; the buds and blossoms, and rich ripe fruit in the harvest time—upon a mountain or an atom; a leviathan or an insect; the world within us or the world without; the conclusion is irresistible, and consoling as true, there is, there must be, a God in whom we live, and move, and have our being.

It is an absurdity equalled only by the day-dream of a maniac, to suppose that we are only what we seem, mere flesh and blood, a branching channel, and a mazy flood—"that a cluster of pretty, thin, round atoms, as Democritus conceited—that a well-mixed combination of elements, as Empedocles fancied—that a harmonious contemporation of humors, as Galen would persuade us, should become the subject of so rare capacities and endowments; the author of actions so worthy and works so wonderful; capable of wisdom and virtue; of knowledge so vast, and works so lofty; apt to contemplate truth and affect good; able to recollect things past, and foresee things future; to search so deep into the causes of things, and disclose so many mysteries of nature ; to invent so many arts and sciences, to contrive such projects of policy, and achieve such feats of prowess; briefly, should become capable to design, undertake, and perform all those admirable effects of human wit and industry which we daily see or hear of."

"The power, wisdom, and design conspicuous in the whole system of nature; the signs of divine workmanship visible in the heavens; the structure of the earth allotted for our habitation, and so well fitted up and furnished for the use of the various tribes of creatures, and of man its principal inhabitant; the exquisite skill and amazing art that appear in the forms and properties of vegetables, in the organs and faculties of animals, in the mechanism of the human body, so fearfully and wonderfully made; and above all, in the human soul, with its various intellectual and moral susceptibilities and powers, are clear proofs of an original, creating mind. Is it possible to conceive that all these effects, these evident appearances of counsel and wisdom, can proceed from undirected, fortuitous motions of unconscious matter? Can we imagine that all the regularity, harmony, and order we see in the general system of things can be the result of chance? If, when we survey a palace, and observe the grandeur and symmetry of the whole, and the elegance and just disposition of its parts, we never fail to infer the skill and ability of the architect: shall we not much more when we contemplate the universe; when we view the beauty and magnificence that everywhere appear; when we see all the characters of infinite wisdom and power in the design and execution, and all the expressions of such art as no art can surpass, shall we not discern an all-wise, omnipotent Architect, who planned and erected the amazing fabric? In short, all the works of creation bear such evident testimony to the agency of a divine inteliigence, that it scarce seems credible that atheism should ever find admission into the human understanding."

But while unbelief in the divine existence is rare, and hardly possible, unbelief in the particular providence of God is but too common; and yet this is atheism in one of its most ruinous, because one of its most seductive and practical forms. This scheme of folly, while professing the most exalted conceptions of the greatness and grandeur of God, in reality denies him his essential attributes, and degrades him beneath human relations; nay, beneath that of the beasts of the field. Parents live and labor for their children, and brutes deny themselves to gratify their young; but the unbeliever's God, with power to create and give form and beauty to stars and central suns, wrapped in the isolation of his nature knows not and cares not for the multitudinous wants of the creatures his own almighty hand has formed! A God that does not know us, or care for us, is tantamount to no God at all. God's providence cannot be separated from his creation; the one necessarily implies the other, for it is not conceivable that God should create all things, and not govern all things. We can as readily believe that God did not create, as we can that he does not govern, for the same power that created is necessary to preserve and direct to the fulfilment of his own great intention. The theory of mechanism wholly fails to illustrate the order of divine Providence. The machine may be made, and wound up, and go for a time, without the presence of the artist; but no machine can exist without something external to itself; and what is external to the creation, but the Creator? His presence is at least as necessary to uphold the creation as the earth is to uphold the machine; and if he uphold the whole, he upholds all the parts; and is it conceivable that he upholds all, and does not govern and direct all to certain definite ends, consistent with his own purposes, and declarative of his wisdom and love? It is not by a system of springs and weights, and checks and balances, that creation is upheld, and moves with infinite regularity in the fulfilment of great purposes, and for the accomplishment of great ends; but by an infinite Intelligence, who sees the end from the beginning, and knows how to reconcile things apparently the most irreconcilable, and to bring order out of confusion.

He who in the beginning created the heaven and the earth; who said, "Let there be light, and there was light—let the earth bring forth grass; the herb yielding seed, and the fruit-tree yielding fruit after his kind; let the waters bring forth abundantly the moving creature that hath life; and let us make man in our image, after our likeness," cannot want ability to supervise and govern all that his power has made. All must be dependent on Him, who created them from nothing; and to him it must be infinitely easy to preside over all things and all events; to direct all natural causes; to govern all contingencies, and to provide for all creatures. And as he cannot be wanting in power to govern the world, so neither can he be defective in disposition to do so. "As certain then as it is that there is a God who created all things, so certain is it that he acts as Sovereign of the Universe; that his supreme providence ruleth over all things, and has the care and superintendence of his creation. He who gave us being, must be concerned for our well-being too. He who is perfect wisdom and goodness, will, in every instance, take such care of us as perfect wisdom and goodness require. And, indeed, far from supposing in God any disinclination to superintend and govern the world, we cannot form to ourselves an employment more glorious in itself, or more worthy of his infinite perfections, than from his throne in heaven to inspect the immeasurable dominions of his universal empire; to have the administration of all its affairs; the appointment of all events; and to conduct the whole with unerring wisdom and unrestricted goodness." What can be more worthy of God, or more conducive to virtue and piety in his children? The doctrine of divine providence is taught in Holy Scripture, not as a theory, about which we may speculate, but as a fact, in which we are personally interested, and which is designed to influence our lives, and promote our peace and happiness. It is taught with the greatest distinctness, to deter men from vicious and criminal practices; to encourage virtue and piety; to support and console amid the disappointments and distresses of life, and to assure all men of a final adjustment of all the inequalities, sufferings, and wrongs of the present life.

To quote all the passages which teach and illustrate this deeply interesting and infinitely important doctrine, would be to transcribe a large part of the Bible. A few will suffice: "Do not I fill heaven and earth? saith the Lord." "The eyes of the Lord are in every place, beholding the evil and the good." "All things are naked and opened unto the eyes of him with whom we have to do." "O Lord, thou preservest man and beast;" and "the hairs of your head are all numbered." Other passages teach the doctrine of a particular providence over nations, kingdoms, families, and individuals, in their prosperity and adversity; in their rise and fall; in rewards and in punishments. But it is enough to say, the fact is distinctly and emphatically asserted, as extending to the little and the great; the minute and the magnificent; the near and the remote; the quick and the dead; the rational and irrational; so as to accomplish all the good purposes of his will, in the creation and preservation of the world.

"In what manner Providence interposes in human affairs; by what means it influences the thoughts and counsels of man, and, notwithstanding the influence it exerts, leaves to them the freedom of will and choice,—are subjects of dark and mysterious nature, and which have given occasion to many an intricate controversy. But, though the mode of the Divine operation remains unknown, the fact of an overruling influence is equally certain, in the moral, as it is in the natural world. In cases where the fact is clearly authenticated, we are not at liberty to call its truth in question merely because we understand not the manner in which it is brought about. Nothing can be more clear from the testimony of Scripture, than that God takes part in all that happens among mankind, directing and overruling the whole course of events, so as to make every one of them answer the designs of his wise and righteous government. Throughout all the sacred writings, God is represented, as on every occasion, by various dispensations of his providence, rewarding the righteous, or chastening them, according as his wisdom requires, and punishing the wicked. We cannot, indeed, conceive God acting as governor of the world at all, unless his government were extended to all the events that happen. It is upon the supposition of a particular providence, that our worship and prayers to him are founded. All his perfections would be utterly insignificant to us, if they were not exercised on every occasion, according as the circumstances of his creatures required. The Almighty would then be no more than an unconcerned spectator of the behavior of his subjects, regarding the obedient and the rebellious with an equal eye."

Our inability to comprehend, explain, and reconcile a particular Providence with human freedom, is not a question of the Divine Sovereignty, but of human weakness. The facts are independent of our strength or weakness, and whether we can reconcile them or not, they are reconcilable, for they are true, and all truth is in harmony. Whether the attempts to reconcile them, which have been so profoundly argued and ably maintained, by great and good men of different creeds, be satisfactory or not, it would ill become us to decide. It is enough for us to know, and with this, for the present, we must rest satisfied: God reigns; and man is free, a responsible subject to his Sovereign. And instead of perplexing ourselves with questions of little practical value, it better becomes us, adoring with the royal Solomon, to say: "Thine, O Lord, is the greatness, and the power, and the glory, and the victory, and the majesty; for all that is in heaven and in the earth is thine; thine is the kingdom, O Lord, and thou art exalted as head above all. Both riches and honor come of thee, and thou reignest over all; and in thine hand is power and might; and in thine hand it is to make great, and to give strength unto all. Now therefore, our God, we thank thee, and praise thy glorious name."

The following pages are designed to teach and illustrate, in a manner the most interesting to all classes, the ways of God with men. The articles are short and pertinent, and may be read at leisure moments; and, with little expense of time, lessons of great practical value may be gathered. It is a book for the parlor, the study, or the school-room, and will interest children, and instruct old age. From the care and ability with which the articles have been collected, through a series of years, we can confidently recommend this book to all Christian people as one that will do them good.

JOSEPH CASTLE.

PHILADELPHIA, Oct. 20th, 1858.

PART I.

ILLUSTRATIONS OF DIVINE PROVIDENCE IN THE PRESERVATION OF HUMAN LIFE.

"The Lord shall preserve thee from all evil: He shall preserve thy soul. The Lord shall preserve thy going out and thy coming in from this time forth, and even for ever more."—PSALM cxxi. 7, 8.

SECTION I.

Life Preserved by Intelligent Agents.

CHILD CARRIED AWAY BY AN EAGLE.

A PEASANT, with his wife and three children, had taken up his summer quarters in a chalet, and was pasturing his flock on one of the rich Alps which overhang the Durance. The oldest boy was an idiot, about eight years of age; the second was five years old, and dumb; and the youngest was an infant. It so happened, that the infant was left one morning in charge of his brothers, and the three had rambled to some distance from the chalet before they were missed. When the mother went in search of the little wanderers, she found the two elder, but could discover no traces of the babe. The idiot boy seemed to be in a transport of joy, while the dumb child displayed every symptom of alarm and terror. In vain did the terrified parent endeavor to collect what had become of the lost infant. The antics of the one and the fright of the other explained nothing. The dumb boy was almost bereft of his senses, while the idiot appeared to have acquired an unusual degree of mirth and expression. He danced about, laughed, and made gesticulations as if he were imitating the action of one who had caught up something of which he was fond, and hugged to his heart. This, however, was some slight comfort to the poor woman; for she imagined that some acquaintance had fallen in with the children, and had taken away the infant. But the day and night wore away, and no tidings came of the lost child. On the morrow, when the parents were pursuing their search, an eagle flew over their heads, at the sight of which the idiot renewed his antics, and the dumb boy clung to his father, with shrieks of anguish and affright. The horrible truth then burst upon their minds, that the miserable infant had been carried off in the talons of a bird of prey, and that the half-witted elder brother was delighted at his riddance of an object of whom he was jealous.

On the morning of this occurrence, an Alpine yager had been watching near an eagle's seat, with the hope of shooting the bird on her return to the nest. The yager, waiting in all the anxious perseverance of a true sportsman, beheld the eagle slowly winging her way toward the rock, behind which he was concealed. Imagine his horror, when, upon her nearer approach, he heard the cries and distinguished the figure of an infant in her fatal grasp. In an instant his resolution was formed—to fire at the bird at all hazards, the moment she should alight on her nest, and rather to kill the child, than leave it to be torn to pieces by the horrid devourer. With a silent prayer, and a steady aim, the mountaineer poised his rifle. The ball went directly through the head of the eagle, and, in a moment after, the gallant hunter was bearing away the child in triumph. It was torn in the arms and sides, but not mortally wounded. Twenty-four hours after it was first missed, it was happily sleeping in its mother's arms.

PROVIDENTIAL RESCUE.

TRANSLATED FROM THE GERMAN.

ONE day, in harvest time, my mother sent me into the cellar to fetch a pitcher of beer for the reapers. I was about ten years old, and of a lively temper, always going with a hop and a bound rather than walking. On coming into the dark cellar I felt a little timid, and, to keep up my courage, sprang and danced about at a greater rate than usual.

Now it happened that Harrach, my native town, was built over old mines, which had fallen in a long time before. All around the place lie great fragments of stone from the abandoned works, and in many of the houses are found half-opened passages, which are sometimes used as cellars. Our house, likewise, was built over a shaft, but this was either not known or not thought of. But while I was capering about, and had just seized the pitcher which stood in the corner, suddenly the earth opened under me, and I was gone, I knew not where.

I went down to a great depth, and should have plunged to the very bottom of the abyss, had not a hook, which probably had been used for fastening the mining ladder, caught me by the coat. At the instant of falling I had uttered a fearful shriek, which reached the ears of my mother, who was busy in the kitchen. She came running down with a light, and when she saw the opening in the ground, and could neither find me nor hear answer to her call, she could not doubt that I had perished.

My mother has often told me that she was beside herself with terror, and was near plunging down after me. It became so dark before her eyes that she could hardly sustain herself upon her trembling knees. But the thought that possibly I might yet be rescued, brought her to herself.

She hastened up stairs and called for help; but no one heard her, for all the household were at work in the harvest field. It was not until she had run down the street that some women heard her, and hastened to the spot. They stood around wringing their hands and looking down into the aperture, but knew not what to do.

In falling I had lost my consciousness, and it would have been a happy thing to have remained thus till the moment of my deliverance. But after a time I came to myself. I knew not where I was, but I felt that I was hanging between heaven and earth, and that the next moment might plunge me into the bottomless abyss. I hardly ventured to make a sound, so great was my terror: but when I heard voices and piteous lamentations above me, I begged in God's name for help. At this the lamentations ceased for a moment, and then burst out more violently than before; for to know that I was alive, and yet no way to help me, only added to their misery.

There was no lack of counsel. Each one had something to propose. But it was soon seen that nothing was to be effected in this way. They tried to let down cords, but they did not reach me. Poles were still more useless. Indeed, how could it have been possible for me to hold on to a cord or a pole long enough to draw me up to that height?

At length they called in the aid of an old miner, who at once saw what was to be done. His first business was carefully to enlarge the aperture. He then set up a windlass beside it, with a long rope coiled upon it, and to this fastened a bucket. The compassionate neighbors watched every movement with agonizing impatience. Many prayed aloud.

And in those terrible moments of consciousness which now and then broke in upon my swoon, for I had swooned after my fall, my ear caught single words of hymns and prayers for the dying, which I understood too well.

At length all was ready; and the old miner, with a light attached to his cap, having first given warning that perhaps he might drag me down with him in his descent, stepped into the bucket. Slowly and cautiously was the rope unwound. I saw the burning light, and it seemed to me like a star descending from heaven for my help. Above was the silence of death. Without knowing what I did, I shrank up as close as possible to the damp wall. The movement loosened a bit of stone, and I heard the reverberation of its fall in the depth below. My groans indicated the place where I hung. The old man now began to comfort me, saying that I must keep up a good heart, for he hoped that, with God's help, he should deliver me.

Now I saw the bucket hovering far over my head; then nearer and nearer; but the opening was so narrow that it could not pass by me. My deliverer, therefore, gave a sign for those at the top to stop unwinding. He then reached down to me a cord with a noose tied to it. I seized hold of this, and, by raising myself a little, grasped the edge of the bucket, first by one, and then by both hands. At this instant the frail threads, which had thus far sustained me, gave way. The bucket swayed with my weight, but I was already grasped by my old friend. He drew me into the bucket, and called aloud :

"Thank God, there above; I have the child; I have the child!"

As I sat in the miner's lap and felt myself safe, the first thing that came into my head was the pitcher, which, in my fall, had slipped from my hand. I began to weep bitterly.

"Why do you weep, my boy?" said the old man; "the danger is all over; we are just at the top."

"Ah, the pitcher, the pitcher!" I sobbed out. "It was bran new, and the very best we had!"

We were at the brink of the chasm. My mother leaned over it, reaching toward me with yearning arms. The old miner lifted me out to her. With trembling hands she caught me and drew me to her bosom. All the bystanders shouted for joy. They crowded around, and each one wished to embrace me; but my mother trusted me not out of her arms. The dear, good mother! She had always loved me dearly; but from that time I was the apple of her eye.

I have heard my mother more than once relate that when she heard the words of the miner— "Thank God, there above; I have the child"—a thrill of horror ran through her heart. Then it seemed to her impossible that it could be true; she fell with her face to the ground, and could only weep. But when the light reappeared, and by its weak rays she could discern her child, and see that he was alive, heaven seemed to open to her in all its glory. Never did she forget the blessed moment. My mother was a very pious woman; and was, on this account, held in great esteem by all who knew her. God laid many trials upon her, but I never saw her faint-hearted, never heard her murmur. In all her sorrows she acknowledged the fatherly love of God. But she often told her children that it was in that day of agony, when I was lost and again restored, that she was first fully established in her faith, and knew what it was to trust in the goodness of God.

REMARKABLE PROVIDENCE.

About Christmas, in the year 1840, a Russian clergyman was going home from a place at some distance from the village where he lived. Evening was coming on, and it was growing so bitterly cold that it was almost dangerous for any one to be out. He was wrapped in a fur cloak, and travelled in a sledge, which went fast over the hard, smooth snow. As he went along he saw something lying on the ground, and stopped to see what it was. He found that it was a soldier, who seemed to have fallen down exhausted with the cold, and to all appearance was dead. The good clergyman, however, would not leave him on the road, but lifted him into the sledge, with his gun, which lay beside him, and drove as fast as he could to the next inn, which it took about half an hour to reach. He was not satisfied with leaving the poor soldier in the care of the people there; but, although he was very anxious to reach his home, he stayed for an hour directing and helping them to do all that was possible in order to bring the man to conscious life again in case he was not really dead. And at length their endeavors were successful, and his senses and the use of his limbs gradually returned. Then the clergyman set off homeward, having first rewarded the people of the inn, and also given them money to pay for a good meal for the poor man, before he should go forward on his journey. As soon as the man was refreshed and felt able to go, he insisted upon doing so, although the people did all they could to persuade him not to venture out again that night.

But he said that he was carrying letters which were important, and he must not delay any longer than was quite necessary. So, taking his gun, he proceeded on his way, which he found would very soon bring him to the village where the clergyman lived to whom he owed his life. He reached the place before long, and, though it was now very late at night, he could not forbear going to the clergyman's house, that he might, if possible, see and thank him for what he had done.

As he went up to the house, he saw that, though

it was late, there was still a light in it; and as he came nearer, he heard loud voices and great confusion within. He hastened to the door, but it was fastened; and without waiting to knock, he ran to the window close by, and, looking in, saw the clergyman surrounded by four armed robbers. They had just tied his hands and feet, and were threatening to murder him if he would not tell where his money was to be found. The soldier instantly forced his way in, fired his gun at one of the robbers, and killed him on the spot. The others attacked the soldier, but he disabled one with his bayonet, and the other two were then seized with fear, and rushed out of the house, leaving the clergyman, as may be supposed, overpowered by astonishment and gratitude for his sudden deliverance. And then his still deeper and happier feelings may be imagined when he found that the poor man, whose life he had saved only a few hours before, had now been made the means of preserving his own.

Captain H. and crew sailed some time since from the port of ———. After having been at sea for several days, they were assailed by an unusually severe storm, which continued forty-five days and nights in succession. They were driven far from their course by the violence of the wind. Nature had become nearly exhausted by hard and long toiling; and, to add to their affliction, famine began to threaten them with a death far more appalling than that of a watery grave.

The captain had with him his wife, two daughters, and ten persons besides. As their provisions grew short, his wife became provident and careful of the pittance that fell to their family share. She would eat but little, lest her husband should starve. The children would eat but little, for fear the mother would suffer, and the captain refused to eat any, but left his portion for his suffering family. At length they were reduced to a scanty allowance for twenty-four hours in the midst of a storm, and one thousand miles from land. Captain H. was a man who feared God. In this his extremity he ordered his steward to bring the remaining provision on deck, and spread the same on the tarpauling which covers the hatch, and falling down beside the fragments of bread and meat before him, he lifted up his voice in prayer to Him who heareth out of the deep, and said, "O, thou who didst feed Elijah by a raven while in the wilderness, and who commanded that the widow's cruse of oil and barrel of meal should not fail, look down upon us in our present distress, and grant that this food may be so multiplied that the lives now in jeopardy may be preserved." After this he arose from his knees, went to the companion-way, and found his wife and children engaged in the same holy exercise. He exhorted them to pray on, and assured them that

God had answered his prayer, and that not one soul then on board should perish. Scarcely had he uttered these words, when his mate, who had been at the mast-head for some time on the look-out, exclaimed, "Sail O! sail O!" At this crisis the captain shouted with swelling gratitude, "What, has God sent the ravens already!"—and in one hour from that time, through the friendly sail, barrels of bread and meat were placed upon the deck.

"Thus one thing secures us, whatever betide;
The Scripture assures us the Lord will provide."

WHO CAN TELL?

"I HAVE heard," says Mr. Daniel Wilson, in a sermon of his, "of a certain person, whose name I could mention, who was tempted to conclude his day over, and himself lost; that, therefore, it was his best course to put an end to his life, which, if continued, would but serve to increase his sin, and consequently his misery, from which there was no escape; and seeing he must be in hell, the sooner he was there the sooner he should know the worst; which was preferable to his being worn away with the tormenting expectation of what was to come. Under the influence of such suggestions as these, he went to a river, with a design to throw himself in; but as he was about to do it, he seemed to hear a voice saying to him, *Who can tell?* as if the words had been audibly delivered. By this, therefore, he was brought to a stand; his thoughts were arrested, and thus began to work on the passage mentioned: *Who can tell* (Jonah iii. 9,) viz., what God can do when he will proclaim his grace glorious? *Who can tell* but such an one as I may find mercy? or what will be the issue of humble prayer to heaven for it? *Who can tell* what purposes God will serve in my recovery? By such thoughts as these, being so far influenced as to resolve to try, it pleased God graciously to enable him, through all his doubts and fears, to throw himself by faith on Jesus Christ, as able to save to the uttermost all that come to God by him, humbly desiring and expecting mercy for his sake, to his own soul. In this he was not disappointed; but afterwards became an eminent Christian and minister; and from his own experience of the riches of grace, was greatly useful to the conversion and comfort of others."

THE MARTYR SAVED.

It is related, in the memoirs of the celebrated William Whiston, that a Protestant, in the days of Queen Mary, of the name of Barber, was sentenced to be burned. He walked to Smithfield, was bound to the stake, the fagots were piled around him, and the executioner only waited the word of command to apply the torch. At this crisis, tidings came of the queen's death; the officers were compelled to stay proceedings till the pleasure of Elizabeth should be known; and thus the life of the good man was spared, to labor, with some of his descendants, successfully in the service of the Lord Jesus and his church.

WONDERFUL DELIVERANCE OF PETER THE GREAT.

ALEXANDER MENZIKOFF, who rose to the highest offices of state in Russia, during the reign of Peter the Great, was born of parents so excessively poor, that they could not afford to have him taught to read and write. After their death, he went to Moscow to seek for employment, where he found an asylum with a pastry cook. He had a very fine voice, and soon became known through that great city by the musical tone of his cry when vending his master's pastry in the streets. His voice also gained him admission into the houses of many noblemen; and he was fortunate enough one day to be in the kitchen of a great lord with whom the emperor was to dine. While Menzikoff was there, the nobleman came into the kitchen, and gave directions about a particular dish, to which he said the emperor was very partial; into this dish he dropped (as he thought unperceived) a powder. Menzikoff observed it, but taking no notice, immediately left; and when he saw the emperor's carriage coming, he began to sing very loud. Peter, attracted by his voice, called him, and bought all the pies he had in his basket. He asked some questions of Menzikoff, and was so much pleased with his answers that he commanded him to follow him to the nobleman's house, and wait behind his chair. The servants were surprised at his order, but it proved of the greatest importance to Peter; for when the nobleman pressed his royal guest to take of this favorite dish, his new servant gently pulled him by the sleeve, and begged he would not touch it until he had spoken to him. The emperor immediately withdrew with Menzikoff, who informed his imperial master of his suspicions. The czar returned to his company, and, suddenly turning to his host, pressed him to partake of the favorite dish. Terrified at this command, he said, "It did not become the servant to eat before his master." It was then given to a dog, who shortly after expired in great pain. The nobleman's execution and Menzikoff's elevation complete the story.

PROVIDENTIAL RESCUE OF SEVEN PERSONS FROM A WHALE-BOAT IN THE NORTH PACIFIC.

At daylight on the morning of the 5th of February, 1850, one of the hands of the schooner Wanderer (Royal Yacht Squadron), on her passage from the Society Islands to the Hawaiian, reported what appeared to him to be a boat; but this was for some time considered to be impossible, as no boat, it was thought, could have lived in such a sea—the Wanderer herself being under storm canvas, it blowing a severe gale. A man having been, however, sent aloft with a glass, it proved to be a whale-boat, about three miles to the windward, with signal of distress flying; the schooner then beat up to her near enough to hail; but at first the only intelligible word that could be heard was "water! water!" Her canvas was blown away, and her rudder gone; and having no steering oar she was unmanageable. After three attempts, the Wanderer succeeded in passing sufficiently near to heave the end of a whale-line to the boat. A running bowline was then passed to them, by which means one after another of the people were hauled on board the schooner over the taffrail. The party consisted of Jose Davis, a Brazilian man of color, two men and three women, natives of the Sandwich Islands, one of the latter being the wife of Davis. It appeared that they had left the island of Molokai, where they had called on their passage from Oahu to Maui, and had nearly reached the latter island, where they resided; but being caught in a heavy gale, and their boat disabled, had driven three hundred miles to the southward. They had been nine days without water—subsisting entirely by sucking small pieces of pumpkins, a few of which they had on board, and which Davis doled out to them sparingly; as he said he had determined, if the boat survived the gale, to have made sails out of the women's dresses, and endeavored to rig a new rudder, and steer by a particular star of his acquaintance, which would bring him to the coast of South America; how this was to be accomplished in the teeth of the strong easterly trades, was above, rather, the range of Davis's philosophy. The poor creatures were so exhausted from cold and continued bailing (the garboard streak of the boat having started), that it was some time before hot tea, mixed with a little spirits, revived them, and enabled them to give a distinct account of their misfortunes.

For some time an endeavor was made to get some of their goods out of the boat, for their worldly all was on board of her, consisting of clothes, squashes, and about $100; but by this time the water had gained so much upon her, that she gave one heavy roll, carrying away the mast to which the warp was attached, and when the Wanderer left her she was evidently settling. Poor Jose, whose hair was nearly white with the snows of some sixty winters, took his last fond look; a tear came trickling down his wrinkled cheek; he drew a deep sigh and exclaimed: "There goes my all; I am again a beggar;" and, taking his wife around the neck, kissed her, and said: "Thank God, however, we are safe, and will see our boys again." Jose proved himself quite a character. It was evident that it was not the first time that he had been in a long-keeled craft, as he called her. He surveyed her with the eye of a master spirit; and, when he saw long Tom and other guns, he said, with a knowing expression: "They know nothing of the old trade here; but I have no doubt you will do well dodging off San Francisco;" evidently considering that the schooner was bent on no very honest calling. He and his party remained with us during our stay at Hawaii, where he formerly lived for seventeen years. We found he was universally respected by the inhabitants, who desired him and his family to come again and reside with them; but Jose, having his eldest boy at one of those excellent schools founded by the American Missionaries at Maui, said that he was determined his children should have a good education, and declined their offer. When the Wanderer called at Lahaina to land them, it was ascertained that the boat and party were long since given up as lost; and the maternal uncle of the children had taken charge of them. Nothing could exceed the gratitude of the poor people; and old Jose presented the Wanderer with a fine large hog, cocoanuts, &c., for which he would not accept of any payment; the affair was with difficulty arranged by giving some calico to his wife; and when they left the ship they carried with them the kind wishes of all on board.—*Polynesian*.

SECTION II.

Life Preserved by Unintelligent Agents.

ALL IS FOR THE BEST.

That great and good man, Bernard Gilpin, whose pious labors in the north of England procured for him the title of "The Apostle of the North," when exposed to losses or troubles, was accustomed to say, "Ah, well, God's will be done; it's all for the best."

Toward the close of Mary's reign, Mr. Gilpin was accused of heresy; and being speedily apprehended, he left his happy home, "nothing doubting," as he said, "that it was all for the best;" though fully expecting, when he bid his family farewell, that, instead of returning, he should die at the martyrs' stake.

While on his way to London, by some accident he broke his leg. This, for a time, put a stop to his journey. While thus detained, some malignant persons took occasion to retort on him his habitual remark. "What," said they, "is this all for the best?" "Sirs, I make no question but it is," was his meek reply. And so it actually proved; for, before he was able to travel, Queen Mary died, the persecution ceased, and he was restored to liberty.

SAVED FROM A ROBBER BY RAIN.

A MERCHANT was one day returning from market. He was on horseback, and behind him was a valise filled with money. The rain fell with violence, and the good old man was wet to his skin. At this he was vexed, and murmured because God had given him such bad weather for his journey.

He soon reached the borders of a thick forest. What was his terror on beholding on one side of the road a robber, with levelled gun, aiming at him and attempting to fire! But, the powder being wet by the rain, the gun did not go off, and the merchant, giving spurs to his horse, fortunately had time to escape.

As soon as he found himself safe, he said to himself: "How wrong was I, not to endure the rain patiently, as sent by Providence! If the weather had been dry and fair, I should not, probably, have been alive at this hour, and my little children would have expected my return in vain. The rain which caused me to murmur, came at a fortunate moment, to save my life and preserve my property." And thus it is with a multitude of our afflictions; by causing us slight and short sufferings, they preserve us from others far greater, and of longer duration.

LIFE SAVED BY A TRACT.

A MINISTER from Exeter stated "that not far from the place where he lived, and quite in the country, there were two young ladies residing, and both were pious. It so happened that a poor American sailor, having taken up the employment of a pedlar, passed that way, called at the house of these young ladies, and taking his box of small wares from his shoulders, requested one of them to purchase some tracts. She replied, that there was a certain tract which she was anxious to find, and that she would look over his parcel, and if it contained the one referred to, she would take it. She did so, and finding the tract she wanted, paid the man, and ordered the servants to provide him some refreshments, and went in haste to the door to receive a friend who had come from a distance to visit her. The poor man, in the mean time, gathered up his scattered wares, proceeded a considerable distance on his way, and having reached a very retired spot, sat down by the side of the road, and taking his jack-knife from his pocket, began to appease his hunger with the food so kindly provided for him. It so happened that in the course of the day a most horrible murder and robbery had been committed near this spot, and officers had been despatched to seek out the criminal and bring him back to justice. A party of them approached this poor sailor, and finding him employed with a jack-knife (the very instrument with which the murder was supposed to have been perpetrated), they seized him at once and put him in prison, where he remained three months awaiting his trial. During the whole period of his confinement he was employed in reading the Bible and religious books to his fellow-prisoners, and was so exemplary in his whole conduct as to attract the attention of the jailor, who kindly interested himself for him, listened to his tale of woe, and believed him innocent. When the trial came on the case was of such an interesting nature that it drew together a vast concourse of people; and after the examination had been passed, and the judge had called for the verdict of guilty or not guilty, a voice was heard to issue from the crowd, *Not guilty!* Every eye was directed to the spot from whence the sound proceeded; and immediately a young lady advanced, with a paper in her hand, and appeared before the judge. Her feelings at first overcame her, and she fainted; but recovering herself, and being encouraged to proceed, if she had anything to say in defence of the prisoner at the bar, she stated to the judge the circumstances of having the tract of the poor man, presenting it at the same time, bearing the date of the day and hour when it was purchased. She stated further, that just as the man was about leaving her, a sister whom she had not seen for many years arrived from a distance, and as she was anxious, for a particular reason, to remember the day and hour of her arrival, she made a memorandum of it upon this tract, which she happened to have in her hand. While she was making this statement to the judge, the poor prisoner bent forward with earnestness to discover what gentle voice was pleading in his behalf; for he had thought himself friendless and alone in the world, and was comforted that any one should take a part in his sorrows, even though it should not avail to the saving of his life. But it did avail; for the hour of the murder having been ascertained, and being the same as that recorded upon the tract, it was evident the prisoner must have been in a different place at the time it was committed. He was accordingly discharged; and in a moment was upon his knees, pouring forth the grateful feelings of his heart to his kind benefactress. And this, said the reverend gentleman, holding up a tract, is the very tract which saved that man's life."

DELIVERED FROM DEATH BY A DOG.

Sir Harry Lee, in Ditchlong, in Oxfordshire, ancestor of the late Earl of Litchfield, had a mastiff which guarded the house and yard, but had never met with the least particular attention from his master, and was retained for his utility only, and not for any special regard. One night as his master was retiring to his chamber, attended by his valet, an Italian, the mastiff silently followed him up stairs, which he had never been known to do before, and, to his master's astonishment, presented himself in his bedroom. Being deemed an intruder, he was instantly ordered to be turned out; which being complied with, the poor animal began scratching violently at the door, and howling loudly for admission. The servant was sent to drive him away. Discouragement could not check his labor of love, or rather providential impulse; he returned again, and was more importunate than before to be let in. Sir Harry, weary of opposition, bade the servant open the door, that they might see what he would do. This done, the mastiff, with a wag of his tail, and a look of affection at his lord, deliberately walked up, and crawling under the bed, laid himself down as if desirous of taking up his night's lodging there. To save farther trouble, but not from any partiality for his company, the indulgence was allowed. About the hour of midnight the chamber door opened, and a person was heard stepping across the room. Sir Harry started from his sleep; the dog sprung from his covert, and, seizing the unwelcome disturber, fixed him to the spot! All was dark, and Sir Harry rung his bell in great trepidation, in order

to procure a light. The person who was pinned to
the floor by the courageous mastiff roared for assistance. It was found to be the *valet*, who little
expected such a reception. He endeavored to apologize for his intrusion, and to make the reasons
which induced him to take the step appear plausible; but the importunity of the dog, the time, the
place, and the manner of the valet, all raised suspicion in Sir Harry's mind, and he determined to
refer the investigation of the business to a magistrate. The perfidious Italian, alternately terrified
by the dread of punishment, and soothed with the
hope of pardon, at length confessed that it was his
intention to murder his master, and then rob the
house. This diabolical design was frustrated only
by the dog, who had perhaps providentially overheard some expressions in soliloquy or conversation, from the valet, respecting his contemplated
crime.

THE FALLEN TREE.

About the year 1830, while a young man of the
town of Wells, Maine, was at work in the woods
alone, he felled a tree which struck a large log,
lying up some distance from the ground. When
the tree struck the log, the butt bounded, struck
the man, carried him some distance, plunged him
into a deep snow, and fell across his stomach, con-

fining him there. The log across which the tree fell, served as a fulcrum, being so near the middle of the tree as to prevent it from lying so heavily upon him as to give much immediate distress. His feet were so completely confined that he had no power to move them; his hands being the only means with which he could do the least towards extricating himself, which he used in the best possible manner he was capable of; but he was utterly unsuccessful in his efforts to raise the body of the tree, or beating away the snow. Now feeling in some degree that all hopes of being delivered from that state of confinement also were vain, he cast his eyes toward heaven, when he saw a large limb, which had broken from the tree while falling, suspended in the air by the branch of another tree, and at the distance of thirty or forty feet above him, apparently directly over his head. What must have been his feelings while thus confined, and viewing that threatening death hanging directly over him, and expecting every moment it would fall and terminate his existence?

While he thus lay, with his eyes fastened upon the limb, waiting for the result he thought must soon take place, the twig by which it was suspended gave way—the limb fell and struck the snow about one foot from his head. He immediately thought to use that as a lever, by which to raise the tree. He proved successful.

SINGULAR PRESERVATION—GREENLANDERS.

The United Brethren relate the following account of two converted pagans in Greenland, who, in their heathen state, gave them much trouble by their wild dances and outrageous behavior.

On July 4th, 1827, the assistant Nathaniel arrived here with his family. He immediately called upon us both to make a report of his success in the seal fishery, and of the remarkable preservation of his life; the narrative of which might almost appear fabulous, had he not related it himself; and he is a man of unimpeached veracity. First, he exclaimed: "I have now experienced what it is to be near death;" and then related the following adventure:

Being in company with another brother, who was yet inexperienced in the management of a kayak, he met a neitsersoak, the largest kind of seal, which he killed. He then discovered his companion on a flake of ice, endeavoring to kill another of the same species, and in danger. He therefore left his dead seal, kept buoyant by the bladder, and hastened to help his brother. They succeeded in killing the seal; but suddenly a strong north wind arose, and carried off both the kayaks to sea. They now with terror beheld themselves left on a small flake of ice, far from the land, driving about in the open sea; nor could they discover any kayaks in the neighborhood. They cried aloud for help, but in vain. Meanwhile, the wind rose in strength, and carried both the kayaks, and also the piece of ice, swiftly along with the waves. Having lost sight of the former, they now saw themselves without the least hope of deliverance. Nathaniel added: "I continued praying to my Saviour, and thought with great grief of the situation of my poor family; but felt a small degree of hope arising in my breast." Unexpectedly, he saw his dead seal floating towards him, and was exceedingly surprised to see it approaching against the wind, till it came so near the flake of ice that they could secure it. But how should a dead seal become the means of their deliverance? And what was now to be done? All at once, Nathaniel resolved, at a venture, to seat himself upon the floating seal, and, by the help of his paddle, which he had kept in his hand when he joined his companion on the ice, to go in quest of the kayaks. Though the sea and waves continually overflowed him, yet the body of the seal being sufficiently buoyant to bear his weight, he kept his seat, made after the kayaks, and succeeded in overtaking his own, into which he crept, and went in quest of that of his companion, which he likewise found. He also kept possession of the seal; and now hastened in search of the flake of ice, on which his companion was most anxiously looking out for him. Having reached it, he brought him his kayak, and enabled him to secure the other seal, when both returned home in safety.

We were thankful that Nathaniel had received no harm from so dangerous an adventure. During this affecting narrative, he ascribed his preservation, not to his own clever contrivance, but to the mercy of God alone; and added: "When I found myself delivered from death, and sat again in my kayak, I shed abundance of tears of gratitude to our Saviour; for in my greatest distress my only hope was placed on him. I ascribe to him alone my deliverance!" We could not refrain from tears on hearing the undisguised and simple account he gave of this event; and joined in his thanksgiving to the Lord, who has thousands of means at his command of saving them who call upon him in trouble.

A REMARKABLE DELIVERANCE.

In 1672, the Dutch were saved by an extraordinary event, at a time when nothing but the interposition of Providence could have preserved them. In that memorable year, when Louis XIV. came down upon that country like a flood, he proposed that at the same time he should enter the province of Holland by land, his fleet, in conjunction with that of Great Britain, should make a descent on the side of the Hague by sea. When the united fleets came up within sight of Scheveling, the tide, though very regular at other times, just when they were preparing to land, changed its usual course, and stopped for several hours. The next morning the French and English fleets were dispersed by a violent storm.

Those who hate the very name of a miracle (although in reality they suppose the greatest of all miracles, that is, the tying up the hands of the Almighty from disposing events according to his will), pretend, "This was only an extraordinary ebb." But this very ebb was an extraordinary providence, as the descent, which must have terminated in the destruction of the republic, was to be punctually at that and no other time. But that this retrogradation of the sea was no natural event, is as certain as anything in nature.

Many writers of unquestionable veracity might be produced to confirm the truth of the fact. I shall only cite one, who was at the Hague but three years after it happened. "An extraordinary thing lately happened at the Hague: I had it from many eye-witnesses. The English fleet appeared in sight of Scheveling, making up to the shore. The tide turned: but they made no doubt of landing the forces the next flood, where they were like to meet no resistance. The states sent to the prince for men to hinder the descent, but he could spare few, having the French near him. So the country was given up for lost; their admiral, De Ruyter, with their fleet being absent. The flood returned, which the people expected would end in their ruin; but, to the amazement of them all, after the sea had flowed two or three hours, an ebb of many hours succeeded, which carried the fleet again to sea. And before the flood returned, De Ruyter came in view. This they esteemed no less than a miracle wrought for their preservation."—*Bishop Burnet's History of his own Times.* Book II.

SECTION III.

Life Preserved by Mental Impressions, Dreams, &c.

REMARKABLE DELIVERANCE OF THE REV. R. BOARDMAN.

"I PREACHED one evening at Mould, in Flintshire, and next morning set out for Parkgate. After riding some miles, I asked a man if I was on the road to that place. He answered, 'Yes; but you will have some sands to go over, and unless you ride fast you will be in danger of being enclosed by the tide.' It then began to snow to such a degree that I could scarcely see a step of my way. I got to the sands, and pursued my journey over them for sometime as rapidly as I could; but the tide then came in, and surrounded me on every side, so that I could neither proceed nor turn back, and to ascend the perpendicular rocks was impossible. In this situation I commended my soul to God, not having the least expectation of escaping death. In a little time I perceived two men running down a hill on the other side of the water, and by some means they got into a boat, and came to my relief, just as the sea had reached my knees, as I sat on my saddle. They took me into the boat, the mare swimming by our side till we reached the land. While we were in the boat, one of the men said, 'Surely, sir, God is with you.' I answered, 'I trust he is.' The man replied, 'I know he is;' and then related the following circumstance: 'Last night I dreamed that I must go to the top of such a hill. When I awoke the dream made such an impression on my mind that I could not rest. I therefore went and called on this man to accompany me. When we came to the place we saw nothing more than usual. However, I begged him to go with me to another at a small distance, and there we saw your distressed situation.' When we got ashore I went with my two friends to a public-house not far distant from where we landed; and as we were relating the wonderful providence, the landlady said, 'This day month we saw a gentleman just in your situation; but before we could hasten to his relief he plunged into the sea, supposing, as we concluded, that his horse could swim to the shore; but they both sank, and were drowned together.' I gave my deliverers all the money I had, which I think was about eighteen pence, and tarried all night at the hotel. Next morning I was not a little embarrassed how to pay my reckoning, for the want of cash, and I begged my landlord would keep a pair of silver spurs till I should redeem them; but he answered, 'The Lord bless you, sir, I would not take a farthing from you for the world.' After some serious conversation with the friendly people, I bade them farewell, and recommenced my journey, rejoicing in the Lord, and praising him for his great salvation."

ESCAPE OF GENERAL WASHINGTON.

Major Ferguson, who commanded a rifle corps in advance of the hussars under Kniphausen, during some skirmishing a day or two previous to the battle of Brandywine, was the hero of a very singular incident, which he thus relates in a letter to a friend. It illustrates, in a most forcible manner, the overruling hand of Providence in directing the operations of a man's mind, in moments when he is least of all aware of it.

"We had not lain long, when a rebel officer, remarkable by a hussar dress, pressed towards our army, within a hundred yards of my right flank, not perceiving us. He was followed by another, dressed in dark green and blue, mounted on a bay horse, with a remarkably high cocked hat. I ordered three good shots to steal near to them, and fire at them; but the idea disgusting me, I recalled the order. The hussar, in returning, made a circuit, but the other passed within a hundred yards of us, upon which I advanced from the wood towards him. Upon my calling, he stopped; but after looking at me, he proceeded. I again drew his attention, and made signs to him to stop, levelling my piece at him; but he slowly cantered away. As I was within that distance at which, in the quickest firing, I could have lodged half a dozen balls in or about him, before he was out of my reach, I had only to determine; but it was not pleasant to fire at the back of an unoffending individual, who was acquitting himself very coolly of his duty; so I let him alone.

"The day after, I had been telling this story to some wounded officers who lay in the same room with me, when one of the surgeons, who had been dressing the wounded rebel officers, came in, and told us, that they had been informing him that General Washington was all the morning with the light troops, and only attended by a French officer in a hussar dress, he himself dressed and mounted in every point as above described. I am not sorry that I did not know at the time who it was."

THE DROWNING LADY.

A GAY lady in New England once had occasion to go to a neighboring town, where she had often been before. In the immediate vicinity was a stream which she had to go near, and which at this period was high. With a view of showing her courage to a young person whom she had taken with her as a companion, she went into the stream with her horse, and in a very little time was thrown into the water—had already sunk once or twice to the bottom, and felt that she was within a few moments of an eternal world, without being prepared for so great a change.

It so happened, that a young man in another neighboring town had felt a powerful impression on his mind that morning, that he would visit the same place. He had no business to transact; but, being forcibly impressed with the importance of going thither, he invited a young man to accompany him. Arriving at the side of the stream just as the young ladies were about to cross it, they saw it was improbable that they could ford it; yet, as the ladies went, they determined to follow.

By the time the young lady was thrown from her horse, the others had nearly reached the opposite shore; but, perceiving her danger, one of them immediately followed her on his horse, and in the last moment of life, as it then appeared, she caught hold of the horse's leg; he thus secured her, and snatching hold of the other drowning young lady, she was saved also. After the use of proper remedies they recovered; and the young gentlemen, believing that the design of their coming from home was now answered, returned back.

The impressions made on the mind of this young lady were permanent, and she was led to reflect on the sins she had committed against God, to pray for the pardon of her guilt, and to devote herself to the Divine service. She embraced the mercy of the Lord, believing in the Redeemer, who alone saves from the wrath to come.

In the same town with herself lived a young gentleman, who had often spent his hours in vain conversation with her. On her return home, he went to congratulate her on her escape, and to his surprise, found she attributed her deliverance to the power of God, and urged him to seek that grace which they had both neglected. Her serious conversation was blest to his conversion, and he became a faithful minister of Jesus Christ.

HE CRUCIFIED NOT HIMSELF.

A GENTLEMAN was known by his nearest and dearest friend, his wife, never to lie down upon his pillow, some years before his death, or raise his head from it in the morning, without repeating the short hymn annexed to this anecdote; and sometimes he would inadvertently burst into ejaculations in company, when two or three lines of it were distinctly heard before he could recollect himself. The cause at that time was unknown; but after his decease a paper was found in his bureau to the following purport:—" You will no longer be surprised at my involuntary effusions of feeble gratitude to the Almighty, when you shall read that many years since the dread of approaching poverty, disgrace, and desertion of friends, had brought me to the fatal resolution of ending my existence. Conscious that I had brought misfortune upon a numerous family by my own imprudence, dissipation, and pride, I considered my punishment as an act of justice. The destined moment arrived; already had I loaded, primed, and cocked—when, strange to relate! though I had not read a page in the Bible for years, a reflection came suddenly across my mind—'Jesus of Nazareth,' said I to myself, 'was a man (for I disbelieved in his divinity) acquainted with sorrows, endured a life of poverty, was exposed to public scorn and derision, suffered pain of body and agony of mind, and had nothing to reproach himself with—yet this reformer of the morals of mankind, this benefactor to society, this illustrious pattern of fortitude, patience, and humanity, was by an unthankful world put to death: he was crucified! But *he crucified not himself!*' Repeating these last words with unusual energy, my inability humbly to imitate his example of bearing afflictions manfully, produced a passionate conflict of pride, shame, and contempt, in which paroxysm I madly flung the pistol some distance from me; to add to the affecting scene, it went off, unheard but by my affectionate wife, who religiously kept the secret; her consolations restored me to temporary tranquillity. But the work of Providence was not yet completed; not a week had elapsed, and settled melancholy was again taking possession of my soul, when a letter announced the death of a distant relation and summoned me to the reading of his will, by which he bequeathed me sufficient to clear me of embarrassment, and start me upon a career of prosperity, which, by God's blessing, has resulted in independence."

>Rise, O my soul! the hour review,
> When, awed by guilt and fear,
>Thou durst not heaven for mercy sue,
> Nor hope for pity here!
>
>Dried are thy tears, thy griefs are fled,
> Dispelled each bitter care;
>For heaven itself did send its aid,
> To snatch thee from despair.
>
>Then hear, O God, thy work fulfil,
> And from thy mercy's throne
>Vouchsafe me strength to do thy will,
> And to resist my own.
>
>So shall my soul each power employ,
> Thy mercies to adore,
>Whilst heaven itself proclaims with joy,
> One rescued sinner more.

THE VICIOUS HORSE.

Mr. McK——, of Talbot county, Md., told me, that once he owned a young horse, which he desired to break for a carriage-horse, for the use of his family. On one occasion, he concluded to try the horse in a cart, previous to using him in the carriage. He took him to the field to gather in the fodder, and here the animal worked so gently and kindly through the day, that he became satisfied with the trial, and determined on putting him to the carriage, and taking his family out riding. Hauling in the last load of fodder, however, an impression was made on his mind, that he had better try the horse still further. But this suggestion seemed so unreasonable, after the trial already made, that he endeavored to dissipate it from his mind. It, however, strengthened on him, in spite of his resistance; and, by the time he reached the stack-yard, where the fodder was to be deposited, he concluded to yield to it. Throwing down the load, he drove the horse through the gate into the public road; hardly had he gone three hundred yards, when the horse commenced kicking in a manner so furious and terrible, that but for a chain which he had the precaution to fasten across its back, everything must have been destroyed. Had he been allowed to carry out his determination to take his family out, it is hardly possible that they should all have escaped with their lives. But he who controls all things had determined differently. Man proposes, but God disposes.

THE ROBBERS.

A NEIGHBORING farmer, Mr. Reed, had the reputation in the country of being exceedingly rich. Several attempts had been made to rob his house, but they had all failed. At last, a servant, who had lived with him, and knew the way of the house, plotted with one Cain, a cooper, and one Digny, a schoolmaster, and a fellow of the name of McHenry, to rob the house on a Sabbath evening. Neither of them lived in that neighborhood: they rendezvoused in a town called Garvah, about a mile and a half from the place, where they purchased a couple of candles. They left that about eleven o'clock at night, and concealed themselves somewhere in the fields, till about two in the morning. They then came to the house, and had a consultation, which was the best method of entering. At first they got a long ladder, and reared it against the house, intending to strip off some of the thatch above the kitchen, and enter that way, as there was no flooring above it. This they afterwards gave up as too tedious, and likely to lead to a discovery. They were now about to abandon their design, when Digny, a man of desperate courage, upbraided them with cowardice, and said: "Will you resign an enterprise in which you are likely to acquire so large a booty, because there appear to be some difficulties in the way?" After a little parley, they came to the resolution to take the house by storm, and Digny agreed to enter first, by suddenly dashing the kitchen window in pieces. He stripped off his coat and waistcoat, tied a garter round each arm to confine his shirt, and one about each knee to render him more firm, and one around his waist, in which he stuck his pistols, and tied a handkerchief over his face, with three holes cut in it, one for his mouth, and two for his eyes. He then, in a moment, dashed the window to pieces, passed through it, and leaped down from the sill, and, though he lighted on a spinning-wheel, and broke it in pieces, yet he did not stumble. He flew in a moment to the door, unlocked it, and let two of the gang in, the fourth, McHenry, standing without as sentry. The lock being a very good one, the bolt went back with so loud a noise as to awaken Mr. Reed, who lay in a room off the kitchen, on the same floor. A young man of the name of Kennedy, a servant in the family, lay in a room next to that of his master, only separated from it by a narrow passage, which divided two sets of rooms on the right and left.

Cooper Cain, and the other accomplice, went immediately to the fire, which, being in that country formed of turf, was raked up in its own ashes, and began to pull out the coals in order to light their candle. Mr. Reed, having been awakened, as before related, jumped out of bed, and ran up the passage towards the kitchen, and cried out: "Who is there?" Digny, who was standing ready with his hanger drawn, waiting for the light, which the others were endeavoring to procure, hearing the voice, made a blow at the place whence it came, but did not see that the old man had not yet passed through the door into the kitchen; the hanger caught the bricks above the doorhead, broke out more than a pound weight off one of them, above the lintel, slided down, and laid Mr. Reed's right cheek open from the eye to the lower jaw. Had he been six inches more advanced, the blow would have cleft his head in two. The old man, feeling himself wounded, sprang desperately forward, and seized the assassin, who immediately dropped his hanger, which he could no longer use (for Mr. Reed, who was a powerful man, had seized him by both arms), closed in and grappled with Mr. R. Kennedy, who had been awake even before the window was broken, arose, and, while his master and Digny were struggling in the passage, got past them, went into the kitchen, where a loaded gun was hanging on hooks high up on the wall, ascended a large chest, seized the gun, which, he not being able to get readily out of the hooks, with a desperate pull brought the hook out of the wall, descended from the chest, squeezed by his master and the assassin still struggling in the passage, cocked it, and was going to fire, but could not discern his master from the robber. With great presence of mind he delayed till, Cain and his confederate having succeeded in lighting their candle (which they found very difficult, not having a match), he was able to discern between his master and Digny. In that moment he fired, and shot the latter through the heart, who instantly fell, and Mr. Reed on the top of him. Kennedy having discharged his piece, immediately cried out: "I've shot one of them; hand me the other gun!" Cain and his accomplice, hearing the report, and seeing what was done, extinguished their candle, and, with McHenry, fled.

All this was crowded into two or three minutes. Kennedy flew to the door, relocked it, threw chairs, tables, &c., against it and the window, reloaded his gun, and stood ready to meet another attack. At length, after several hours of the deepest anxiety, daylight returned, and brought assurance and confidence to this distressed family. The issue was, McHenry turned king's evidence, and the old servant was taken and hanged; but Cooper Cain fled, and was never heard of more.

The most remarkable feature in the case was, Mr. R. had lent his gun to a man who lived several miles off; on Saturday evening, Kennedy asked liberty from his master to go and bring it home, which was with difficulty granted. Had not the gun been brought home that night, there is no doubt the house would not only have been robbed, but every soul murdered; as it is evident they had intended to leave no person alive to tell tales.—*Life of Dr A. Clarke.*

STRANGE PRESERVATION OF DR. GILL.

In 1752, Dr. Gill was, one day, strongly impressed to leave his study. He could neither account for the impression, nor drive it from his mind; and finally, with some degree of hesitancy, yielded to the strange feeling, and retired from the room. But a short time after he had left, the chimney fell, and crushed the very table at which he was accustomed to sit. Then he saw the hand of God in it, and praised him for his mercy.

KNOX SAVED FROM DEATH.

An incident, somewhat similar to the above, occurred in the case of the celebrated divine J. Knox. He was accustomed to sit at the hearthside in the evenings with his family; his chair always occupying one particular spot. One evening, without explaining his reasons, he would neither sit in that place himself, nor allow any of his family to occupy it. The chair was in its accustomed place, but no one was suffered to fill it. In the course of the evening a shot was fired into the house and passed directly through the back of the empty chair. God had a work for his servant, and saved him from the hand of the assassin.

CASE OF WICKLIFF.

At one period of his life, this eminent reformer's health was considerably impaired by the labor of producing his numerous compositions, and the excitements inseparable from the restless hostilities of his enemies. Being supposed to be in dangerous circumstances, his old antagonists, the mendicants, conceived it next to impossible that so notorious a heretic should find himself near a future world without the most serious apprehensions of Divine anger. While they declared that the dogmas of the reformer had arisen from the suggestions of the great enemy, they anticipated some advantages to their cause, could the dying culprit be induced to make any recantation of his published opinions. Wickliff was in Oxford when this sickness arrested his activity, and confined him to his chamber. From the four orders of friars, four doctors, who were also called regents, were gravely deputed to wait on their expiring enemy; and to these the same number of civil officers, called senators of the city, and aldermen of the wards, were added. When this embassy entered the apartment of the rector of Lutterworth, he was seen stretched on his bed. Some kind wishes were first expressed as to his better health, and the blessing of a speedy recovery. It was presently suggested, that he must be aware of the many wrongs which the whole mendicant brotherhood had sustained from his attacks, especially in his sermons, and in certain of his writings; and, as death was now apparently about to remove him, it was sincerely hoped that he would not conceal his penitence, but distinctly revoke whatever he had preferred against them to their injury. The sick man remained silent and motionless until this address was concluded. He then beckoned his servants to raise him in his bed; and fixing his eyes on the persons assembled, summoned all his remaining strength, as he exclaimed aloud, "I shall not die, but live; and shall again declare the evil deeds of the friars." The doctors and their attendants now hurried from his presence, and they lived to feel the truth of his saying; nor will it be easy to imagine another scene more characteristic of the parties composing it, or of the times in which it occurred.

PROVIDENTIAL DELIVERANCE FROM DANGER.

The following article, lately handed to the editor of the Imperial Magazine, was written by a lady, whose danger it describes. The occurrence took place at Parr, in Cornwall, and is here presented to the reader without fiction or exaggeration.

I THINK it was in the year 1796, or 1797, during the month of November, being then about twenty-five years of age, that I met with the following occurrence. On the day in question, I had been at a town about five miles from my father's house, to which I was returning about five o'clock in the evening. In order to shorten my journey, the weather being cold and boisterous, I crossed a river near the sea, and travelled over a sandy beach, which was a usual route when the tide permitted; but at its farther extremity I had to pass under a cliff, which at high water the influx of the waves renders dangerous, and sometimes impracticable. On approaching this place, I found that the tide had made greater advances than I had anticipated; yet, thinking myself safe, being within half a mile of my home, I entered the water without any apprehension; but I had not proceeded far before I found it much deeper than I expected.

Having discovered my error, the cliff being on my left hand, and the turbulent sea on my right, I endeavored to turn my horse and retreat; but, in doing this, the poor animal fell over a projecting rock, which both the water and the darkness conspired to hide. By this fall I was thrown on the opposite side next the sea, and in an instant was buried in the waves. I, however, retained my senses—and, aware of my danger, held fast by the horse, which, after some struggling, drew me safely on a sandy beach.

But although I had thus far escaped the violence of the surf, my situation was dreadfully insecure. I now found myself hemmed in between two projecting points, with scarcely the possibility of getting round either. The tide was also encroaching rapidly on me, and the cliff it was impossible to scale. The wind, which had been blowing in an angry manner, now increased its fury, and the waves partook of the commotion. Thunder began to roll; and the vivid lightning, gleaming on the surface of the water, just interrupted the dominion of surrounding darkness, to show me the horror of my situation. This was accompanied with tremendous showers of hail, from the violence of which I could find no shelter. Thus circumstanced, I made a desperate effort to remount my horse, resolving to get round one of the projecting points, as my only chance of safety, or perish in the attempt; but all my efforts proved unsuccessful, and to this inability it is probable that I owe my life.

The tide gaining fast upon me, the poor animal, impelled by instinct, mounted a rock; and, taught by his success, as well as driven by necessity, I with difficulty followed the example. In this forlorn condition, I had time for a little reflection,— and but little, and in its first impulses it was exercised to less purpose; for I again made another ineffectual effort to remount, without duly considering the inevitable destruction that awaited me in case I had succeeded.

The waves, urged on by the tempest, to the whole rigor of which I stood exposed, soon told me that my retreat was unsafe. The rock on which myself and horse stood was soon covered with the rising tide, so that at times we were so nearly overwhelmed, that I could literally say, "thy waves and thy billows are gone over me." Surrounded thus by water, and rendered partially buoyant by its encroachment, my horse made another desperate effort, and happily gained a still more elevated crag. I soon followed, but with considerable difficulty; and as all further ascent appeared impracticable, in this place I at first expected to meet my fate.

Under this impression, with "but a step between me and death," I began seriously to reflect on the solemnities and near approach of eternity, into which, perhaps, a few minutes might hurry my disembodied spirit. In these awful moments, I can truly say, "I cried by reason of mine affliction unto the Lord, and he heard me;" for in the midst of the waters I knelt on a rock, and commended my soul to Him who hath all power in heaven and earth, well knowing that he was able to say to the turbulent ocean, "Hitherto shalt thou come, but no further, and here shall thy proud waves be stayed." For some time I felt a gleam of hope that I should survive the calamities of this disastrous night; but this was speedily destroyed by the increasing waters, which, nearly overwhelming us in this forlorn retreat, convinced me that the tide had not yet reached its utmost height.

Conceiving my own deliverance to be scarcely

possible, I felt anxious for the escape of my horse, and with this view endeavored to disencumber him of the bridle and saddle; that, in attempting to swim, he might find no impediment to prevent his reaching the shore. But while I was thus engaged, to my utter astonishment, by another violent exertion, my horse partially ascended on another crag, sufficiently so to keep his head above the water. I was not long in attempting a similar effort, in which I happily succeeded. This, however, was our last retreat, for just over our heads projected a large shelving rock, above which it was impossible for us to ascend. Here I sat down, with a mind somewhat composed, to wait the event which was hastily approaching, and with an expectation suspended between the hope of life and the fear of death.

After remaining in this situation for some time without being increasingly annoyed by the roaring waves, I began to hope that the tide had reached its height, and in this I was at length confirmed by the light of the rising moon, which, gleaming against the rocks, showed, to my inexpressible joy, that the water had actually begun to subside. I was now convinced that if we could retain our position until the water had retired, and I could survive the cold, we might both be preserved; but this was exceedingly doubtful, as the posture in which my horse stood was approaching to a perpendicular, and I was cherished by the warmth which proceeded from his breath, as I kept his head near my bosom, and derived from it a benefit which experience only can explain.

As the tide retired, and the moon became more elevated, I discovered, by its increasing light, to what a fearful height we had ascended, and the difficulty of getting down in safety appeared not less formidable than the means of getting up had been extraordinary. This, however, through a watchful Providence, was at last with care effected, without any material accident. On reaching the beach, from which the waves had now retired, I endeavored to walk towards my home, but found myself so benumbed that I was unable; and my voice was so nearly gone that I could not call for help, although I was not far from my father's house, and near many kind neighbors, who would have risked their lives to render me assistance, if they had known of my situation.

Being unable to proceed, I seated myself upon a rock, and expected, from the intense cold, that here I must perish, although I had escaped the fury of the tempest and the drenching of the waves. How long I remained here I cannot say with certainty, but, when almost reduced to a state of insensibility, I was providentially discovered in this position by my father's servant, who had been sent out to search for me, as from the lateness of the hour the family had anticipated some misfortune, and become alarmed.

I had been in the water about three or four

hours, and exposed to the disasters of the tempest from about five in the evening to half past eleven at night, at which time I reached my comfortable dwelling, much exhausted, but to the great joy of my affectionate parent, who, I doubt not, had been offering up petitions in my behalf to Him who hears the ardent whispers of the soul, when presented to him in sincerity.

For this preservation I desire to thank my God, but my words are poor and insufficient for this purpose. May all my actions praise him, and may my lengthened life be devoted to his glory!

T. K——N.

STRANGELY WARNED.

"I LEFT," said the Rev. E. J. Way, "the camp-meeting, on the river P——, on the morning of the last day. About two miles out from the ground I met the stage which was going up to the camp for persons who were to leave. Having been up all the preceding night, and laboring hard for several days, I was both tired and sleepy. As the horse was going along steadily, I fell into a doze. How long I slept, I know not, but I was greatly oppressed with a sense of danger. Rousing from sleep, I discovered myself in a narrow piece of road, with a high embankment on each side, but everything was safe. I looked to see what had so strangely excited my fears, but found nothing. Happening to look behind me, I saw the stage, which had passed awhile before, coming back. The vehicle was empty, and the horses were running furiously. The road was too narrow for them to pass without tearing my sulky into pieces. Escape seemed impossible. But suddenly turning my horse, I drove him up the steep bank, just in time to save my life. I could not but lift my heart in gratitude to God, who had so strangely warned, and timely delivered me."

DIVINE RETRIBUTION.

A YOUNG farmer, who lived at Belton near Epworth, in Lincolnshire, about the year 1720, being at breakfast in his house, started up, and cried, "I must go into the barn!" One asked him, "For what?" He said, "I cannot tell;" and ran away with his knife in his hand. The first thing he saw, when he came into it, was his father, who had just hanged himself on one of the beams. He immediately cut him down, took him in his arms, brought him into the house, and laid him on a bed. It was not long before he came to himself. He then looked upon his son, and said, "Now God has requited me! Three and twenty years ago I cut down my own father, who had hanged himself on that very beam!"

PART II.

ILLUSTRATIONS OF DIVINE PROVIDENCE IN THE RELIEF OF SUFFERING, DELIVERANCE FROM DANGER, &c.

"Surely he shall deliver thee from the snare of the fowler, and from the noisome pestilence. He shall cover thee with his feathers, and under His wings shalt thou trust: His truth shall be thy shield and buckler." — PSALM xci. 3, 4.

SECTION I.

Relief sent by Intelligent Agents.

REMARKABLE ANSWER TO PRAYER.

He made darkness his secret place; his pavilion round about him were dark waters and thick clouds of the skies.—PSAL. xviii. 11.

WHEN stationed on the island of Nantucket, in 1821, Brother V., from Connecticut, came there for the benefit of his health. He had passed through a furnace of affliction, and found God to be a strong tower and deliverer. It grieved him even to speak of his sad history. He was a charming singer; but sorrow had given each tone a plaintive air, which found a response in a sympathetic heart. As he spake of *sustaining grace*, a chastened cheerfulness would play upon his countenance, which was commonly marked with sadness; he was yet in very feeble health.

On one occasion he gave a number of us a sketch of his affliction, which sunk deep into my heart, and

I think it might be of special benefit to those who are passing through tribulations.

He had been master of a schooner in the West India trade, and, on his last voyage, left a most affectionate and lovely wife and child. With a valuable cargo, he started for home; but when in the Gulf Stream, I think in the night, a sudden squall struck them, and threw the schooner upon her beam-ends, and they were obliged to cut away her masts. She righted; but only the stern remained above the water. They secured a spar, which they lashed to the rails for their support. Some oranges washed from the hold which they caught, and bread also; but it was so salt, it greatly aggravated their thirst. When they had lashed themselves to the spar, I think seven in all, Brother V. requested them to get upon their knees, and he would ask God to have mercy on them. He also desired the mate to pray, who was a pious man. He did so, and they often had such prayer-meetings while on the wreck. One orange a day, and a little bread sufficed. They often saw vessels, but as they were so low, and could set no *signal*, they passed by. One came so near, they hoped to hail them, and all raised a feeble cry,—thirst had parched their mouths,—and they sank almost in despair. Large sharks were playing around them, coming on deck, and as near them as the water would permit, and pause, and look wishfully at them. On the sixth day, I think, a passenger died, and they could only put him overboard to the sharks. The oranges and bread had been consumed, and their strength exhausted, when, on the eighth day, towards night, they saw a black cloud arising, with forked lightnings darting in different directions. All said we can never survive *that*, except Brother V., who still felt a secret hope that they might be saved. He said, Let us get upon our knees once more, which they had hardly strength to do, and he was only able to whisper by reason of thirst. While praying he felt an overwhelming power come upon him, with liberty to come very near the mercy-seat, and ask what he would. His voice returned, and he cried out, *If thou* WILT, *thou* CANST *deliver us! Take us, Lord, and do with us as seemeth good in thy sight!* The Holy Spirit testified *deliverance shall come!* This mighty energy quickened both soul and body, and he started upon his feet, and sang with a clear voice what rushed upon his mind:—

> Ye fearful saints, fresh courage take;
> The clouds ye so much dread,
> Are big with mercy, and shall break
> In blessings on your head.

They were all deeply affected, as reviving hope inspired each heart. He exhorted them to look to God who had undertaken their cause, and see that they were faithfully lashed to the spar, and have no fear of the storm. Soon the horrors of darkness covered them; the lightning's glare, the thunder's roar, the sea raging, and themselves at times submerged in the angry waves,—all, all threatened instant death. But Brother V. was calm; he had hold of the promise of God, and held it fast. Yes, he was happy in the God of his salvation, and could say Glory to God!

The storm had spent its fury, and about the dawn of the ninth day, all was a dead calm. They saw, as the light increased, a brig near by them to the south. With the rising sun, came a gentle breeze from the south, and they saw them unfurling their sails, and the brig came slowly *close by the wreck*, before they saw it. The sufferers were soon on board, though unable to stand, and the captain exclaimed: "I cannot tell by what means you have lived through the night; but if it had not been for this storm, I should not have been within one hundred miles of this place."

Very few, if any, *real infidels* are found among sailors. They see and acknowledge the hand of the Lord in the mighty deep. There was not one there to sneer at the idea that our God is a hearer of prayer. When they heard of *that* prayer, and of the blessing of God upon them, and the assurance of deliverance, they were satisfied why they could not bear up against that tornado; but to save their lives must scud before it. It seemed as though the Lord's hand was upon them to bring them to the spot, and there waited for the morning.

A. K.

New Bedford, 1856.

THE CAPTIVE'S RELEASE.

In the war called Braddock's War, says a writer in the Christian Advocate, my father was an officer in the British navy. One night, as they were running close to the coast of Barbary, the officers on deck heard some person singing. A moment convinced them that he was singing the Old Hundred psalm tune. They immediately conjectured that the singer was a Christian captive, and determined to attempt his rescue. Twenty stout sailors, armed with pistols and cutlasses, manned the ship's boats, and approached the shore. Directed by the voice of singing and prayer, they soon reached the abode of the Christian captive. It was a little hut at the bottom of his master's garden, on a small river. They burst open the door, and took him from his knees, and, in a few moments, he was on the ship's deck frantic with joy. The account he gave of himself was, that his name was McDonald; that he was a native of Scotland, and had been a captive eighteen years; he obtained the confidence of his master, and had the privilege of living by himself. He said that he was not at all surprised when they broke open his door; for the Turks had often done so, and whipped him when on his knees.

THE LITTLE CAPTIVES STRANGELY DELIVERED.

In the year 1754, a dreadful war broke out in Canada, between the French and the English. The Indians took part with the French, and made many excursions as far as Pennsylvania, where they plundered and burnt the houses and murdered the people. In 1755, they reached the dwelling of a poor family from Wirtemberg, while the wife and one of the sons were gone to a mill, four miles distant, to get some corn ground. The husband, the eldest son, and two little girls, named Barbara and Regina, were at home. The father and son were killed by the savages, and the two little girls carried into captivity, with a great many other children, who were taken in the same manner. They were led many miles through woods and thorny bushes, that nobody might follow them. In this condition they were brought to the habitations of the Indians, who divided among themselves all the children whom they had taken captive.

Barbara was at this time ten years old, and Regina nine. It was never known what became of Barbara; but Regina, with a little girl of two years old, whom she had never seen before, were given to an old widow, who was to them very cruel. In this melancholy state of slavery these children remained nine long years, till Regina reached the age of nineteen, and her little companion was eleven years old. While captives, their hearts seemed to have been drawn towards what was good. Regina continually repeated the verses from the Bible, and the hymns which she had learnt when at home, and she taught them to the little girl. They often used to cheer each other with one hymn from the hymn-book used at Halle, in Germany:—

"Alone, yet not alone am I,
Though in this solitude so drear."

They constantly hoped that the Lord Jesus would, some time, bring them back to their Christian friends.

In 1764, the hope of these children was realized. The merciful providence of God brought the English Colonel Bouquet to the place where they were in captivity. He conquered the Indians, and forced them to ask for peace. The first condition he made was, that they should restore all the prisoners they had taken. Thus the two poor girls were released. More than four hundred captives were brought to Colonel Bouquet. It was an affecting sight to see so many young people wretched and distressed. The colonel and his soldiers gave them food and clothes, brought them to the town of Carlisle, and published in the Pennsylvania newspapers, that all parents who had lost their children might come to this place, and, in case of their finding them, they should be restored.

Poor Regina's sorrowing mother came, among

many other bereaved parents, to Carlisle; but, alas! her child had become a stranger to her: Regina had acquired the appearance and manner, as well as the language of the natives. The poor mother went up and down amongst the young persons assembled, but by no efforts could she discover her daughters. She wept in bitter grief and disappointment. Colonel Bouquet said: "Do you recollect nothing by which your children might be discovered?" She answered that she recollected nothing but a hymn, which she used to sing with them, and which was as follows:—

> "Alone, yet not alone am I,
>   Though in this solitude so drear;
> I feel my Saviour always nigh,
>   He comes the weary hours to cheer.
> I am with him, and he with me,
> Even here alone I cannot be."

The colonel desired her to sing this hymn. Scarcely had the mother sung two lines of it, when Regina rushed from the crowd, began to sing it also, and threw herself into her mother's arms. They both wept for joy, and the colonel restored the daughter to her mother. But there were no parents or friends in search of the other little girl; it is supposed they were all murdered: and now the child clung to Regina, and would not let her go; and Regina's mother, though very poor, took her home with her. Regina repeatedly asked after "the book in which God speaks to us." But her mother did not possess a Bible; she had lost everything when the natives burned her house.

THE PERSEVERING PURITAN.

Old Mr. Studley was a lawyer in Kent, of about £400 a year. He was a great enemy to the power of religion, and a hater of those that were then called Puritans. His son followed his steps, until the Lord awakened him as followeth. The young man was at London, and being drunk in company, and going late at night to his lodgings, fell into a cellar, and in the fall was seized with horror, for he thought he fell into hell. It pleased God he took little harm, but lay there sometime in a drunken state, his body being heated with what he drank, and his soul awakened, so that he thought he was actually in hell.

After he was come to himself, and had returned home to Kent, he fell into melancholy, and betook himself to read and study the Scriptures, and to much prayer; which at length his father perceived, and fearing he would turn Puritan, was troubled, and dealt roughly with him, making him dress his horses, which he humbly and cheerfully submitted to do. When his father perceived he sat up late at night reading his Bible, he denied him candle-light; but being allowed a fire in his chamber, he was wont to read by fire-light; and long after told a friend, that while he was dressing his father's horses in his frock, and reading by fire-light, he had those comforts and joys from the Lord, that he had scarce experienced since.

His father, seeing these means ineffectual, resolved to send him into France, that by the lightness of that country his melancholy might be cured. He went, and being at his own disposal, the Lord guiding, he placed himself in the house of a godly Protestant minister; and between them, after they were acquainted (and such is the likeness of saving grace in different subjects, that a little time will serve for Christians to be acquainted), there grew great endearments. He made great progress in speaking the language, and his father expecting an account from the gentleman with whom he lived of his speaking French, he sent it to him: but soon after, he had orders to return home. The father directing, or the son entreating, his landlord came with him into England, and both were welcomed at the father's house, he not knowing that his son's landlord was a minister. At last, the father found the French gentleman and his son at prayers, was angry, and sent him away.

Then Mr. Studley, having interest in a person of honor, a lady at White-hall, and his son now by his education being accomplished for such an employment, prevailed with her to take him for her gentleman to wait upon her in her coach. The father thought by a court life to drive away his son's melancholy, as he called his seriousness in religion. The lady had many servants, some given to swearing and rudeness, whom this young gentleman would take upon him to reprove with that prudence and gravity, that sin was abashed before him. If any of the servants were ill employed, and heard him coming, they would say, Let us cease, or be gone, for Mr. Studley is coming. After a year's time, his father waited on the lady to inquire of his son's behavior. She answered that she was glad she had seen his son, he had wrought such a reformation in her family. She that had formerly been troubled with unruly servants, by his prudent carriage was now as quiet in her house, as if she had lived in a private family in the country. Upon receiving this information the father stormed, "What, will he make Puritans in Whitehall?" He told the lady that was no place for his son, that he would take him with him, which, to her trouble, he did. When he had him at home in Kent, as his last refuge, he thought of marrying him; and to this end found out a match which he thought fit for his ends, to stifle the work of religion in his son. One evening, he bade him put on his best clothes the next morning, and ordered his servant to make ready their horses, and himself to wait on them. When they were riding on the way, he bade the servant ride before, and spoke to his son to this purpose: "Son, you have been a great grief to me, and having used much means to reclaim you from this way you are in, to no purpose, I have one more remedy to apply, in which, if you comply with me, I shall settle my estate upon you, else you shall never have a groat of it. I am riding to such a gentleman's house, to whose daughter I intend to marry you." The son said little, knowing that family to be profane, but went with his father, who before had been there on the same errand. They were entertained nobly: he had a sight of the young lady, a great beauty, and fell much in love with her. When they had taken their leave, and were on their way home, the father asked the son what he thought of the young lady? He answered, "There is no man living but must be taken with such an one;" but he feared she would not like him. The father bid him take no care for that. The wooing was not long: at three weeks' end they both went to London to buy things for the wedding.

The father had charged, that in the time of wooing at the house of the young lady's father, there should be no swearing nor debauchery, lest his son should be discouraged. Wedding clothes were bought, the day came, and the young couple were married. At the wedding dinner at the young lady's father's house, the mask was taken off; they fell to drinking healths, and swearing among their cups, and among others, the bride swore an oath; at which the bridegroom, as a man amazed, rose from the table, stepped forth, and went to the stable, took a horse, none observing it (all were

busy within), and rode away, not knowing what to
do. He bewailed himself, as he rode along, as
undone, and deservedly; for he had been so taken
in love, and business so hurried on his design, he
said he had at that time restrained prayer, and
slackened his communion with God; when, as in
that grand affair of his life, he should have been
doubly and trebly serious; and so might thank himself that he was utterly undone. He sometimes
thought of riding quite away; at last, being among
the woods, he led his horse into a solitary place,
tied him to a tree in his distress, and betook himself
to prayer and tears, in which he spent the afternoon.
The providence of God had altered his argument of
prayer, which was now for the conversion of his
new-married wife, or he was undone. This he
pressed with tears a great part of the afternoon,
and he did not rise from prayer without good hope
of being heard.

At the house of the bride there was hurry enough;
messengers (after they missed the bridegroom)
were sent every way. No news of him could be
obtained; he was wrestling, as Jacob once was,
at Peniel. In the evening he returned home, and
inquiring where his bride was, went up to her, and
found her in her chamber pensive enough. She
asked him if he had done well to expose her to
scorn and derision all the day. He entreated her
to sit down upon a couch there by him, and he
would give her an account of what he had been

doing, and tell her the story of his whole life, and what the Lord, through grace, had done for him.

He went over the story here above mentioned with many beautiful particulars, with great affection and tears, the flood-gates of which had been opened in the wood, and often in the relation would say, *Through grace,* God did so and so for me. When he had told her his story, she asked him what he had meant by those words so often used in the relation of his life, "*through grace,*" so ignorantly had she been educated; and asked him if he thought there was no grace for her, who was so wretched a stranger to God. Yes, my dear, said he, there is grace for you, and that I have been praying for this day in the wood, and God hath heard my prayer and seen my tears; let us now go together to him about it. Then they kneeled down by the couch side, and he prayed, and such weeping and supplication was there on both sides, that when they were called down to supper, they had hardly eyes to see with, so swelled were they with weeping. At supper the bride's father (according to his custom) swore. The bride immediately said, "Father, I beseech you, swear not." At which the bridegroom's father in a rage rose from the table; "What," says he, "is the devil in him? Hath he made his wife a Puritan already?" and swore bitterly, that he would rather set fire, with his own hands, to the four corners of his fair-built house, than ever he should enjoy it; and accordingly he did: for when he made his will, he gave his son (when he should die) ten pounds, to cut off his claim, and gave his estate to several persons of whom a Dr. Reeves was one; and not long after died.

Dr. Reeves sent for the gentleman, paid him his ten pounds, told him he had been a rebellious son, and had disobliged his father, and might thank himself. He received the money, and meekly departed.

His wife (the match was huddled up) had no portion promised, at least that he knew of; so that she was also deserted by his friends, only having £200 in her hands that had been given her by a grandmother, with which they stocked a farm in Sussex, where the writer of these memoirs hath often been and seen her, who had been highly bred, in her red waistcoat milking her cows. She was exceedingly cheerful, and was now become the great comforter and encourager of her husband. "God," said she, "hath had mercy on me, and any pains I can take are pleasant."

There they lived some years with much comfort, and had several children. After about three years, he was met in Kent, on the road, by one of the tenants of the estate, and saluted by the name of landlord. "Alas!" said he, "I am none of your landlord." "Yes you are," said the tenant, "I know more of the settlement than you do. Your father, though a cunning lawyer, could not alienate the estate from you, whom he had made joint purchaser. Myself and some other tenants know it, and have refused to pay any amount to Dr. Reeves. I have sixteen pounds ready for you, which I will pay to your acquittance, and this will serve you to wage law with them." He was amazed at this wonderful providence, received the money, sued for his estate, and in a term or two recovered it. "He that loseth his life for my sake and the Gospel's shall find it."

DELIVERANCE FROM STARVATION.

In 1662 Oliver Haywood, one of the rejected ministers, was reduced to the greatest distress. His large family was on the point of starvation. One morning he sent his servant to a gentleman's for relief. As there seemed to be no reasonable encouragement for such an appeal, the servant was afraid to go in. While he was walking to and fro before the house, he was discovered by the gentleman, and called in. Without being interrogated as to his business, five guineas were placed in his hands, with the remark, that some person had left them there for the use of his master.

FOX RELIEVED.

Fox, the martyrologist, was once in great straits. As he was one day passing through the streets in great dejection, and very weak from long-protracted hunger, an unknown person, without saying a word, slipped some money in his hands, sufficient to relieve his necessities, and comfort his desponding heart.

TEXT FOR A DISCOURAGED MINISTER.

AFTER the Rev. John Clark, of Trowbridge, had been engaged in the ministry for a few years, his mind became greatly depressed with a view of its responsibility, a sense of his own inability, and the want of more success. At length these discouragements were so oppressive, that he assured some Christian friends, one Sabbath afternoon, that he could preach no longer. In vain did they try to remove his difficulties, or to persuade him at least to address the congregation that evening, as no supply could be obtained. He declared his positive inability to preach any more. At this moment a pious old woman applied to speak to the minister. Being admitted, she requested him to preach from that text, "Then I said, I will speak no more in his name: but his word was in my heart as a burning fire shut up in my bones, and I was weary with forbearing, and I could not stay." (Jer. xx. 9.) She stated that she did not know where the words were, but that her mind was so much impressed with them, that she could not forbear to request him to preach from them that evening. Being satisfied that she was entirely unacquainted with the circumstances which had just transpired, Mr. Clark was assured that Providence had thus interposed that he should continue his ministry. He preached that evening from the text thus given, and never afterwards was greatly distressed on the subject.

REMARKABLE ANSWER TO PRAYER.

The following circumstance was related to me by the late Brother P., who was one of the most deeply pious men I ever knew, and for many years a class-leader in one of the Methodist churches in Philadelphia. This brother and myself were conversing one day on God's dealings toward his children, and how far we might expect the interposition of Divine Providence in answer to prayer, in the prosecution of the ordinary business of life, when, with tears of joy rolling down his cheeks, he related to me the following:—

After I had served out my time, and had married, which was about thirty-five years ago, I moved with my little family to Wilmington, about thirty miles below Philadelphia, and opened a small jewelry store, which was my business, trusting in God to prosper me. But, for several years, business was dull, and frequently, for weeks, I would not take in enough to keep my family in bread. This state of things continued so long, that I began to be discouraged, and to look around for some way of escape, but none appeared to offer. To make my difficulties worse, if possible, a very deep snow had fallen; it was midwinter, and, with the exception of a watch or two to repair, I had taken nothing in for many days. The wants of myself and family were pressing upon me, and two notes were coming due in Philadelphia in a few days for over $400. I was almost beside myself. I tried to borrow of my friends; but those who would have gladly assisted me, were, in consequence of the stringency of the times, unable to do so. I then tried to get the notes renewed, but this was positively refused; so that, apparently, my little all in a few days would be sold out by the sheriff. In this emergency I resolved to lay my case before the Lord, and, in order to do this, I set apart a day for fasting and prayer. This was on Friday; the next Monday the payment of the notes fell due; and my creditors told me plainly, if they were not paid they would immediately proceed against me.

Under these discouraging circumstances, I arose very early on the morning which I had devoted to prayer and fasting, and, locking myself in my room, commenced to pray. All day I stayed there; now reading some encouraging chapter in God's blessed book, then earnestly pressing my case at the throne of grace. Having thus passed the day, in the twilight of the evening I received what I believed to be a clear evidence that the Lord had heard my prayer, and that deliverance was at hand. I left the room happy in God. Frequently on Saturday, and also on the Sabbath, would my mind turn to my approaching difficulties; but, if I attempted to pray about it, the same evidence would be renewed that deliverance was at hand. On Monday morning I arose three hours before day. It had been snowing, and everything outward was dreary. I fell on my knees, and attempted to lay my case before the Lord again, when, with such power that I was thrown flat on my face on the floor, the evidence was again renewed—deliverance is at hand. I went to my store, made a fire, and sat down behind the counter. It was now nearly daylight. I would here state, that in my window there hung, as a show-set, an antiquated set of silver-ware, of English make, very heavy, having the English coat of arms engraved on it. It had been owned by my last employer for some twenty years, and by me for several. No one ever asked its price: it was simply in the window for a show. As the day began to dawn, I heard the creak of a wagon, and, on looking out, I perceived an old-fashioned gig drive up and stop, when a tall and venerable-looking man, whose locks were almost as white as the snow that lay on the ground, stepped down, and, after looking in my window for a moment, entered the store, and immediately asked the price of the silver-set in the window. I told him, with a faltering voice, five hundred dollars. He asked me, with a benevolent look, if I had a box that would hold it; and, on my answering in the affirmative, he told me he would take it. In a few minutes it was safely boxed, and put into his gig; the money in gold paid down, and he, with a smile, drove off. No one was ever able to tell from whence he came, or whither he went; nor have I ever been able to tell to this day. Suffice it to say, I procured a good horse, mounted him, and, a few minutes before three o'clock, was in Philadelphia, paid my notes, and returned the next day to my family, strong in faith, giving glory to God.

SINGULAR ANSWERS TO PRAYER.

The person to whom this anecdote refers, when speaking to the writer of the goodness of God, said: God never gave me what I wanted. He always gave me more. As a proof, I will tell you the following anecdote:—

When I married, I was a working man, and consequently, I had not much money to spare. In about three months after my marriage, I fell ill, and my illness continued for more than nine months. At that period, I was in great distress. I owed a sum of money, and had no means to pay it: it must be paid on a certain day, or I must go to jail. I had no food for myself or wife; and, in this distress, I went up to my room, and took my Bible. I got down on my knees, and opened it, laid my fingers on several of the promises, and claimed them as mine. I said: "Lord, this is thine own word of promise: I claim thy promises." I endeavored to lay hold of them by faith. I wrestled with God for some time in this way. I got up off my knees, and walked about some time. I then went to bed, and took my Bible, and opened it on these words: "Call upon me in the time of trouble: I will deliver thee, and thou shalt glorify me." I said: "It is enough, Lord." I knew deliverance would come, and I praised God with my whole heart. Whilst in this frame of mind I heard a knock at the door. I went and opened it, and a man handed me a letter. I turned to look at the letter; and when I looked up again, the man was gone. The letter contained the sum I wanted, and five shillings over. It is now eighteen years ago: and I never knew who sent it: God only knows. Thus God delivered me out of all my distress. To Him be all the praise!

G. A. was a very intimate acquaintance of mine, when he was living in the city of C——. I heard the story which I am about to relate from his own lips. He had been out of employment for a considerable time, and was, in consequence, so circumstanced as only to be enabled to keep himself from dying of hunger; in fact, he was left with but eightpence halfpenny in the world. Nor had he one friend, but the Friend that "sticketh closer than a brother." He went to chapel, thanking God for that which was past, and trusting him for that which was to come, and heard Dr. Newton preach a sermon in aid of a society that was under perplexing circumstances. Sensibly feeling the solemn appeal which the Rev. Doctor made to the liberality of the audience in behalf of the society, he at once gave the whole of his eightpence halfpenny. But he still trusted in Him who delivered the Israelites out of the hands of Pharaoh. He rose next morning penniless. But very soon after terminating the duties of his closet, a message came to him, saying that he was to commence work that morning. He has been in constant employment ever since; and God, in his infinite goodness and mercy, has raised him to a state of respectability. Truly the words of the Lord were verified in this man: "Them that honor me I will honor." 1 Sam. ii. 30.

UNEXPECTED DELIVERANCE.

One day, having business to transact with a person living in Broad Street, I was standing at his door-knocking for admittance. I was not heard until I had used the knocker a number of times. During this short interval, an important particular, which demanded of me five dollars more than I possessed, was brought to my mind with great force. A sigh of regret escaped me, followed by an ejaculatory prayer for relief. Turning round I saw a man, an Englishman, and an apparent stranger, walking fast down the street towards me. He came directly up to me, and with his hand thrust something into my vest pocket without saying a word. I felt in my pocket and found he had deposited a guinea, which was sufficient for my present need. He told me afterwards that he had fallen heir to an estate in England, and as he had realized spiritual benefit from my conversation on the subject of religion with some of his friends, he wished to show me a token of kindness for it, and therefore gave me the gold.—*Life of Scarlett.*

WONDERFUL DELIVERANCE.

THE *Watchman and Reflector* furnishes the following extraordinary incident:—

A clergyman, whom I personally knew, was charged by a woman with crime. A council, consisting of seven clergymen, with other persons, was convened. Two days were consumed by a long detail of circumstances, all of which bore the semblance of guilt, and which were sustained by the solemn affidavit and oath of the accusing party. Some time about ten o'clock of the closing day, the evidence being all adverse, although the minister solemnly protested his perfect innocency, a resolution was introduced to depose him. To this, he requested simply that the action upon it might be deferred till the next morning; which request was granted. He then proposed that the night should be devoted to special prayer, saying, "I believe there is a righteous God in heaven, and who, in his providence, governs upon earth. I believe I am his servant, and am willing to commit my case to him, after such an exercise in prayer." The clergymen were much exhausted, nevertheless two of them agreed to his proposition. He proposed that they should occupy distinct rooms till twelve. This being done, they met for social supplication. The two remarked as they met, one to the other, "I have had remarkable freedom in prayer, and I believe light will beam from some quarter, I know not where." While they were in prayer a loud rap was heard upon the door of the house. A messenger from the dwelling of the accuser was there, with an urgent entreaty that they would come immediately thither. On entering her apartment, she addressed them, saying, "I have sinned. He is perfectly innocent." By circumstances which she related, all were convinced that she then told the truth. She had been suddenly prostrated by disease, which terminated fatally. Her statements were given to the public. Great fear fell upon the people. A most powerful revival of religion ensued. The man of God was heard with great effect long after, as he ministered at the altar, living in the respect of all, and died in the sweetness of Christian assurance, leaning his head upon the arm of Jesus. And to this day many remember well the emphasis with which these words were quoted in that region; namely, "Verily there is a reward for the righteous; verily he is a God that judgeth in the earth."

REMARKABLE PROVIDENCE.

> God moves in a mysterious way,
> His wonders to perform;
> He plants his footsteps in the sea,
> And rides upon the storm.—COWPER.

There are few employments in which we can engage, more calculated to raise our hearts in gratitude to God, or encourage us to exercise resignation to his will, than an enlarged view of the dispensations of his providence. Who can turn to the sacred volume, and read the histories of Joseph, of Ruth, or of Esther, without recognising in the events connected with them the Divine hand, and saying with the devout Psalmist, "what time I am afraid I will trust in thee?" O, it is a delightful thought to the Christian, that all the affairs of the world are under the direction of Him who is the friend of those who love him, and who has engaged that "all things shall work together for their good." This holds true in reference to the most painful and adverse events, as well as those of a pleasing and prosperous kind.

The reader, in all probability, has long been acquainted with the history of the hymn from which I have selected a stanza as motto for this paper; and has often admired the good hand of God, that in so singular a manner delivered his dejected servant from self-destruction. The narrative I have now to give, in some of its parts, is not very dissimilar to that. The facts I received but a few evenings ago from an amiable lady of my congregation, and may be fully depended on, though I am not at liberty to mention names. I will give the account as nearly as possible in her own words:

"One afternoon, in the winter of about the year of 1808, I had occasion to go from F——— to S———, a distance of about two miles, and was unexpectedly detained till late in the evening, when I set out to return home alone. The night was very frosty and cold, and the ground was covered with a deep snow: when I had proceeded some short distance on the road, I was stopped by two Irishmen, who were, I believe, employed in some of the military works in the neighborhood. They asked me if I was going to F———: I gave them an evasive answer, and proceeded, not a little sensible of the dangerous circumstances in which I was placed. I went on a little distance, when they again accosted me, and once more I found means to give them an evasive reply. They passed on before me, and hid themselves in the hedge, and as I came near to them, I heard them engaged in a conversation that roused all my fears; I paused a moment, and then resolved to return to S——— with all possible speed. I set off to run, with one of these men almost immediately behind me. Once I fell on the ice almost exhausted, but remembering that my very life was at stake, I arose, and with aid communicated from on high, I pursued my journey till I reached the turnpike house, into which I ran, and fell in a state of exhaustion into one of the chairs. At some times during the pursuit the man was not more than three yards behind me.

"In about two hours I was in some degree recovered from my fright; and that I might not alarm my friends at S—— with my return, I resolved to spend the night with a pious old lady, a member of your church, who at that time was keeping the house of a baronet in S——, who was then, with all his family, absent from home.

"Late at night, probably at ten o'clock, I arrived at the house, and still terrified with what I had passed through, I knocked at the different doors with all my might, but it was long before I received an answer. At length the old lady, who was quite alone, came to a small back door situated among the stables, to inquire who was there. I mentioned my name, and she opened the door for my admission; I related the circumstances in which I was placed, and she begged me to stay over night, to which I very cheerfully assented, and accompanied her into the house.

"As we passed through the different parts of the house, I could not help remarking the circumstance, that *every* door, even those we had to enter, and from which I supposed the old lady had just passed, were all carefully made secure, nor was I a little surprised to find that she had no refreshment to offer me, except a little bread. But as my heart overflowed with gratitude for the deliverance I had experienced, I felt but little concern on that account. We retired to rest, and in the morning I left my friend with the feelings of thankfulness to the great Preserver of my life, for the escape I had on the past night, which I can never forget.

"From this period I could not but be struck with the attention and kindness which the good old lady manifested towards me. She seemed almost to regard me with an idolatrous regard, and I sometimes felt grieved at the trouble she gave herself to promote my comfort whenever I paid her a visit.

"Mark the sequel of these events.—About the year 1818, as her husband was dead, it was judged desirable that she should leave S—— to go to reside with her son in London. She came, therefore, to take her leave of me; and, after some general conversation, she said—'Miss——, I have somewhat particular to say to you. Do you remember coming to Sir —— ——'s house to me ten years ago?'—'Certainly I do,' I replied; 'nor can I ever forget the deliverance I then experienced.' —'Do you remember that you found all the doors bolted and barred?—that I came to you at a door among the stables,—and that I had nothing to offer you for your supper but a morsel of bread?'—'Yes, I remember it all.' Here she burst into tears, and as soon as she could, she told me, that at that time she had long labored under very heavy depression of spirits; that she had been tempted to destroy herself;—and that when I went to the house, she had fastened all the doors, and was passing down the yard with a determination to drown herself in the sea; but that my coming in the way I did, had clearly shown her the interposing hand of God had removed the temptation, and scattered the gloomy feelings of her mind. She added, that she had ever since endured much pain on account of the painful event:—that as she was not likely to live very long, and in all probability should never see me again, she had come to the determination, however painful the task, to disclose the whole affair, begging me never to relate the circumstance as long as she lived. I acceded to her request, nor was the affair known, even to her own family, till that event had taken place.

"A few months after this conversation had taken place, she passed, with a hope full of immortality and joy, very suddenly, from a world of sorrow and temptation, to enter on a state of bliss, where, I doubt not, she shall for ever enjoy all the blessedness connected with eternal life."

Such are the leading circumstances of the case as detailed to me. It needs no comment. How many such providences occur to prevent greater evils, will only be known by us at the great day, when all events shall be disclosed. If the relation of these circumstances should be the happy means of leading any of the children of distress to cast their burdens on the Lord, and should enable them to resist the temptations of Satan, and to triumph over bodily and mental disease, the purposes for which they are mentioned will be fully answered.

SEASONABLE RELIEF.

THE following is from the Life of Thomas Cranfield:—

The year 1789 was one of peculiar suffering, owing to a great stagnation of business. His children often cried for bread, when there was none to give them. His distress of mind, under such circumstances, can only be conceived by those who have endured a like affliction; but he was enabled to wrestle hard with God in prayer, and he found him faithful to his promise—"Call upon me in the day of trouble, and I will deliver thee." Sometimes, however, when his mind was filled with doubts and fears, his affectionate wife would inspire him with fresh confidence, by bidding him to remember the goodness of the Lord towards them in former days, and would repeat to him the verse—

> "His love in times past forbids me to think
> He'll leave me at last in trouble to sink;
> Each sweet Ebenezer I have in review
> Confirms his good pleasure to help me quite through."

On one of these occasions he had remained at

home the whole of the morning, praying with his wife and children. Dinner time arrived, but they had no food to place upon the table. His confidence in God was, however, unabated. "Let us pray again," he said, "for the Lord *will* answer prayer." They did so, and scarcely had arisen from their knees, when a knock was heard at the door. It was a female friend, a pious woman, who owed him a shilling. "Come in," said Mr. C., "thou blessed of the Lord! I know what you are come for." "Do you?" said she; "then it is almost more than I know." "Why," said he, "you have some money for me. I am in necessity, and the Lord has sent you to relieve me." "Well," said the woman, "that is singular enough; I was sitting at home by myself, when the thought struck me that I would go and see Mr. Cranfield. I had got part of the way on my journey, when I remembered I owed you a shilling, so I turned back for it, and here it is." He took the money, exclaiming to his wife, "O what a blessed thing it is to live by faith upon the Son of God! Who ever trusted in him, and was confounded?"

SECTION II.

Relief sent by Unintelligent Agents.

THE FRENCH ARMAMENT.

The destruction of the French armament, under the Duke d'Anville, in the year 1746, ought to be remembered with gratitude and admiration by every inhabitant of this country. This fleet consisted of forty ships of war; was destined for the destruction of New England, was of sufficient force to render that destruction, in the ordinary progress of things, certain; and sailed from Chebucto, in Nova Scotia, for this purpose.

In the mean time, our pious fathers, apprised of their danger, and feeling that their only safety was in God, had appointed a season of fasting and prayer to be observed in all their churches. "While Mr. Prince was officiating" in this church (Old South Church) on this fast day, and praying most fervently to God, to avert the dreaded calamity, a sudden gust of wind arose (the day had till now been perfectly clear and calm), so violent as to cause a loud clattering of the windows. The reverend pastor paused in his prayer, and looking round upon the congregation with a countenance of hope, he again commenced, and with great devotional ardor, supplicated the Almighty God to cause that wind to frustrate the object of our enemies, and save the country from conquest and popery. A tempest ensued in which the greater part of the French fleet was wrecked on the coast of Nova Scotia. The Duke d'Anville the principal general, and the second in command, both committed suicide. Many died with disease, and thousands were consigned to a watery grave. The small number that remained alive, returned to France without health and without spirits. "And the enterprise was abandoned, and never again resumed."

VESSEL SAVED BY A DOLPHIN.

Mr. Colstone, an eminent merchant of Bristol, who lived a century ago, was remarkable for his liberality to the poor, and equally distinguished for his success in commerce. The providence of God seemed to smile, in a peculiar manner, on the concerns of one who made so good a use of his affluence. It has been said that he never insured, nor ever lost a ship. Once, indeed, a vessel belonging to him, on her voyage home struck on a rock, and immediately sprang a leak, by which so much water was admitted as to threaten speedy destruction. Means were instantly adopted to save the vessel, but all seemed ineffectual, as the water rose rapidly. In a short time, however, the leak stopped without any apparent cause, and the vessel reached Bristol in safety. On examining her bottom, a fish, said to be a dolphin, was found fast wedged in the fracture made by the rock when she struck; which had prevented any water from entering during the remainder of the voyage. As a memorial of this singular event, the figure of a dolphin is carved on the staves which are carried in procession, on public occasions, by the children who are educated at the charity schools founded by Mr. Colstone.

A PRAYER-ANSWERING GOD.

A COMPANY of Moravian missionaries were on their voyage from London to St. Thomas, on board the ship Britannia. Nothing remarkable occurred till they discovered a pirate.

The pirate ship approached till it came within gun-shot of the Britannia; and then, from the cannon ranged along its deck, began to pour out a heavy fire. There were grappling irons on board, or strong sharp hooks, fixed to long ropes ready to throw into the Britannia, and hold her fast, while the pirates should board her, and do their work of destruction. It seemed that there was little chance of escape from such an enemy. But the captain, whose heart was sinking at the fearful prospect before him, did not know what powerful helpers he had below, in the few peaceable missionaries, whose fervent prayers were then ascending, through the noise of the fight, to heaven.

The moment the pirates tried to throw their grappling irons across to the other ship, their own was tossed violently, and the men who held the ropes were thrown by force into the sea. Vexed by this disaster, the pirate captain sent others who shared the same fate. Seeing that he could not succeed in this manner, he resolved to fire at the Britannia, till she sunk with repeated blows. But this effect strangely failed also; for the balls missed their aim, and fell into the sea. The smoke of the frequent charges was very dense, and hung about the vessels for some minutes, hiding them from each other's view. At last a sudden gust of wind cleared it away; and, to the amazement of the pirate captain, the Britannia was seen at a distance with all her sails spread to the wind, speeding swiftly away from the attack, and they were forced in great anger to abandon their cruel purposes. Thus wonderfully had God appeared, and saved the vessel in answer to prayer. The missionaries' prayers had been greatly honored, but they were to have a further fruit still.

Five years afterward, during which the missionaries had been diligently preaching the Gospel at St. Thomas, they, and the other missionaries on the island, agreed to meet together to celebrate the anniversary of their deliverance from the pirates, and to thank God for his other mercies. As they sat together, word was brought that a stranger wished to speak to them, and, at their permission, a tall man entered, with fine bold features, and a bold expression of face. The missionaries wondered, and one asked what was the stranger's business with them.

"First answer me one question," said he. "Are you the men who came to this island five years ago, in the English ship Britannia?"

"We are," replied the missionary who had spoken.

"And you were attacked upon the sea by pirates?"

"Exactly, but why are these questions?"

"Because," answered the stranger, "I am the captain who commanded the vessel which attacked you." Then the missionaries looked at one another in silent wonder, as their former enemy continued: "The miraculous way in which your vessel escaped was the cause of my own salvation from the power of sin, through faith in Christ."

It would be too long to tell you all his words; but you may imagine with what unspeakable joy the missionaries listened to his tale, as he went on to tell them how, in his vexation at their strange escape, he had made inquiries for the captain of the Britannia, and learned that it was through the prayers of the Moravian missionaries of St. Thomas, and how, not understanding how a vessel could be saved from pirates by prayer, he resolved to know the Moravian brothers. He sold his vessel, and in the United States of America one day visited a Moravian chapel, and heard a sermon from the words, "Work out your own salvation with fear and trembling." He sought the preacher, and heard from him the way of salvation through Jesus Christ, "and thus," he concluded, "from a pirate captain I am a poor sinner, justified by the grace and mercy of Christ, and my chief hope has been that I might one day be able to see you, and relate to you my miraculous conversion. This joy is granted to me to-day."

He ceased, and you may imagine the feelings of the missionaries. They were met to celebrate their deliverance from the pirates on that day five years ago, through prayer, and there stood before them the pirate captain himself, not fierce now, but humble and pious, who traced his own deliverance from the bondage of Satan to the same prayer that rescued them from him! They all knelt down together before God, and thanked him for his great mercies.

THE PIOUS CAPTAIN AND THE PIRATE SHIP.

Captain S——, of W——, Massachusetts, relates, that on a voyage to Brazil, in the spring of 1833, while sailing near Cape St. Roque, he descried, one morning, in the distance, a suspicious-looking vessel, under a press of canvas, standing toward him. From several circumstances, he was led to imagine that she was occupied by pirates, who were advancing to plunder and murder. Still, not being certain of the fact, he concluded to keep the vessel on her course. The suspicious schooner continued to gain upon him, and soon, by the help of the glass, he saw her deck covered with men, and a long eighteen pounder on a swivel, so prepared as to turn in any direction desired. She was evidently a faster sailer than his own vessel; he concluded, therefore, that if he turned out of his course, he would at length be overtaken, and from the pirates, excited and exasperated by a long chase, little mercy could be expected. The captain was a professed Christian, a strong believer in the *providence of God*, and emphatically a *man of peace*. Instead of fighting with carnal weapons, he determined to fight him with spiritual ones. Having religious tracts on board, he determined, as soon as the schooner came alongside, to go on board, and present his tracts to the captain and crew, and preach to them in a bold, but affectionate manner, appropriate truths from the Gospel of Christ. He ordered all the hands to go down below, but the man at the helm. This he did partly to keep them from being agitated and from agitating his own mind, and partly to do away with all appearance of opposition against the approaching foe. Then, committing his men and himself to God, he patiently awaited the pirate's arrival. The schooner came nearer and nearer, till at length even the figures of the men could be distinctly seen by the naked eye. A fearful crisis was fast coming. But still the captain never shrunk nor veered from his course for a moment. Suddenly the pirates altered their course, hauled the vessel upon the wind, and stood away as rapidly as sail and surge could carry them! From the fact that they saw no men on board but Captain S—— and the helmsman, and no manifestations of fear, the pirates might have been led to suspect that there was a large armed force below, or some other decoy prepared; and thus concluded it dangerous to attempt their hostile design. Whatever process of thought it was, however, which led them to retreat, who will fail to recognise in that process an overruling Providence, protecting in this instance, as in many others, the man who resists not evil, but in the hour of threatened violence depends not on his own arm, but on God's?

DELIVERANCE FROM CAPTIVITY.

This day, in the evening, Brother K—— was called on to perform the funeral solemnities of Mrs. Scott. Perhaps she has been as great a female sufferer as I have heard of. The following account, in substance, was taken from her own mouth, some time ago, by J. Kobler, who performed her funeral rites :—

Her maiden name was Dickenson. She was married to a Mr. Scott, and lived in Powell's Valley; at which time the Indians were very troublesome, often killing and plundering the inhabitants. On a certain evening, her husband and children being in bed, eight or nine Indians rushed into the house; her husband being alarmed, started up, when all that had guns fired at him. Although he was badly wounded, he broke through them all, and got out of the house. Several pursued him and put an end to his life. They then murdered and scalped all her children before her eyes, plundered her house, and took her prisoner. The remainder of the night they spent around a fire in the woods, drinking, shouting, and dancing. The next day they divided the plunder, with great equality; among the rest of the goods was one of Mr. Wesley's hymn-books; she asked them for it, and they gave it to her; but when they saw her often reading in it, they were displeased, called her a conjurer, and took it from her. After this they travelled several days' journey towards the Indian towns; but, said she, my grief was so great, I could hardly believe my situation was a reality, but thought I dreamed. To aggravate my grief, one of the Indians hung my husband's and my children's scalps to his back, and would walk the next before me. In walking up and down the hills and mountains, I was worn out with fatigue and sorrow; they would often laugh when they saw me almost spent, and mimic my panting for breath. There was one Indian who was more humane than the rest; he would get me water, and make the others stop when I wanted to rest; thus they carried me on eleven days' journey, until they were all greatly distressed with hunger; they then committed me to the care of an old Indian in the camp, while they went off hunting.

Whilst the old man was busily employed in dressing a deer-skin, I walked backward and forward through the woods, until I observed he took no notice of me; I then slipped off, and ran a considerable distance, and came to a cane-brake, where I hid myself very securely. Through most of the night I heard the Indians searching for me, and answering each other with a voice like that of an owl. Thus was I left alone in the savage wilderness, far from any inhabitants, without a morsel of food, or a friend to help, but the common Saviour and Friend of all: to Him I poured out my com plaint in fervent prayer, that He would not forsake in this distressing circumstance. I then set out the course I thought Kentucky lay, though with very little expectation of seeing a human face again, except of the savages, whom I looked upon as so many fiends from the bottomless pit; and my greatest dread was that of meeting some of them whilst wandering in the wilderness.

One day, as I was travelling, I heard a loud human voice, and a prodigious noise, like horses running; I ran into a safe place and hid myself; and saw a company of Indians pass by, furiously driving a gang of horses which they had stolen from the white people. I had nothing to subsist on but roots, young grape-vines, and sweet-cane, and such like produce of the woods. I accidentally came near a place where a bear was eating a deer, and drew near, in hopes of getting some, but he growled and looked angry; so I left him, and quickly passed on. At night, when I lay down to rest, I never slept but I dreamed of eating. In my lonesome travels, I came to a very large shelving rock, under which was a fine bed of leaves; I crept in among them, and determined there to end my days of sorrow. I lay there several hours, until my bones ached in so distressing a manner that I was obliged to stir out again. I then thought of, and wished for, home; and travelled on several days, till I came where Cumberland river breaks through the mountains.

I went down the cliffs a considerable distance, until I was affrighted, and made an attempt to go back; but found the place down which I had gone was so steep that I could not return. I then saw but one way that I could go, which was a considerable perpendicular distance down the bank of the river. I took hold of the top of a little bush, and for half an hour prayed fervently to God for assistance; I then let myself down by the little bush till it broke, and I fell with great violence to the bottom. This was early in the morning; and I lay there a considerable time determined to go no further. About ten o'clock I grew so thirsty, that I concluded to crawl to the water and drink; after which I found I could walk. The place I came through, as I have been since informed, is only two miles, and I was four days in getting through it. I travelled on till I came to a little path, one end of which led to the inhabitants, and the other to the wilderness; I knew not which end of the path to take; after standing and praying to the Lord for some time, I turned to the wilderness; immediately there came a little bird of a dove color to my feet, and fluttered along the path which led to the inhabitants. I did not observe this much at first, until it did it a second and third time; I then understood this as a direction of Providence, and took the path which led me to the inhabitants.—
From the Journal of Bishop Asbury.

THE LORD KINDLY PROVIDES.

Rev. Charles S. Robinson, a missionary at St. Charles, Missouri, who lately deceased, is said to have suffered during his missionary labors, the privations which few ever have suffered. But his Heavenly Father, in whom he trusted, and who is ever mindful of the wants of his children, watched over him, and kindly provided relief when he had been driven to the greatest extremity. The following is from his own pen on the subject:—

"I went to the store for necessary food, and was refused, because I had not money to pay for it. I returned to my destitute family; you may imagine with what feelings. None knew of our distress but those who felt it. It was in November. The cold wind found a ready entrance to our cabin, and we had no wood. I procured a spade, with a view of remedying the evil, as well as I could, by throwing up a bank around the house. I had scarcely dug into the earth a foot, when, to my surprise, I threw up a *silver dollar*, which had long been buried beneath the surface! The goodness of God filled my heart, and I wept plentifully at the sight of it. This served to furnish us with a little wood and a few necessaries."

THE SOLDIER AND THE POOR WOMAN.

A POOR woman, who owed her landlord fourteen pounds, scraped seven together, which she brought him. He absolutely **refused to take less than** the whole, yet detained her in talk till the evening. She then set out on a cart. When she was within a mile of home, she overtook a soldier, who said he was exceedingly tired, and earnestly entreated her to let him ride with her on the cart, to which she at last consented. When they came to her house, finding there was no town within two miles, he begged he might sit by the fireside till morning. She refused at first, as hers was a lone house, and she alone with her girls, but at last consented. At midnight, two men, who had blackened their faces, broke into the house and demanded her money. She said: "Then let me go into the next room and fetch it." Going in, she said to the soldier: "You have requited me well for my kindness, by bringing your comrades to rob my house." He asked: "Where are they?" She said: "In the next room." He started up and ran thither. The men ran away with all speed. He fired after them, and shot one dead, who proved to be her landlord! So that a soldier was sent to protect an innocent woman, and punish a hardened villain.—*Rev. John Wesley's Journal.*

SECTION III.

Relief sent by Mental Impressions, Dreams, &c.

TAUGHT BY A DREAM.

It has been well observed that we may place too little, as well as too much, dependence upon dreams. For while many foolishly regard every trifling imagination of the thought in sleep to be either the prognostication or the revelation of an important event, there are others who believe that all dreams should be entirely disregarded, and think it a mark of profound ignorance and superstition, if not of sin, to suppose that dreams can have any connection with our line of duty. Yet our own experience, and the testimony of many men of sound judgment, extensive learning, and deep piety, sufficiently confute the latter opinion. In the Holy Scriptures, we are informed of people having been warned of God in dreams (Gen. xx. 3; Matt. ii. 22, &c.); and if we deny that any spiritual agency is in operation, do we not deny the truth of divine revelation? How such communications are made, we know not; but that they have been made, even in our own days, we know full well. We hear the sound caused by the wind, "but cannot tell whence it cometh, and whither it goeth:" so are all the communications of the Spirit of God. The following fact not only establishes the truth of our position, but manifests the care of Divine Providence towards his helpless creatures.

Some years ago, Ann Jane M——, then about fourteen years of age, residing with her parents at L——, near Belfast, received a slight injury in one of her toes. Little attention was paid to the wound at first; and, as was customary for children in that country, she wore no shoes. As might have been expected, the injury became worse; the swelling increased, and extended rapidly in the foot and leg. The tumor afterwards broke, and discharged, giving excessive pain, and exhibiting an alarming appearance. The nail of the toe dropped off; and the sufferings of the little girl became so violent that surgical advice was resorted to. When the doctor examined it, he said it was then too late to apply any remedy for the purpose of attempting to heal it; that the inflammation was so great, that its progress could only be arrested by amputation, and if that were not immediately done, the consequence would soon be fatal. This step, generally so repugnant to our feelings, the parents were unwilling to allow, and applied to another surgeon.

Poulticing was then tried, but without success: the whole limb became inflamed, and the swelling increased. A consultation of surgeons took place on the matter, and they unanimously agreed that nothing could save the poor sufferer's life but the amputation of the toe. It was then decided that the operation should take place upon an appointed day, when the girl was to be brought to town, and a car provided to take her home again.

The patient had passed a sleepless night: the agony she suffered was so excruciating that she could not obtain a moment's repose. "Tired nature's sweet restorer, balmy sleep," came not to her relief: how true the words of the poet,—

"The wretched he forsakes!"

She was prepared for the journey, and sat waiting the arrival of the car, holding her limb with her hands, attempting to allay her torture. While in this position she dropped asleep, and seemed to enjoy a short cessation from pain. In about an hour she awoke, and with a happy smile said, "O, I dreamed that my leg was well! I thought that I was taken to Dr. B——, in Belfast; that when we went to his house, I saw him standing in his room, with his coat off, and his shirt-sleeves rolled up. He had red hair, and wore a black apron. I thought he cured me without cutting off my toe." The fond parents were puzzled how to act: the child's dream appeared remarkable, for she had never heard of Dr. B——; yet in the anxious hope that there might be such a person, and that he could heal the sore, they went to Belfast and inquired for him. After some search, they found there was a surgeon of that name attending the dispensary of —— Lane. Thither they repaired, and, on entering the room, were astonished to see a man answering precisely the description in the child's dream. He examined the toe, and immediately applied a remedy, putting a tight bandage on the seat of pain. She was ordered to return again to have it dressed. She did so, and the third visit was her last. Restoration rapidly took place; in less than a month the pain and sore were completely gone; and she has continued well to this day

---

"I HAVE JUST MET WITH A WONDERFUL MANIFESTATION OF DIVINE PROVIDENCE."

Thus spake a venerable man of God, some months since, on meeting me upon one of the streets of our city. He was aged, though active; had a wife and children to provide for, and withal was poor. After introducing the subject in the manner, and with the words at the head of this article, he proceeded to narrate the following facts. That morning as he sat down at his table with his wife and children, to partake of a very scanty breakfast, his partner told him it was the very last in the house, and said,

"Husband, where is the dinner to come from?" He replied that he knew not, and added, "God will provide." After finishing their humble meal, instead of offering thanks to God in the customary manner, they bowed down upon their knees, and by "prayer and supplication, with thanksgiving," made known their requests. Before concluding their devotions, a knock was heard at the front door of his house. On finishing the prayer, he went to the door, and much to his surprise, there stood before him a most excellent and pious brother, a member of one of the Presbyterian churches of this city; a gentleman and Christian, whose worth was "known and read" of many, but whose numerous acts of noble charity will never be fully manifested, until the "judgment of the great day." His astonishment at seeing this excellent man was the greater, because he had but a partial personal acquaintance with him, and he had never before visited his dwelling. Upon invitation he entered, and after being seated, asked the old gentleman how it was with him and his family. After telling him, in reply, that physically they were well, and spiritually they were at "peace with God and all mankind," he apologized for keeping him at the door for a short time, and told him of what his wife had said at the commencement of their meal, and further remarked that when he knocked, they were engaged in fervent prayer to God, commending themselves in their necessitous state to his fatherly care.

After listening to his simple and affecting narrative, this brother told him that he had left his home thus early for the purpose of visiting a poor widow, who lived some distance beyond him, and without the most remote thought of calling on him or his family. On passing his door, the impression was made strongly upon his mind, that he ought to stop and inquire after his health. He resisted it, and went on, because of not being, as he supposed, sufficiently intimate with him to justify such a visit, and particularly so early in the day. He had not, however, progressed very far, before the impression became so strong, that he stopped, and after reflecting for a moment or two, determined to yield to it. He had done so. Whilst in the act of saying a few words of encouragement to this aged servant of God, he took leave of him, at the same time pressing into his hand a *ten dollar gold piece.*

Reader, your judgment now is, this was truly a direct and "wonderful manifestation of Divine Providence," in behalf of his needy child. The "eye of the Lord" was over him for good, and thus sent help from a quarter least expected, and at the very time in which it was most called for. Christian reader, in straitened circumstances, have you ever been led, like old Jacob, to say, "all these things are against me?" If so, be ashamed, heartily ashamed, of having thus dishonored your God. He has never failed you, or ceased to "care for you." Remember his plain, pointed, and all-comprehensive command, "Trust in the Lord." "It is better to trust in the Lord than to put confidence in men; it is better to trust in the Lord than to put confidence in princes." Write these blessed Scriptures upon the tablet of your memory. Give them a permanent lodgment in the innermost recesses of your heart's warmest affections. Now in spirit, and if possible, upon your knees, consecrate yourself fully to your God, and resolve from this moment never again to succumb in the day of clouds and darkness; never again to doubt the good Providence that has thus far always been over you. Resolve that NOW, *henceforth* and *for ever*, you will, "by prayer and supplication, with thanksgiving, let your requests be made known unto God." Then may you realize the fulfilment of the promise annexed, viz.: "The peace of God, which passeth all understanding, shall keep your heart and mind through Jesus Christ."

REMARKABLE INSTANCE OF DIVINE PROVIDENCE IN THE CASE OF A SCOTCH CLERGYMAN.

In the year 1681, a gentleman who lived near Aberdeen, came to town on purpose to ask advice of some of the ministers. He told them he had an impression continually following him, to go to Rotterdam. They asked him, "For what reason?" But he could tell none: on which they advised him to stay at home. Some time after he came again, and informed them, "Either I must go to Rotterdam, or die; for this impression follows me day and night, so that I can neither eat, nor drink, nor sleep." They then advised him to go. Accordingly he embarked and came to Rotterdam. As he was landing, his foot slipped, and he fell into the sea. A gentleman who was walking on the quay, leaped in and caught hold of him, brought him out, and conducted him to an inn. He then procured some dry linen for him, and a warm bed, in which he slept sound for several hours. When he awoke, he found the gentleman sitting by his bedside, who, taking it for granted he would be hungry, had bespoke a dinner, which, to his great satisfaction, was immediately served up. The Scotch gentleman desired the other to ask a blessing, which he did in such a manner as quite surprised him. But he was still more surprised, both at the spirit and language in which he returned thanks; and asked him, "Sir, are not you a minister?" He answered, "I am: but I was, some time since, banished from Scotland." The other replied, "Sir, I observed, though you behaved quite decently, you seemed to be extremely hungry. Pray, permit me to ask, how long is it since you took any food?" He said, "Eight and forty hours;" on which the Scot started up and said, "Now I know why God sent me to Rotterdam. You shall want for nothing any more: I have enough for us both." Shortly after the revolution ensued: and he was reinstated in his living.

REMARKABLE CURE OF DISEASE.

A FRIEND once told me that, amongst other symptoms of high nervous excitement, he had been painfully harassed by the want of sleep. To such a degree had this proceeded, that if, in the course of the day, any occasion led him to his bed-chamber, the sight of his bed made him shudder at the idea of the restless hours he had passed upon it. In this case, it was recommended to him to endeavor, when he lay down at night, to fix his thoughts on something at the same time vast and simple—such as the wide expanse of ocean, or the cloudless vault of heaven; that the little hurried and disturbing images that flitted before his mind might be charmed away, or hushed to rest, by the calming influence of one absorbing thought. Though not at all a religious man at the time, the advice suggested to his mind, that if an object at once vast and simple was to be selected, none could serve the purpose so well as that of God. He resolved then to make the trial, and to think of Him. The result exceeded his most sanguine hopes: in thinking of God he fell asleep. Night after night he resorted to the same expedient. The process became delightful; so much so, that he used to long for the usual hour of retiring, that he might fall asleep, as he termed it, in God. What began as a mere physical operation, grew by imperceptible degrees into a gracious influence. The same God who was his repose at night, was in all his thoughts by day. And at the same time this person spoke to me, God, as revealed in the gospel of his Son, was "all his salvation," so inscrutable are the ways by which God can "fetch home again his banished."

REMARKABLE INTERPOSITION OF DIVINE PROVIDENCE.

THOMAS HOWNHAM, the subject of the following providence, was a poor man, who lived in a lone house or hut upon a moor, called Baramourmoor, about a mile from Lowick, and two miles from Doddington, in the county of Northumberland. He had no means to support a wife and two children, save the scanty earning obtained by keeping an ass, on which he used to carry coals from Baramour coalhill to Doddington and Wooler; or by making brooms of the heath, and selling them around the country. Yet, poor and despised as he was in consequence of his poverty, in my forty years' acquaintance with the professing world, I have scarce met with his equal, as a man that lived near to God, or one who was favored with more evident answers to prayer. My parents then living at a village called

Hanging Hall, about one mile and a half from his hut, I had frequent interviews with him, in one of which he was solicitous to know whether my father or mother had sent him any unexpected relief the night before. I answered him in the negative, so far as I knew: at which he seemed to be uneasy. I then pressed to know what relief he had found; and how? After requesting secrecy, unless I should hear from any other quarter (and if so, he begged I would acquaint him), he proceeded to inform me, that, being disappointed in receiving money for his coals the day before, he returned home in the evening, and to his pain and distress found that there was neither bread nor meal, nor anything to supply their place, in his house; and that his wife wept sore for the poor children who were both crying for hunger; that they continued crying till they both fell asleep; that he put them to bed, and their mother with them, who likewise soon went to sleep, being worn out with the sufferings of the children and her own tender feelings. Being a fine moonlight night, he went out of the house, to a retired spot, at a little distance, to meditate on those remarkable expressions in Hab. iii. 17–19. Here he continued, as he thought, about an hour and a half, found great liberty and enlargement in prayer; and got such a heart-loathing and soul-humbling sight of himself, and such interesting views of the grace of God, and the love of his adorable Saviour, that though he went on purpose to spread his temporal wants before his Lord, yet, having obtained a heart-attracting and soul-captivating view of him by faith, he was so enamored with his beauty, and so anxious to have his heart entirely under his forming hand, that all thought about temporals was taken away.

In a sweet, serene, and composed frame of mind, he returned into his house; when by the light of the moon, through the window, he perceived something upon a stool or form (for chairs they had none) before the bed; and after viewing it with astonishment, and feeling it, he found it to be a joint of meat roasted, and a loaf of bread about the size of our half-peck loaves. He then went to the door to look if he could see anybody; and after using his voice, as well as his eyes, and neither perceiving nor hearing any one, he returned, awoke his wife, who was still asleep, asked a blessing, and then awoke the children, and gave them a comfortable repast; but could give me no further account. I related this extraordinary affair to my father and mother, who both heard it with astonishment; but ordered me to keep the secret as requested; and such it would have ever remained, but for the following reason. A short time after this event I left that country; but on a visit about twelve years after, at a friend's, the conversation one evening took a turn about one Mr. Strangeways, commonly called Stranguage, a farmer, who lived at Lowick-Highsteed, which the people named Pinchmenear, on account of this miserly wretch that dwelt there. I asked what had become of his property, as I apprehended he had never done one generous action in his lifetime. An elderly woman in company said I was mistaken; for she could relate one which was somewhat curious: She said, that she had lived with him as a servant or housekeeper; that about twelve or thirteen years ago, one Thursday morning, he ordered her to have a whole joint of meat roasted, having giving her directions a day or two before to bake two large loaves of white bread. He then went to Wooler market, and took a piece of bread and cheese in his pocket as usual. He came home in the evening in a very bad humor, and went soon to bed. In about two hours after he called up his man-servant, and ordered him to take one of the loaves, and the joint of meat, and carry them down the moor to Thomas Hownham's, and leave them there. The man did so, and finding the family asleep, he set them at their bed-side and came away.

The next morning her master called her and the man-servant in, and seemed in great agitation of mind. He told them that he intended to have invited a Mr. John Mool, with two or three more neighboring farmers (who were always teasing him for his meanness), to sup with him the night before; that he would not invite them in the market place, as he purposed to have taken them by surprise near home, as two or three of them passed his house; but a smart shower of rain coming on, they rode off and left him before he could get an opportunity; that going soon to bed he did not rest well, fell a dreaming, and thought he saw Hownham's wife and children starving for hunger; that he awoke and threw off the impression; that he dreamed the second time, and endeavored again to shake it off, but that he was altogether overcome with the nonsense the third time; that he believed the devil was in him, but that since he was so foolish as to send the bread and meat, he could not now help it, and charged her and the man never to speak of it, or he would turn them away directly. She added, that since he was dead long ago, she thought she might relate it, as a proof that he had done one generous action, though he was grieved for it afterwards.

RELIEF SENT THROUGH A DREAM.

I WILL give an incident, in which I thought I saw a mark of divine interposition in some small degree. I owed a man a sum of money, which came due on a certain day specified, on which I was particularly anxious not to disappoint my friend. When the day arrived, notwithstanding all my care, I lacked twenty dollars to meet the amount I owed. This was rather strange to me, as I thought I had done my best. On the morning of that day I arose early and meditated on the matter. Some might think twenty dollars a small matter to meditate upon; but I wished to see where, if at all, I had erred. True, I had given away some money to the poor. I had not kept account how much. Had I displeased God in this? Or why was Providence seemingly suffering me to feel the regret of a broken promise made to my neighbor? I took no breakfast, but went from home fasting, to see what God was about to unfold to me. In a secluded place I bowed to God in mighty prayer. Before I rose from my knees, I was impressed with a strong assurance that the twenty dollars would be in my possession by the hour I needed it. I had not gone far before I was accosted by a man—a good Methodist—with these words: "My brother, just stop: I have something for you. I had a dream last night. In it I was told to let you have twenty dollars, the extra profit of my business last week." Saying which, he took from his pocket-book four five-dollar notes, and laid them down before me on a full sack that stood on the sidewalk. I took the money and paid my debt, with an increased confidence in the Providence of God, not regretting that I had given a few shillings to the poor.—*Life of Scarlett.*

THE PRAYER OF THE POOR ANSWERED.

A LADY, who had just sat down to breakfast, had a strong impression on her mind, that she must instantly carry a loaf of bread to a poor man, who lived about half a mile from her house, by the side of a common. Her husband wished her either to postpone taking it till after breakfast, or to send it by a servant; but she chose to take it immediately herself. As she approached the hut, she heard the sound of a human voice, and wishing to discover what was said, she stepped unperceived to the door. She heard the poor man praying, and among other things he said, "O Lord, help me; Lord, thou wilt help me; thy promise cannot fail: although my wife, myself, and children, have no bread to eat, and it is now a whole day since we had any, I know thou wilt supply me, though thou shouldst again rain down manna from heaven." The lady could wait no longer, but opening the door, "Yes," she replied, "God has sent you relief. Take this loaf, and be encouraged to cast your care upon Him who careth for you; and whenever you want a loaf of bread come to my house."

THE BUTCHER AND HIS WIFE.

RELATED BY MR. JOHN FLETCHER.

ONE Sunday I went up into the pulpit, intending to preach a sermon, which I had prepared for that purpose: but my mind was so confused, that I could not recollect either my text, or any part of my sermon. I was afraid I should be obliged to come down without saying anything. But having recollected myself a little, I thought I would say something on the first lesson, which was the third chapter of Daniel, containing the account of the three young men cast into the fiery furnace. I found, in doing it, such an extraordinary assistance from God, and such a peculiar enlargement of heart, that I supposed there must be some special cause for it; I therefore desired, if any of the congregation found anything particular, they would acquaint me with it in the ensuing week.

In consequence of this, the Wednesday after, a woman came, and gave me the following account: "I have been for some time much concerned about my soul. I have attended the church at all opportunities, and have spent much time in private prayer. At this, my husband, who is a butcher, has been exceedingly enraged, and threatened me severely what he would do, if I did not leave off going to John Fletcher's church, yea, if I dared to go to any religious meeting whatever. When I told him I could not in conscience refrain from going at least to our parish church, he grew quite outrageous, and swore dreadfully, that if I went any more, he would cut my throat as soon as I came home. This made me cry mightily to God, that he would support me in the trying hour: and, though I did not feel any great degree of comfort, yet, having a sure confidence in God, I determined to go on in my duty, and leave the rest to Him. Last Sunday, after many struggles with the devil and my own heart, I came down stairs, ready for church. My husband asked me whether I was resolved to go thither? I told him I was. 'Well, then,' said he, 'I shall not, as I intended, cut your throat, but will heat the oven, and throw you into it the moment you come home.' Notwithstanding this threatening, which he enforced with many bitter oaths, I went to church, praying all the way that God would strengthen me to suffer whatever might befall me. While you were speaking of the three persons whom Nebuchadnezzar cast into the burning fiery furnace, I found it all belonged to *me*, and God applied every word of it to my heart. And when the sermon was ended, I thought if I had a thousand lives, I could lay them all down for God. I felt my whole soul so filled with the love of Christ, that I *hastened* home, fully determined to give myself to whatever God pleased: nothing doubting but that either he would take me to heaven, if he suffered me to be burnt to death, or that he would somehow deliver me, even as he did his three servants who trusted in him. When I had got almost to my own door, I saw the flames issuing out of the mouth of the oven; and I expected nothing else but that I should be thrown into it immediately. I felt my heart rejoice, that if it were so, the will of the Lord would be done. I opened the door, and, to my utter astonishment, saw my husband upon his knees, wrestling with God in prayer, for the forgiveness of his sins. He caught me in his arms, earnestly begged my pardon, and has continued diligently seeking the Lord ever since."

I now know (adds Mr. Fletcher) why my sermon was taken from me, namely, that God might thus magnify his mercy.

THE PROVIDENCE OF GOD ASSERTED.

Many years ago a fact came to my knowledge, which I have intended preserving by sending an account of it to your magazine.

About thirty years ago, Mr. Floyd, who had been educated in the medical and surgical line, and was then an itinerant preacher, was stationed in Bristol. Breakfasting one morning at Miss Chapman's, he related to us the following story of a pious young man in the North of Ireland, which happened while

Mr. Floyd was in those parts. The young man was afflicted with epileptic fits, and found no relief from the means used. One night he dreamed that a person bade him go to a bridge about a mile from his dwelling, gather some herbs, which he would find growing at the side, pound them, and take a table-spoonful of the juice, fasting, for nine or ten mornings, and it would remove his fits.

This dream was repeated more than once, and made such an impression on his mind that he believed it to be sent of God. Therefore he arose and went, found the herbs, used them as he was directed, and was cured. The herb was that which we call *Pellitory of the Wall*, and grows abundantly in dry places in and near old walls. Mr. Floyd added, that he had mentioned this to a friend in Bristol whose daughter was afflicted with violent fits, of a hysteric kind, and she had been benefited by the use of the herb. At that time I had, in part, the care of a young person who had epileptic fits, and I immediately tried the remedy, which was happily successful; nor did the fits return. If you think, sir, this account worth preserving, you may depend on its authenticity, as far as I have related it.— *London Meth. Magazine,* vol. xxxii.   E. M. B.

THE LITTLE STRANGER.

Though a man of very strict principles, no man ever enjoyed a joke more than Dr. Byron; he had a vast fund of humor, an everyday wit, and, with children, particularly, he loved to chat familiarly and draw them out. As he was one day passing into the house, he was accosted by a very little boy, who asked him if he wanted any SAUCE, meaning vegetables. The doctor inquired if such a tiny thing was a market-man. "No, sir, my father," was the prompt answer. The doctor said, "Bring me in some squashes," and he passed into the house, sending out the change. In a few moments the child returned, bringing back part of the change; the doctor told him he was welcome to it; but the child would not take it back, saying his father would blame him. Such singular manners in a child attracted his attention, and he began to examine the child attentively: he was evidently poor; his little jacket was pieced and patched with almost every kind of cloth, and his trowsers darned with so many colors, it was difficult to tell the original fabric, but scrupulously neat and clean withal. The boy very quietly endured the scrutiny of the doctor, while holding him at arm's length, and examining his face. At length he said:

"You seem a nice little boy; won't you come and live with me, and be a doctor?"

"Yes, sir," said the child.

"Spoken like a man," said the doctor, patting his head as he dismissed him.

A few weeks passed on, when, one day, Jim came to say that there was a little boy with a bundle down stairs wanting to see the doctor, and would not tell his business to any one else. "Send him up," was the answer; and, in a few moments, he recognised the boy of the squashes (but no squash himself, as we shall see); he was dressed in a new, though coarse suit of clothes, his hair very nicely combed, his shoes brushed up, and a little bundle, tied in a homespun checked handkerchief, on his arm. Deliberately taking off his hat, and laying it down with his bundle, he walked up to the doctor, saying:—

"I have come, sir."

"Come for what, my child?"

"To live with you, and be a doctor," said the child, with the utmost *naïveté*.

The first impulse of the doctor was to laugh immoderately; but the imperturbable gravity of the little thing rather sobered him, as he recalled, too, his former conversation, and he avowed he felt he needed no addition to his family.

"Did your father consent to your coming?" he asked.

"Yes, sir."

"What did he say?"

"I told him you wanted me to come and live

with you, and be a doctor; and he said you was a very good man, and I might come as soon as my clothes were ready."

"And your mother, what did she say?"

"She said Doctor Byron would do just what he said he would, and God had provided for me."

"And," said he, "I have on a new suit of clothes," surveying himself, "and here is another in the bundle," undoing the kerchief and displaying them, with two little shirts, white as snow, and a couple of neat checked aprons, so carefully folded, it was plain none but a mother would have done it. The sensibilities of the doctor were awakened to see the fearless, the undoubting trust with which that poor couple had bestowed their child upon him, and such a child. His cogitations were not long; he thought of Moses in the bulrushes abandoned to Providence; and, above all, he thought of the child that was carried into Egypt, and that that divine Saviour had said, "Blessed be little children;" and he called for the wife of his bosom, saying, "Susan, dear, I think we pray in church that God will have mercy *upon all young children?*"

"To be sure we do," said the wondering wife; "and what then?"

"And the Saviour said, 'Whosoever receiveth one such little child in my name, receiveth me;' take this child in his name, and take care of him;" and from this hour this good couple received him to their hearts and homes. It did not then occur to them, that one of the most eminent physicians and best men of the age stood before them in the person of that child; it did not occur to them that this little creature, thus thrown upon their charity, was destined to be their staff and stay in declining age—a protector to their daughters, and more than son to themselves; all this was then unrevealed; but they cheerfully received the child they believed Providence had committed to their care; and if ever beneficence was rewarded, it was in this instance.

THE PRAYER OF FAITH ANSWERED.

I ARRIVED at Mewry one Saturday evening, soon after I came to the Charlemount circuit, and was informed that I must visit a lady who was supposed to be dying, as soon as I could make it convenient. I was informed that she had been ill a considerable time of a dropsical complaint, and had often expressed a wish to converse with our people, and especially to be visited by our preachers; but her husband had refused his consent, dreading the reproach that he thought would follow. He was a Socinian, and a man of some eminence in the town, and in his congregation; but the hopeless case of a wife that he loved had at length roused him to comply with her wishes. I accordingly went, and was introduced to a most interesting person; a young lady whose every look seemed to say, "Who will show me any good?" Her swollen state, with the emaciation of her still beautiful countenance, proclaimed her case to be desperate; and two most lovely children added to the afflictive scene.

Her husband, a fine young man, hung over her with every appearance of strong affection; but I could perceive that there was a feeling concerning me that was not comfortable. I spoke to the lady as to a dying person, and in a way that I supposed he would perhaps account enthusiastic. But I was encouraged to hope for the sufferer, as I found she was indeed "poor in spirit." We engaged in prayer, but I think I never felt myself so embarrassed. I attempted to pray for her as a dying person, but could hardly utter a sentence without hesitation. My prayer had, indeed, no wings; and the thought that the husband was watching over me, so greatly added to my embarrassment, that I thought I must give over. At length the thought of her recovery came with strange force into my mind, and I ventured to indulge it. Immediately words poured upon me faster than I could utter them. I felt that it was indeed "the prayer of faith," which, St. James says, "shall save the sick." I seemed to claim in her behalf a return to life at the Lord's hand. I at length concluded; but was almost immediately tempted to think I had given way to a delusion that would render me ridiculous, and do harm to unprepared minds. I took my leave, the afflicted lady requesting that I would soon call again; and the husband, with an astonished countenance, was hardly able to utter even the common civilities usual at parting.

On returning to my quarters, I had some very painful thoughts; fearing that the tender mind of the sufferer might be wounded by the remarks that would probably be made, in such a family, upon my visionary conduct. The hope of her recovery seemed, however, to abide with me; but I thought I would keep it to myself, and pray for her in the family, as for a dying person. But it was in vain. The same strong influence set my prudence at defiance; and I was constrained to ask life for her as at her own habitation, to the great amazement of my pious host and his family. On the Sabbath evening, after the services were over, I again visited my patient, and again amazed all who were assembled by the strange confidence and importunity of my faith. I took leave of her, however, with a strong exhortation to fix her mind on the divine atonement, and to aim at conformity to the Son of God, in his prayer to the Father—"Not my will, but thine be done."

I returned, in my course, at the end of six weeks, and found my very amiable sufferer in a state rather beyond convalescence, and a member of the society! The husband had dismissed all opposition; he received me with joy, and expressed his gratitude in strong terms. He would have me to dine with him; and I made one of a very happy family. In the afternoon I met my recovering patient at the class, all alive to the things which make for our peace.

She made swift progress, and soon rejoiced in "redemption through his blood, the forgiveness of her sins."—*Life of Rev. H. Moore.*

PART III.

ILLUSTRATIONS OF DIVINE PROVIDENCE IN THE PUNISHMENT OF SIN, DEFEAT OF WICKED PLANS, &c.

"How oft is the candle of the wicked put out? and how oft cometh their destruction upon them? God distributeth sorrows in his anger."—JOB xxi. 17

SECTION I.

Intelligent Agents in the Punishment of Sin, &c.

THE EMIGRANT'S PERSECUTORS.

A NUMBER of persons, in the north of England, once determined to emigrate to South Africa. They had a great dread of what they called *Methodism*, and refused to allow a young man, who was reputed to belong to that body of Christians, to go with them. They had not, however, been many days at sea, before it was discovered, that notwithstanding their most strenuous endeavors to prevent the exportation of Methodism, they had got an excellent old man aboard, who privately exhorted his fellow passengers to fear God, and flee from the wrath to come. The flame of persecution was now lighted up; and Mr. C., the leader of the party, availed himself of every opportunity to annoy and injure poor Mr. P. In the course of the passage, his wife and son were taken alarmingly ill; but, so bitter was the spirit which prevailed against him, that it was with difficulty he obtained even the medicines provided by government, which their state rendered absolutely necessary. The above-mentioned gentleman, who had the affairs of the party almost wholly under his control, frequently threatened not only to deprive him of the land to which he was legally entitled, but of all the privileges of the settlement, unless he kept his religion to himself. In his menaces and designs, this petty Nero was supported by three or four others, who were influenced by a similar spirit. The earth, however, is the Lord's, and "though hand join in hand, the wicked shall not go unpunished." Two only of those persecutors lived to see the settlement. The death of one was occasioned by intemperance and dissipation while at sea. The head of the party himself fell sick immediately after his arrival at Algoa Bay, and there expired, in dreadful agony, both mental and bodily. He therefore never set foot on the land which he had so arrogantly affected to command. Another of his comrades was taken off suddenly, and carried to the grave along with him! A fourth, being some time afterward provoked by his companion, the only survivor of the five, presented his fowling-piece at him, and lodged the contents in his breast; for which he was, of course, arrested, and conveyed to prison in Graham's Town. But his spirit and conduct having apparently rendered life burdensome, and filled his dungeon with insufferable gloom, the unhappy wretch hung himself in his cell! "Woe unto the wicked! it shall be ill with him; for the reward of his hands shall be given him: but say ye to the righteous, it shall be well with him; they shall eat the fruit of their doings."

The poor old Methodist now began, more earnestly than ever, to call all around him to repentance, and actually became the virtual head of the party; he obtained favor in the eyes of the people, and was ever after looked up to as their chief counsellor in all matters of importance. His rustic cottage was no sooner built than converted into a place of worship, wherein Divine service was regularly performed, until, by steady zeal and praiseworthy exertions, they were enabled to erect a neat little chapel, which constitutes a lasting honor to his memory. This good man is now no more; but, although dead, by his works he still speaketh; and his name is held in the highest estimation by all who knew him.

DR. COLE'S COMMISSION.

It is related, in the papers of Richard Earl of Cork, that towards the conclusion of Queen Mary's reign, a commission was signed for the persecution of the Irish Protestants; and, to give greater weight to this important affair, Dr. Cole was nominated one of the commission. The doctor, in his way to Dublin, stopped at Chester, where he was waited upon by the mayor; to whom, in the course of conversation, he imparted the object of his mission, and exhibited the leather box which contained his credentials. The mistress of the inn, where this interview took place, being a Protestant, and having overheard the conversation, seized the opportunity, while the doctor was attending the mayor to the bottom of the stairs, of exchanging the commission for a dirty pack of cards, on the top of which she facetiously turned up the knave of clubs. The doctor, little suspecting the trick, secured his box, pursued his journey, and arrived in Dublin on the 7th of October, 1558. He then lost no time in presenting himself before Lord Fitzwalter and the privy council; to whom, after an explanatory speech, the box was presented, which, to the astonishment of all present, was found to contain only a pack of cards! The doctor, greatly chagrined, returned instantly to London, to have his commission renewed; but while waiting a second time on the coast for a favorable wind, the news reached him of the queen's decease, which prevented the persecution, that would have otherwise proved so awful a calamity. Queen Elizabeth was so much gratified with these facts, which were related to her by Lord Fitzwalter on his return to England, that she sent for the woman, whose name was Elizabeth Edwards, and gave her a pension of forty pounds a year, during her life.

THE MURDERER AND HIS SINGULAR WOUND.

A GENTLEMAN who was very ill, sending for Dr. Lake, of England, told him that he found he must die, and gave him the following account of the cause of his death. He had, about a fortnight before, been riding over Hounslow-heath, where several boys were playing at cricket. One of them, striking the ball, hit him just on the toe with it, looked him in the face, and ran away. His toe pained him extremely. As soon as he came to Brentford, he sent for a surgeon, who was for cutting it off. But, unwilling to suffer that, he went on to London. When he arrived there, he immediately called another surgeon to examine it, who told him his *foot* must be cut off. But neither would he hear of this; and so, before the next day, the mortification seized his *leg*, and in a day or two more struck up into his *body*. Dr. Lake asked him, whether he knew the boy that struck the ball? He answered, "About ten years ago, I was riding over Hounslow-heath, where an old man ran by my horse's side, begged me to relieve him, and said he was almost famished. I bade him begone. He kept up with me still; upon which I threatened to beat him. Finding that he took no notice of this, I drew my sword, and with one blow killed him. A boy about four years old, who was with him, screamed out, 'His father was killed!' His face I perfectly remember. *That boy it was who struck the ball against me, which is the cause of my death.*"

JOHN EYRE'S NEPHEW.

An anecdote is related of John Eyre, a man whose name is recorded in the annals of crime, as possessing £30,000, and yet being sentenced to transportation for stealing eleven quires of writing paper; which shows, in a striking manner, the depravity of the human heart, and may help to account for the meanness of the crime of which he stood convicted. An uncle of his, a gentleman of considerable property, made his will in favor of a clergyman who was his intimate friend, and committed it, unknown to the rest of the family, to the custody of the divine. However, not long before his death, having altered his mind with regard to the disposal of his wealth, he made another will, in which he left the clergyman only £500, bequeathing the bulk of his large property to his nephew and heir-at-law, Mr. Eyre. Soon after the old gentleman's death, Mr. Eyre, rummaging over his drawers, found this last will, and perceiving the legacy of £500 in it for the clergyman, without any hesitation or scruple of conscience, he put it into the fire, and took possession of the whole effects, in consequence of his uncle being supposed to die intestate. The clergyman coming to town soon after, and inquiring into the circumstances of his old friend's death, asked if he had made a will before he died. On being answered by Mr. Eyre in the negative, the clergyman very coolly put his hand in his pocket, and pulled out the former will, which had been committed to his care, in which Mr. Eyre had bequeathed him the whole of his fortune, amounting to several thousand pounds, excepting a legacy of £200 to his nephew.

SECTION II.

Unintelligent Agents in the Punishment of Sin, &c.

AWFUL DEATH OF A PERSECUTOR.

In Cork my reception was very encouraging, and a door was opened to me of great usefulness. At Dunmanway, one of our preaching places, a remarkable event occurred soon after my coming upon the circuit. The whole town was subject to one landlord, Sir R. C——, a young man of the most profligate habits. He had appeared to be much displeased with the change which had taken place in the town, and with the preachers who had caused it; and he had frequently threatened that he would put a stop to such proceedings. A good man observed, "He may certainly do so, if God permit, for no man here can resist him; he is greater in Dunmanway than King George himself." He at length threatened that he would throw the next preacher that came, into the lake which fronted his mansion. When the time of my going there came, I found the Lord had most awfully prevented the execution of his purpose. He had himself been thrown into it the evening before, where he miserably perished. His body was recovered after several hours' search; and when I rode into the town, the corpse lay at the public-house, waiting the coroner's inquest. I went to look at the body; it was a dreadful spectacle. He was a tall, athletic young man, about twenty-two years of age. The body was much swollen by the water, and his countenance dreadfully disfigured by the large eels which abounded in the lake. He was interred the following evening. I received the following information respecting his way of life, and his melancholy end.

He had entered the army at an early age; but, after offending many by his excesses, he was ultimately obliged to quit the regiment in consequence of having challenged his commanding officer. He then, at about nineteen, married a most amiable young lady, who was obliged to leave him on account of his profligacy. Living by himself at the mansion-house, and being at a loss for some amusement on the Lord's day, he determined to have an aquatic excursion on the lake. One of the oars of his boat had been broken, but this could not stop him. Timber was procured, and a piece sawed from it in the churchyard, where the only sawpit was situated, and the oar was thus made during divine service in the forenoon. In the afternoon he embarked, with a young gentleman, the curate of the parish; and after sailing for some time, he resolved to know in how short a time he could make the circuit of the lake. The rowers struck off, and he remained for some time beholding them, with his watch in his hand. The slowness of their motions offended him; and after many oaths and execrations, he pulled one of them from the bench, and sat down himself, saying, he would show them how to row. He dipped too deep, and making a violent pull, the new oar snapped like a twig, and Sir R—— was precipitated backward into the lake. There were above three hundred people soon collected on the shore, and every effort was made to save him, but in vain. The body was not recovered until Monday morning, and in that dreadful state I beheld him soon after I entered the town in the afternoon. The funeral passed on the second evening, close by the place where I was preaching. All opposition was now at an end, and "the word of the Lord had free course, and was glorified in" the conversion of many souls.

DEACON EATON AND THE INFIDEL.

DEACON EATON, a missionary on the Erie canal, once came in contact with an infidel on a canal boat, who urged him into a dispute about the divinity of Jesus Christ. At first he proposed to argue the question on the ground of the Scriptures, but being confounded by Deacon Eaton's reading 1 John, chapter v., he declared that the Bible was nothing but man's invention. "I saw," says Deacon E., "that he appeared to be very angry, and left him; but during the whole afternoon, whenever he had an opportunity, he would vent some of his spite upon me. When we came to Syracuse, where we changed packets, I thought I should stop, and was bidding the passengers farewell. Among the rest I shook hands with the infidel's wife, and said to her, 'I hope you will alter your belief before I see you again.' He saw me talking to her, and coming along, struck off my hand with which I held hers, and said, 'Let the woman alone. If you wish to attack any one, try me, but don't abuse the woman.'

"I asked his pardon, and told him I intended no abuse to any one. I finally concluded to go in the packet, and as the boat started many of the passengers went on deck, and among the rest the infidel and his wife. I was in the cabin when a man came down in great haste, and inquired for a bottle of camphor; he said a man had fainted on deck. Without knowing who it was, it struck me immediately that it was the infidel, and that God had destroyed him. I went on deck, and sure enough the infidel was dead. A gentleman with whom he was conversing, said he was railing against me, and saying I was spunging my living, when he fell in a moment with a half-uttered curse on his lips. They were trying to bring him back to life, but I saw that there were no hopes that he would ever breathe again. He was dead the moment he reached the deck, and then presented the most awful object I had ever looked upon. His eyes were open, and his countenance indicated woful despair. It was a solemn moment, as still as the house of death. One of the boatmen said to me, 'It will not do to fight against God.'"

FALSEHOOD AWFULLY REALIZED.

J—— W—— was a laborer employed on the Liverpool and Manchester railway. During part of the time in which he was thus employed, he lodged at Edge Hill, near Liverpool. There is reason to believe that he was a young man who had "no fear of God before his eyes;" that he was, in the expressive language of an inspired apostle, "without God in the world:" Eph. ii. 12. Becoming acquainted with a young woman, he succeeded in seducing her from the paths of virtue; and soon after, he removed to a new lodging, with a view to avoid the consequences of his conduct. The Almighty, in mercy to the sinner, sent affliction by illness to overtake him, and thus gave him time for repentance, and an opportunity to seek the love and favor of the Lord. But he refused the mercy and hardened his heart. In the course of the last week before he resumed his work, he called upon the person with whom he had formerly lodged, and among other things, asked whether old George (the young woman's father) ever came there to inquire after him. She replied that he did, and mentioned the time of his last inquiry. "Oh," said W——, "when he comes again, tell him that I was killed on the railway; and that I was buried in Childwall churchyard." Childwall is a village about a mile from part of the railway, and about four miles from Liverpool. Within a day or two, old George called, and the above iniquitous and awful assertion was made. Deceived by the falsehood, the poor old man went away mourning over the disgrace of his daughter, and the supposed sad end of her base seducer. But the delusion was soon to be dissipated; the lie told, with a view to evade the consequences of previous guilt, was awfully, singularly, literally realized; and the wretched man, who had so impiously trifled with death, was hurried, in a moment, before the bar of his Maker.

On the following Monday morning, May 17, 1830, the laborer returned to work, and on the same day entered upon his everlasting state. Being on the road at the time when an engine, to which several wagons employed to convey rubbish were attached, was passing, he was entangled with the apparatus, felled to the earth, and his body so dreadfully mangled, as to occasion instantaneous death. Thus the most affecting, and, to him, important part of his wicked fabrication, was made, by the mysterious providence of God, a solemn reality; and that of which he had no idea when he uttered the language above related, turned out, within a few days, to be a fact, namely, "That he was killed on the railway!"

But there was to be a further literal accomplishment of his words, which, although to him a matter of no consequence after the spirit had quitted the body, should not be passed over unobserved, as it tends to show, in a still more striking manner, that the Supreme Arbiter of life and death does indeed sometimes take men at their word, and fulfil their imprecations, their thoughtless wishes, or their blasphemous expressions, even to the very letter. J—— W—— had no immediate relations in the neighborhood in which he so unexpectedly expired. But, since his removal to Edge Hill, he had lodged with a family who possessed a burial-place in Childwall churchyard. Some of his fellow workmen proposed his interment at Walton, a village three miles north of Liverpool: but others, on account of the nearness of Childwall, urged his burial there; and in little more than a week after he had deliberately uttered a falsehood to deceive one he had deeply injured, his own awful words were fulfilled.

THE TRAVELLER AND THE DOG.

A GENTLEMAN being benighted, in a lonely place, stopped at an inn. After supper he retired to rest. When he opened his room door, he was surprised to see a strange dog, which had followed in the afternoon, rush in. After several fruitless efforts to drive him out, the gentleman concluded to let him stay, thinking he would do no harm. When the gentleman began to prepare for bed, the dog ran to a closet door, and then ran back to him, looking very wistfully at him. This the dog did several times, which so far excited the curiosity of the gentleman, that he opened the closet door; and to his great terror, saw a person laid with his throat cut. Struck with horror, he began to think of his own state. To attempt to run away he supposed would be unsafe. He therefore began to barricade the door with the furniture of the room, and laid himself on the bed with his clothes on. About midnight two men came to the door and requested admittance, stating that the gentleman that slept there the preceding night, had forgotten something and was returned for it. He replied, the room was his, and no one should enter his room until morning. They went away, but soon returned with two or three other men, and demanded entrance; but the gentleman, with an austere voice, threatened if they did not desist, he would defend himself.

Awed apparently by this bold reply, they left him and disturbed him no more.

In the morning he inquired for a barber; one was immediately sent for, when the gentleman took the opportunity of inquiring into the character of his host. The barber replied, he was a neighbor, and did not wish to say anything to his disadvantage. The gentleman still urged his inquiry, assuring him he had nothing to fear, till the barber said, "Sir, if I must tell the truth, they bear a very bad character, for it has been reported, that persons have called here, who have never been heard of afterwards." "Can you," said the gentleman, "keep a secret?" On his answering in the affirmative, the gentleman opened the closet door, and showed him the person with his throat cut; he then directed the barber to procure a constable, and proper assistance with all speed, which was done immediately, and the host and hostess were both taken into custody, to take their trial at the next assize. They took their trial and were found guilty of the murder, condemned and executed. The dog was never seen by the gentleman afterwards.

SECTION III.

Dreams and Mental Exercises in the Punishment of Sin, &c.

MURDER CONFESSED IN A DREAM.

The following is translated from a respectable publication at Basle, Switzerland:—

A person who worked in a brewery quarrelled with one of his fellow-workmen, and struck him in such a manner that he died upon the spot. No other person was witness to the deed. He then took the dead body and threw it into a large fire under the boiling-vat, where it was in a short time so completely consumed, that no traces of its existence remained. On the following day, when the man was missed, the murderer observed, very coolly, that he had perceived his fellow-servant to have been intoxicated, and that he had probably fallen from a bridge which he had to cross in his way home, and been drowned. For the space of seven years after no one entertained any suspicion of the real state of the fact. At the end of this period, the murderer was again employed in the same brewery. He was then induced to reflect on the singularity of the circumstance that his crime had remained so long concealed. Having retired one evening to rest, one of the other workmen, who slept with him, hearing him say in his sleep, "It is now fully seven years ago," asked him, "What was it you did seven years ago?" "I put him," he replied, still speaking in his sleep, "under the boiling-vat." As the affair was not entirely forgotten, it immediately occurred to the man that his bedfellow must allude to the person who was missing about that time, and he accordingly gave information of what he had heard to a magistrate. The murderer was apprehended; and, though at first he denied that he knew anything of the matter, a confession of his crime was at length obtained from him, for which he suffered condign punishment.

MURDER REVEALED BY A DREAM.

In the village of Manchester, Vermont, R. Colvin, a man of respectable connexions and character, suddenly and mysteriously disappeared; all search and inquiry proved in vain, until a person dreamed that he had appeared to him, and informed him that he had been murdered by two persons, whom he named, and that he had been buried in such a place, a few rods distant from a sapling, bearing a particular mark, which he minutely described. The same dream occurred three times successively before he awoke, and each time the deceased seemed very solicitous for him to follow. Upon awaking, his feelings were wrought up to such a degree, and he was so impressed with a belief of the fact, that he determined to collect some friends, and follow the directions laid down in the dream. He did so, and discovered, to his great surprise, not only a tree marked precisely as described, but also the appearance of a grave; and, upon digging, found a human skeleton! After this discovery, Stephen and Jesse Brown, the persons implicated in the dream, were apprehended and put in confinement, and, after a few days, confessed their crime. They were tried, convicted, and sentenced to be executed, on the 18th of January, 1820.

BUNYAN AND THE JAILER.

THE respectability of Bunyan's character and the propriety of his conduct, while in prison at Bedford, appear to have operated very powerfully on the mind of the jailer, who showed him much kindness, in permitting him to go out and visit his friends occasionally, and once to take a journey to London.

The following anecdote is told respecting the

jailer and Mr. Bunyan:—It being known to some of his persecutors, in London, that he was often out of prison, they sent an officer to talk with the jailer on the subject; and, in order to discover the fact, he was to get there in the middle of the night. Bunyan was at home with his family, but so restless that he could not sleep; he therefore acquainted his wife that, though the jailer had given him liberty to stay till the morning, yet, from his uneasiness, he must immediately return. He did so, and the jailer blamed him for coming in at such an unseasonable hour. Early in the morning the messenger came, and interrogating the jailer, said, "Are all the prisoners safe?" "Yes." "Is John Bunyan safe?" "Yes." "Let me see him." He was called, and appeared, and all was well. After the messenger was gone, the jailer, addressing Mr. Bunyan, said, "Well, you may go in and out again just when you think proper, for you know when to return better than I can tell you."

A REMARKABLE DREAM.

The proof of the truth of the following statement, taken from the *Courier de l'Europe*, rests not only upon the known veracity of the narrative, but upon the fact that the whole occurrence is registered in the judicial records of the criminal trials of the Province of Languedoc. We give it as we heard it from the lips of the dreamer, as nearly as possible in his own words.

As the junior partner of a commercial house at Lyons, I had been travelling for some time. In the month of June, 1761, I arrived at a town in Languedoc, where I had never before been. I put up at a quiet inn in the suburbs, and being very much fatigued, ordered dinner at once, and went to bed almost immediately after, determined to begin very early in the morning my visit to the different merchants.

I was no sooner in bed than I fell into a deep sleep, and had a dream that made the strongest impression upon me.

I thought that I had arrived at the same town, but in the middle of the day instead of the evening, as was really the case—that I had stopped at the very same inn, and gone out immediately as an unoccupied stranger would do, to see whatever was worthy of observation in the place. I walked down the main street, crossing it at right angles, and apparently leading into the country. I had not gone very far when I came to a church, the Gothic portal of which I stood to examine. When I had satisfied my curiosity, I advanced to a bypath which branched off from the main street. Obeying an impulse which I could neither account for nor control, I struck into this path, though it was winding, rugged, and unfrequented, and presently reached a miserable cottage, in front of which was a garden covered with weeds. I had no difficulty in getting into the garden, for the hedge had several gaps in it wide enough to admit four carts abreast. I approached an old well which stood, solitary and gloomy, in a distant corner, and looking down into it I beheld distinctly, without any possibility of mistake, a corpse which had been stabbed in several places. I counted the deep wounds and the wide gashes whence the blood was flowing.

I would have cried out; but my tongue clove to the roof of my mouth. At this moment I awoke with my hair on end, trembling in every limb, and cold drops of perspiration bedewed my forehead,—awoke to find myself comfortably in bed, my trunk standing beside me; birds warbling cheerfully around the window; while a young clear voice was singing a provincial air in the next room, and the morning sun was shining brightly through the curtain.

I sprang from my bed, dressed myself, and as it was yet very early, I thought I would seek an appetite for my breakfast by a morning walk. I went accordingly into the street and strolled along. The further I went the stronger became the confused recollections of the objects that presented themselves to my view. "It is very strange," I thought, "I have never been here before, and I could swear that I have seen this house and the next, and that other on the left." On I went till

I came to the corner of the street crossing the one down which I had come. For the first time I had remembered my dream, but put away the idea as too absurd; still at every step I took, some fresh point of resemblance struck me. "Am I still dreaming?" I exclaimed, not without a momentary thrill through my whole frame. "Is the agreement to be perfect to the very end?" Before long I reached the church with the same architectural features that had attracted my notice in the dream, and then the by-path that had presented itself to my imagination a few hours before—there was no possibility of doubt or mistake. Every tree, every turn was familiar to me. I was not at all of a superstitious turn; and was wholly engrossed in the practical details of commercial business. My mind had never dwelt upon the hallucinations, the presentiments that science either denies or is unable to explain; but I confess that I now felt myself spellbound as by some enchantment—and with Pascal's words on my lips—" A continued dream would be equal to reality"—I hurried forward, no longer doubting that the next moment would bring me to the cottage, and this really was the case.

In all its outward circumstances it corresponded to what I had seen in my dream. Who then would wonder that I determined to ascertain whether the coincidence would hold good in every other point? I entered the garden, and went directly to the spot on which I had seen the well; but here the resemblance failed—well there was none. I looked in every direction, examined the whole garden, went round the cottage, which appeared to be inhabited, although no person was visible, but nowhere could I find any vestige of a well.

I made no attempt to enter the cottage, but hastened back to the hotel in a state of agitation difficult to describe. I could not make up my mind to pass unnoticed such extraordinary coincidences; but how was any clue to be obtained to the terrible mystery?

I went to the landlord, and after chatting with him for some time on different subjects, I came to the point, and asked him directly to whom the cottage belonged that was on the by-road which I described to him.

"I wonder, sir," said he, "what made you take such particular notice of such a wretched little hovel. It is inhabited by an old man with his wife, who have the character of being very morose and unsociable. They rarely leave the house, see nobody, and nobody goes to see them; but they are quiet enough, and I never heard anything against them beyond this. Of late, their very existence seems to be forgotten; and I believe, sir, that you are the first for years, has turned your steps to the deserted spot."

These details, far from satisfying my curiosity, did but provoke it the more. Snatching my hat, I cried, "I will go, come what may!"

I repaired to the nearest magistrate, told him the object of my visit, and related the whole circumstance briefly and clearly. I saw distinctly that he was much impressed by my statement.

"It is, indeed, very strange," said he; "after what has happened, I do not think I am at liberty to leave the matter to further inquiry. I will place two of the police at your command. Go once more to the hovel, see its inhabitants, and search every part of it. You may, perhaps, make some important discovery."

I suffered but a few moments to elapse before I was on my way, accompanied by the two officers, and we soon reached the cottage. We knocked, and after waiting some time an old man opened the door. He received us somewhat uncivilly, but showed no mark of suspicion, nor, indeed, of any other emotion, when we told him we wished to search the house.

"Very well, gentlemen, as fast and as soon as you like," was his reply.

"Have you a well here?" I inquired.

"No, sir; we are obliged to go for water to a spring at a considerable distance."

We searched the house, which I did, I confess, with a kind of feverish excitement, expecting every moment to bring some fatal secret to light. Meanwhile, the man gazed upon us with an impenetrable vacancy of look, and we at last left the cottage, without anything that could confirm my suspicions. I resolved to inspect the garden once more, and a number of idlers having by this time collected, drawn to the spot by the sight of a stranger, with two armed men engaged in searching the premises, I made inquiries of some of them whether they knew anything about a well in that place. I could get no information at first, but at length an old woman came slowly forward, leaning on a crutch.

"A well!" cried she; "is it the well you are looking after? That has been gone these thirty years. I remember as if it were only yesterday, how, many a time when I was a young girl, I used to amuse myself with throwing stones into it, and hearing the splash they used to make in the water."

"And could you tell me where that well used to be?" asked I, almost breathless with excitement.

"As near as I can remember, on the very spot on which your honor is standing," said the old woman.

"I could have sworn it," thought I, springing from the place as if I had trod upon a scorpion.

Need I say that we set to work to dig up the ground? At about eighteen inches deep we came to a layer of bricks, which, being broken up, gave to view some boards which were easily removed, after which we beheld the mouth of the well.

"I was quite sure it was here," said the old woman. "What a fool the old fellow was to stop it up, and then have to go so far for water!"

A sounding-line, furnished with hooks, was let down into the well; the crowd pressing around us, and breathlessly bending over the dark and fetid hole, the secrets of which seemed hidden in impenetrable obscurity. This was repeated several times without result. At length, penetrating below the mud, the hooks caught in an old chest, upon top of which had been thrown a great many large stones, and, after much time and effort, we succeeded in raising it to daylight. The sides and lid were decayed and rotten; it needed no locksmith to open it, and we found within it what I was certain we should find, and which paralyzed with horror all the spectators, who had not my pre-conviction—we found the remains of a human body.

The police who had accompanied me, now rushed into the house, and secured the person of the old man. As to his wife—no one could tell, at first, what had become of her; after some search, however, she was found hidden behind a bundle of faggots.

By this time nearly the whole town had gathered around the spot, and now that this fact had come to light, everybody had some crime to tell of which had been laid to the charge of the old couple. The people who predict after an event are numerous.

The old couple were brought before the proper authorities and privately and separately examined. The old man persisted in his denial most pertinaciously, but his wife at length confessed, that in concert with her husband she had once, a very long time ago, murdered a pedlar whom they had met one night on the high road, and who had been incautious enough to tell them of a considerable sum of money which he had about him, and whom, in consequence, they induced to pass the night at their house. They had taken advantage of the heavy sleep induced by fatigue to strangle him, his body had been put into the chest, the chest thrown into the well, and the well stopped up.

The pedlar being from another country, his disappearance had occasioned no inquiry; there was no witness of the crime; and as its traces had been carefully concealed from every eye, the two criminals had good reason to believe themselves secure from detection. They had not, however, been able to silence the voice of conscience; they fled from the sight of their fellow men; they thought they beheld wherever they turned, mute accusers; they trembled at the slightest noise, and silence thrilled them with terror. They had often formed a determination to leave the scene of their crime, to fly to some distant land, but still some undefinable fascination kept them near the remains of their victim.

Terrified by the deposition of the wife, and unable to resist the overwhelming proofs against him, the man at last made a similar confession, and six weeks after the unhappy criminals died on the scaffold, in accordance with the sentence of the parliament of Toulouse.

They died penitent.

The well was once more shut up, and the cottage levelled to the ground; it was not, however, until fifty years had in some measure deadened the memory of the terrible transaction, that the ground was cultivated. It is now a field of corn.

Such was the dream and its result.

———◆———

A WICKED PROCLAMATION DEFEATED.

The following interesting facts were related to the Rev. Dr. Conder, of London, by an old gentleman, who remembered when a boy to have heard them from the great-grandfather of that gentleman :—

I used, said he, when young to accompany my father to Royston market, which Mr. Conder also frequented. The custom of the worthy men in those days was, when they had done their marketing, to meet together, and take needful refreshment in a private room, where, without interruption, they might talk freely about the things of God— how they had heard on the Sabbath day, and how they had gone on the week past, &c. I was admitted to sit in a corner of the room. One day, when I was there, the conversation turned upon the question, "By what means God first visited

their souls, and began a work of grace upon them?" It was your great-grandfather's turn to speak, and his account struck me so, that I never forgot it. He told the company as follows:—
"When I was a young man, I was greatly addicted to foot-ball playing; and, as the custom was in our parish, and in many others also, the young men, as soon as church was over, took a foot-ball and went to play. Our minister often remonstrated against our breaking the Sabbath, which, however, had but little effect; only my conscience checked me at times, and I would sometimes steal away and hide myself from my companions. But being dextrous at the game, they would find me out, and get me among them. This would bring on me more guilt and horror of conscience. Thus I went on sinning and repenting a long time, but had no resolution to break off from the practice, till, one Sabbath morning, our minister acquainted his hearers that he was very sorry to tell them, that by order of the king (James I.) and his council, he must read them the following paper or relinquish his living. This was the Book of Sports, forbidding the ministers or churchwardens, or any others, to molest or discourage the youth, in what were called their manly sports and recreations on the Lord's day, &c. While our minister was reading it, I was seized with a chill and horror not to be described. Now, thought I, iniquity is established by a law, and sinners are hardened in their sinful ways! What

sore judgments are to be expected upon so wicked and guilty a nation! What shall I do? Whither shall I flee? How shall I escape the wrath to come?—And thus God convinced me that it was high time to be in earnest about salvation. And from that time, I never had the least inclination to take a foot-ball in hand, or to join my vain companions any more: so that I date my conversion from that time, and adore the grace of God in making that to be an ordinance for my salvation, which the devil and wicked governors laid as a trap for my destruction."

This, continued the narrator, I heard him tell: and I hope with some serious benefit to my own soul.

THE JEWELLER AND HIS SERVANT.

A JEWELLER, a man of good character, and considerable wealth, having occasion, in the way of business, to travel some distance from his abode, took along with him a servant: he had with him some of his best jewels, and a large sum of money, to which his servant was likewise privy. The master having occasion to dismount on the road, the servant watched his opportunity, took a pistol from his master's saddle, and shot him dead on the spot; then rifling him of his jewels and money, and hanging a large stone to his neck, he threw him into the nearest canal. With his booty he made off to a distant part of the country, where he had reason to believe that neither he nor his master was known. There he began to trade, in a very low way at first, that his obscurity might screen him from observation; and in the course of many years seemed to rise up, by the natural progress of business, into wealth and consideration; so that his good fortune appeared at once the effect of industry and the reward of virtue. Of these he counterfeited the appearance so well, that he grew into great credit, married into a good family, and, by laying out his hidden stores discreetly, as he saw occasion, and joining to all a universal affability, he was at length admitted to a share of the government of the town, and rose from one post to another, till at last he was chosen chief magistrate. In this office he maintained a fair character, and continued to fill it with no small applause, both as governor and judge; till one day, as he sat on the bench with some of his brethren, a criminal was brought before him who was accused of murdering his master. The evidence came out full; the jury brought in their verdict that the prisoner was guilty, and the whole assembly awaited the sentence of the president of the court (which happened to be himself) in great suspense. Meanwhile he appeared to be in unusual disorder and agitation of mind; his color changed often; at length he arose from his seat, and, coming down from the bench, placed himself just by the unfortunate man at the bar, to the no small astonishment of all present. "You see before you," said he, addressing himself to those who had sat on the bench with him, "a striking instance of the just awards of Heaven, for this day, after thirty years' concealment, presents to you a greater criminal than the man just now found guilty." He then made an ample confession of his heinous offence, with all its peculiar aggravations. "Nor can I," continued he, "feel any relief from the agonies of an awakened conscience, but by requiring that justice be forthwith done against me in the most public and solemn manner." We may easily imagine the amazement of all, especially his fellow-judges. They accordingly proceeded, upon his confession, to pass sentence upon him, and he died with all the symptoms of a penitent mind.

SECTION IV.

Unknown Agents in the Punishment of Sin, &c.

THE PRAYER OF THE WICKED ANSWERED.

A CORRESPONDENT of the London Pulpit gives the following incident, which was well authenticated. A young girl, residing at Exeter, was accused by her mother of having stolen a silver spoon. She repeatedly, and in the most emphatic manner, denied the charge as often as it was reiterated. Her mother still pressed it upon her. At last, determined to conceal her guilt, and hoping to silence all further accusation, the girl exclaimed in a solemn manner, "May God strike me dead if I have the spoon." God heard her. Judgment came. She fell dead upon the spot. On examining her clothes afterwards the spoon was found concealed on her person.

THE CRUCIFIXION CARICATURED.

MELANCTHON, the Reformer, relates the following awful illustration of the judgments of Divine Prodence.

A company of profane wretches undertook to represent, in a farcical way, the death scene of our Lord Jesus Christ, when he, who acted the soldier, instead of piercing a bladder of blood, hid under the garments of the one on the cross, ran the spear into his side, and killed him. The dead man fell from the cross upon the one acting the part of the weeping woman, and killed him. The brother of the man first slain, immediately killed the murderer, and was afterwards tried and hung by sentence of the court. Thus did the judgments of Almighty God speedily overtake these wicked men, who sought to trifle with one of the most solemn scenes known to man.

FEIGNING DEATH.

THE Gazette de Lyons published the following fact; it happened at Chenas, not far from Lyons:—

A rich widow, without children, had promised to make her will in favor of her niece. The aunt fell sick, and the niece, as much through attachment as interest, lavished upon her the tenderest as well as the most assiduous cares; however, the aunt died without making a will. The niece was in despair for the loss of her friend and her hopes. She went around, told her story, and asked what could be done. Her perfidious counsellors engaged her to play the old trick of hiding the death, and placing herself in bed, calling for a notary and witnesses, and dictating a convenient testament. She did her part well, and it succeeded wonderfully in a room that was partially darkened. The young girl, sunk in a pillow and curtains, pronounced with a feeble and broken voice, the last will and testament of the aunt; the notary wrote, and the victory was nearly sure, when one of the witnesses, who knew a little more than the others, declared he would sign no such act; for that the pretended testatrix had been dead for several hours, and he would not be the accomplice of a like deception. The unhappy niece, confounded and overwhelmed, could not support the idea of the consequent shame and punishment of her guilt, and she suddenly expired. She was buried at the same time with her aunt.

A LIAR'S IMPRECATION ANSWERED.

A FEW years since, a woman in the Church Gate, Loughborough, England, went to purchase a bedstead, which was sold to her for thirteen shillings, and change given her out of a one pound note, which she gave in payment. A short time after, she went again to the shop, and asserted that eighteen pence less than the proper change was given her. This the shopkeeper denied, stating the exact coins he had given her. She, however, persisted in her declaration, and said, she wished she might die in his house if she had not spoken the truth. Awful to relate, she was immediately taken ill, was removed to another house, and soon after expired, never once speaking after she had left the shop. The money was found in her pocket, exactly as the shopkeeper had described.

PROFANITY AWFULLY VISITED.

About the year 1793, an awful incident occurred at Salem, in the state of New Jersey. There had been a revival of religion, and the pious part of the community had been disturbed with riots and mobs; but on making application to the civil magistrate, these tumults had been effectually suppressed. The opposers of religion now turned their attention to a new method of entertainment; acting in a farcical way at religious meetings, pretending to speak of their experiences, to exhort, &c., in order to amuse one another in a profane theatrical manner. One evening a young actress stood up on one of the benches, pretending to speak of her experience; and, with mock solemnity, cried out, "Glory to God!

I have found peace; I am sanctified; I am now fit to die." Scarcely had the unhappy girl uttered these words, before she actually dropped dead upon the floor, and was taken up a lifeless corpse. Struck with this awful visitation, the auditors were instantly seized with inexpressible terror, and every face was covered with consternation and dismay.

THE CONSTABLE'S ADMONITION.

In 1682, some soldiers came to break up a meeting where Mr. Browning, who had been ejected from Desborough, in Northamptonshire, was, and to apprehend him. The constable of the place, who was present, admonished them to be well advised in what they did, "For," said he, "when Sir —— was alive, he eagerly persecuted these meetings, and engaged eight soldiers of the country troop to assist him, whereof myself was one. Sir —— himself is dead; six of the soldiers are dead; some of them were hanged, and some of them broke their necks, and I myself fell off my horse and broke my collar-bone, in the act of persecuting them. This has given me such a warning, that, for my part, I am resolved I will never meddle with them more."

THE UNGRATEFUL SONS.

In Birmingham, England, once lived a family in humble circumstances. Some of the younger children and their father died, leaving the aged mother with two sons grown up, and able to assist her. This, however, they refused to do, and she was obliged to apply to the parish for relief; and for some years two shillings a week were allowed her by the overseers, which, with a small sum added by some Christian friends, was all on which she had to subsist.

During this time her youngest son died. He had lived without the fear of God, and died under a sense of his wrath, in deep agonies, both of body and mind, and uttering dreadful expressions.

The eldest son was clever in his business, got forward in the world, and became possessed of considerable property. But he still refused to assist his mother, and even while holding offices of consideration and importance, left her to subsist on her allowance from the parish. This conduct of course was noticed; he was repeatedly spoken to upon the subject; and at length he ordered her name to be taken from the parish books, and allowed her the two shillings a week out of his own pocket, at a time when he possessed thousands of pounds, and was without a family.

One day some friends were assembled, and her

case being mentioned, they proposed to remonstrate with the ungrateful son. "No," said an aged minister, "let him alone; if he dies possessed of the property he is now worth, I shall be deceived. God will never suffer such base *ingratitude* to prosper."

In a short time afterwards, the mother was removed to another world. The circumstances of the son at length began to change; repeated losses ensued, and finally he became a bankrupt, and was reduced to abject poverty.

SUFFERING DEATH WHILE FEIGNING IT.

One day, as Archbishop Leighton was going from Glasgow to Dumblane, there happened a tremendous storm of lightning and thunder. He was observed, when at a considerable distance, by two men of bad character. They had not courage to rob him; but wishing to fall on some method to extort money from him, one said, "I will lie down by the wayside as if I were dead, and you shall inform the archbishop that I was killed by the lightning, and beg money of him to bury me." When the archbishop arrived at the spot, the wicked wretch told the fabricated story: the archbishop sympathized with the survivor, gave him money, and proceeded on his journey. But when the man returned to his companion, he found him really lifeless! Immediately he began to exclaim aloud, "Oh! sir, he *is* dead! Oh! sir, he *is* dead!" On this, the archbishop, discovering the fraud, left the man with this important reflection: "It is a dangerous thing to trifle with the judgments of God!"

THE PERJURER'S IMPRECATION.

A MAN once waited on a magistrate near Hitchin, in the county of Hertford (England), and informed him that he had been stopped by a young gentleman in Hitchin, who had knocked him down and searched his pockets; but not finding anything, he had suffered him to depart. The magistrate, astonished at this intelligence, despatched a messenger to the young gentleman, ordering him to appear immediately, and answer to the charge exhibited against him. The youth obeyed the summons, accompanied by his guardian and an intimate friend. Upon their arrival at the seat of justice, the accused and accuser were confronted; when the magistrate hinted to the man, that he was afraid he had made the charge with no other view than that of extorting money, and bade him take care how he proceeded; exhorting him, in the most earnest and pathetic manner, to beware of the dreadful train of consequences attending perjury. The man insisted upon making oath to what he had advanced; the oath was accordingly administered, and the business fully investigated, when the innocence of the young gentleman was established, by the most incontrovertible evidence. The infamous wretch, finding his intentions thus frustrated, returned home much chagrined; and meeting soon afterwards with one of his neighbors, he declared he had not sworn to anything but the truth, calling God to witness the same in the most solemn manner, and wished, if it was not as he had said, his jaws might be locked, and that his flesh might rot upon his bones; when, terrible to relate, his jaws were instantly arrested, and he was deprived of the use of the faculty he had so awfully perverted! After lingering nearly a fortnight, he expired in the greatest agonies, his flesh literally rotting upon his bones.

THE TWISTED NECK.

At a general muster in one of the Western States, a wicked man being addressed on the subject of religion was filled with rage, and uttered the horrid declaration that if Jesus of Nazareth was there, he would wring his neck! Suddenly a violent spasm seized the neck of the blasphemer, twisted it round, rolled his eyes nearly out of their sockets, and left him in this frightful position, a living monument of outraged omnipotence. "This fact," says a writer in the Vermont Chronicle, "was stated at a public meeting in this vicinity lately by a respectable gentleman of the bar from Ohio." The meeting referred to, took place in Lebanon, Ohio, and the lawyer referred to was Mr. Latham. His statements having been called in question, Mr. Latham procured a full corroboration of them from the Rev. Ahab Jenks, of Delaware, Ohio, who resided in the immediate vicinity where the circumstance took place.

BETTING AND DYING.

THE following relation of facts was presented to the public in several of the London newspapers of February 13, 1814 :—A melancholy event occurred yesterday evening, between seven and eight o'clock, at the cock-pit, St. Giles's. Whilst preparations were making for the setting-to of the cocks, to engage in this cruel sport, a Mr. Thorpe, from the country, a well-known character, had taken his seat in the front of the pit, and not two minutes before his death, had offered to back the Huntingdon birds for ten guineas. He was observed to lean his head forward, and appeared somewhat ill. He made a kind of moan, and instantly his color changed, and he was a corpse. Surgical aid was immediately procured, but the spark of life was extinct. The body was removed to a neighboring public-house, for the inspection of a coroner's inquest. The wife and sister of the deceased soon arrived to see the body, and the reader may judge of their feelings. It is a fact no less singular than true, that the deceased, half an hour before his death, had said, "The last time I was here, I said, if ever I attended the pit again, I hoped I should die there."

THE NEWBURG INFIDELS.

DURING the prevalence of infidelity that occurred in this country after the reign of terror in France, Newburg, New York, was remarkable for its Deism. Through the influence of "Blind Palmer," there was formed a Druidical Society, so called, which had a high priest, and met at stated times, to uproot and destroy all true religion. They descended sometimes to acts the most impious and blasphemous. Thus, for instance, at one of their meetings in Newburg, they burned the Bible, baptized a cat, partook of the sacrament, and one of the number, approved by the rest, administered it to a dog. Now mark the retributive judgments of God towards these blasphemers, which at once commenced falling upon them. On the evening of that very day, he who had administered this mock sacrament was attacked with a violent inflammatory disease; his inflamed eyeballs were protruded from their sockets; his tongue was swollen; and he died before morning in great bodily and mental agony. Dr. H., another of the same party, was found dead in his bed the next morning. D. D., a printer, who was present, three days after fell in a fit, and died immediately; and three others were drowned in a few days. In short, within five years from the time the Druidical Society was organized, it is a remarkable fact, that all the original members died in some strange or unnatural manner. There were thirty-six of them; and these were the actors in the horrid farce described above. Two were starved to death; seven drowned; eight shot; five committed suicide; seven died on the gallows; one was frozen to death; and three died "*accidentally.*"

Of the foregoing statements there is good proof. They have been certified before justices of the peace in New York; and again and again published to the world.

THE BLASPHEMOUS SAILOR.

The following fact took place in the spring of 1812, at a public-house in Rochester, in the county of Kent (England):—

Two wicked sailors meeting at a tavern one day, began to curse and swear, when the more violent of the two, in a tempest of passion, swore that he would kill the other. The awe-struck landlord, raising his voice, said to the sailor who had made the threat, " What if God of a sudden should strike *you* dead, and sink you into hell with his curse upon you!" The sailor replied with a terrible oath, " The Almighty *cannot* do that—give me the tankard of beer—if God *can* do it, I'll go to hell before I drink it up."

With an awful oath he seized the tankard, but instantly fell down and expired!

All blasphemers are not thus suddenly and singularly cut off; but there is a point in every blasphemer's progress in sin, beyond which the forbearance of God cannot be extended to him longer. And how often does God say to such men, in the midst of their awful contempt and mockery of his power, " Thus far shalt thou go, and no farther." We do not suppose that any miracle is wrought in such cases; but God, working in and through natural laws, so often causes sudden and awful deaths in immediate connection with bold and impious blasphemy, that we are justified in regarding such a death as a judgment of God, sent in consequence of the blasphemy.

We mean to say as much as this, that in such cases the sinner's blasphemy and death are so far related to each other, that if the one had not been committed, the other had not occurred; if he had not blasphemed as he did, he had not died as he did.

PART IV.

ILLUSTRATIONS OF DIVINE PROVIDENCE IN THE CONVERSION OF MEN.

"And the Lord added to the church daily such as should be saved."—Acts ii. 47.

SECTION I.

Conversions effected by Human Agency.

THE DELIVERANCE OF THE REV. MR. HOWE.

WHEN the melancholy state of the times compelled this excellent man to quit the public charge of his beloved congregation at Torrington, in Devonshire, impressed with a sense of duty, he embraced every opportunity of preaching the word of life. He and Mr. Flavel used frequently to conduct their secret ministrations at midnight in different houses in the north of Devonshire. One of the principal of these was Hudscott, an ancient mansion belonging to the family of Rolle, between Torrington and Southmolton. Yet, even here, the observant eye of malevolence was upon them. Mr. Howe had been officiating there, in a dark and tempestuous wintry night, when an alarm was made that information had been given, and a warrant granted to apprehend him. It was judged prudent for him to quit the house; but in riding over a large common, he and his servant missed their way. After several fruitless efforts to recover it, the attendant went forward to seek for a habitation, where they might either find directions or a lodging. He soon discovered a mansion, and received a cheerful invitation to rest there for the night. But how great was Mr. Howe's surprise, to find, on his arrival, that the house belonged to his most inveterate enemy, a country magistrate, who had often breathed the most implacable vengeance against him, and, as he had reason to believe, was well acquainted with the occasion of his travelling at such an hour. However, he put the best face he could upon it, and even mentioned his name and residence to the gentleman, trusting to Providence for the result. His host ordered supper to be provided, and entered into a lengthened conversation with his guest; and was so delighted with his company, that it was a very late hour before he could permit him to retire to his chamber. In the morning, Mr. Howe expected to be accosted with a commitment, and sent to Exeter; but, on the contrary, he was received by the family at breakfast with a very hospitable welcome. After mutual civilities, he departed to his own abode, greatly wondering to himself at the kindness of a man from whom he had before dreaded so much.

Not long after, the gentleman sent for Mr. Howe, who found him confined to his bed by sickness, and still more deeply wounded with a sense of sin. He acknowledged that, when Mr. Howe came first to his door, he inwardly rejoiced that he had an opportunity of exercising his malice upon him, but that his conversation and his manner insensibly awed him into respect. He had long ruminated on the observations which had fallen from the man of God, and was become a penitent, earnestly anxious for the blessings of eternal life. From that sickness he recovered, became an eminent Christian, a friend to the conscientious, and an intimate companion of the man whom he had threatened with his vengeance.

THE CONVERTED ACTRESS.

An actress, in one of the English provincial or country theatres, was one day passing through the streets of the town in which she then resided, when her attention was attracted by the sound of voices, which she heard in a poor cottage before her. Curiosity prompted her to look in at an open door, when she saw a few poor people sitting together, one of whom, at the moment of her observation, was giving out the following hymn, which the others joined in singing:—

> "Depth of mercy! can there be
> Mercy still reserved for me?"

The tune was sweet and simple, but she heeded it not. The words had riveted her attention, and she stood motionless, until she was invited to enter, by the woman of the house, who had observed her standing at the door. She complied, and remained during a prayer which was offered up by one of the little company; and uncouth as the expressions sounded, perhaps, to her ears, they carried with them a conviction of sincerity, on the part of the person then employed. She quitted the cottage, but the words of the hymn followed her. She could not banish them from her mind, and at last she resolved to procure the book which contained it. She did so, and the more she read it, the more decided her serious impressions became. She attended the ministry of the gospel, read her hitherto neglected and despised Bible, and bowed herself in humility and contrition of heart, before him whose mercy she now felt she needed, whose sacrifices are those of a broken heart and a contrite spirit, and who has declared, that with such sacrifices he is well pleased.

Her profession she determined at once and for ever to renounce; and for some little time excused herself from appearing on the stage, without, however, disclosing her change of sentiments or making known her resolution finally to leave it.

The manager of the theatre called upon her one morning, and requested her to sustain the principal character in a new play which was to be performed the next week for his benefit. She had frequently performed this character to general admiration; but she now, however, told him her resolution never to appear as an actress again, at the same time giving her reasons. At first he attempted to overcome her scruples by ridicule, but this was unavailing; he then represented the loss he would incur by her refusal, and concluded his arguments by promising, that if she would act on this occasion, it would be the last request of the kind he should ever make. Unable to resist his solicitations, she promised to appear, and on the appointed evening went to the theatre. The character she assumed required her, on her entrance, to sing a song; and when the curtain drew up, the orchestra began the accompaniment. But she stood as if lost in thought, and as one forgetting all around her, and her own situation. The music ceased, but she did not sing; supposing her to be overcome by embarrassment, the band commenced again. A second time they paused for her to begin, and still she did not open her lips. A third time the air was played, and then, with clasped hands, and eyes suffused with tears, she sang, not the song, but,

> "Depth of mercy! can there be
> Mercy still reserved for me?"

It is almost needless to add, that the performance was suddenly ended; many ridiculed, though some were induced from that memorable night to "consider their ways," and to reflect on the wonderful power of that religion which could so influence the heart and change the life of one so vain, and so evidently pursuing "the road to ruin."

It might be satisfactory to the reader to know, that the change in Miss —— was as permanent as it was singular; she walked consistently with her profession of religion for a number of years, and at length became the wife of a minister of the Gospel.

CONVERSION OF THE HALDANES.

The Rev. James Haldane (pastor of one of the Baptist churches in Edinburgh, Scotland), says Rev. Mr. Turnbull, was a junior member of a highly respectable and wealthy family. In his youth he became connected with the British navy, and rose to the post of captain, in one of his majesty's war ships. On one occasion, being engaged in a warmly contested battle, he saw the whole of his men on deck swept off by a tremendous broadside from the enemy. He ordered another company to be "piped up" from below, to take the place of their lost companions. On coming up, they saw their mangled remains strewn upon the deck, and were seized with a sudden and irresistible panic. On seeing this, the captain jumped up, and swore a horrid oath, imprecating the vengeance of Almighty God upon the whole of them, and wishing that they might all sink to hell. An old marine, who was a pious man, stepped up to him, and respectfully touching his hat, said:—"Captain, I believe God hears prayer; and if God had heard your prayer just now, what would have become of us?" Having spoken this, he made a respectful bow, and retired to his place. After the engagement, the captain calmly reflected upon the words of the old marine, and was so deeply affected by them, that he devoted his attention to the claims of religion, and was subsequently converted to God.

Of course he informed his brother Robert of his change of views, but, instead of being gratified by it, his brother was greatly offended, and requested him never to enter his house till he had changed his views. "Very well, Robert," said James, "but I have one comfort in the case, and that is, you cannot prevent my praying for you;" and holding out his hand, he bade him good-bye. His brother Robert was much affected by this; he could not get rid of the idea that his brother was constantly praying for him. He saw the error of his ways, and, after much investigation and reflection, became a decided Christian.

Some years afterwards, Robert Haldane made a journey to the continent, and settled for some time in Geneva. He was much affected with the low spiritual condition of the Protestant church there, which had become infected with the rationalistic and neological views prevalent in Germany. Indeed, the clergy themselves had so far departed from the faith of the Reformation, as to reject almost all the fundamental doctrines of the gospel, particularly the divinity of Christ, and the doctrine of atonement. Mr. Haldane made himself acquainted with the students attending the divinity school in Geneva, and invited a number of them to his house, and, by free conversation, endeavored to teach them the gospel, and the nature of spiritual religion. This he frequently repeated, till, at last, God blessed his efforts to the conversion of ten or twelve of them. Among them were *Felix Neff*, subsequently pastor in the High Alps, and one of the purest and most devoted men that ever lived; *Henry Pyt*, another well known and truly pious man; and *Henry Merle d'Aubigné*, well known throughout the literary and religious world as the author of the History of the Reformation, and President of the New Evangelical School of Theology in Geneva.

THE WRECKED SAILOR LED TO GOD.

A SHIP, says Rev. John Blain, was wrecked amongst the rocks, near Cape Horn. While the winds fiercely blew, and the foaming billows dashed the timbers in pieces, one seaman reached a lonely, barren rock. The day passed slowly away. He stretched his eye to the east and west, to the north and south, over the deep, dark, and ever restless waters—but no friendly sail appeared!

The sun disappeared, and he sat down to pass in solitude the lonely night. His shipmates were cold and silent in their watery graves. The waves dashed against the rock, the winds passed swiftly onward, the lamps of night shed their dismal light on the bosom of the deep—but no human voice sounded in his ear, no brother's hand administered to his wants. Hunger and thirst made strong demands, but he had no means to relieve them. The bread and the water were entombed with his companions. Nor had he any consolation to draw from a future world. The Bible and the Redeemer had been neglected, and he was strangely indifferent. Another day came and passed, and another night. On the third night, as he lay on his back, gazing into the starry heavens, he began to think about *God* and *eternity*, his past life, and the interests of his soul. But all was dark. His skin was peeling from his face, his teeth all loose, his thirst almost intolerable, and death seemed to stand by his side. He had never prayed, nor did he know how to pray. A single commandment was all he remembered, and that commandment his dear mother taught him when a child. And how should he meet that mother and his God in a future world? His sins passed in review, and pressed on his guilty conscience, while bitter tears of repentance began to roll down his scalded cheeks. Without knowing what the Lord required of him, he rose, stood on his knees, lifted his feeble hands towards heaven, and there on that lonely rock, far, far away from home and friends, he submitted all to God, and most solemnly promised, if his life was spared, he would *learn* and do whatever God required. From that consecrated and blessed hour, peace flowed into his soul—Christ was his Saviour, and hope entered within the vail. The next day the life-boat from a passing ship took him from the Bethel rock. He landed in Boston, found the sailor's friend, and the sailor's home, and listened to the gospel of peace. Father Taylor gave him a Bible, which he read with prayerful attention. He came to New York—visited different churches, searched for truth, remembered his solemn vow, and in February, 1843, while I was preaching in the Baptist Tabernacle, he offered himself to the church. On hearing his experience, every heart felt—every eye wept. Brother Wm. W. Evarts baptized him, welcomed him to the church, and *he went on his way rejoicing.*

THE INFIDEL'S CHILD.

The following fact, communicated by a foreign correspondent of the *American Spectator* at Albany, shows alike the blessing of Sunday schools, and the influences which even these "little ones" may exert upon others for good.

In the city of London there lived a little girl,

who attended, for three years, and by stealth, the teaching of a Sabbath school. Coming under the saving influence of truth, she became concerned for her father, a noted infidel and active opposer to Christianity. She obtained a Bible, but knew not how to put it into his hands; for she feared his displeasure, and dreaded any prohibition which might deprive her of the prized advantages of the Sunday school. She retired to seek Divine guidance. Her father passing the door of the apartment, heard the voice of his child; it was the voice of prayer—she prayed for him. He became affected, agitated, distressed. After a little while, the family assembled at tea-table; the beverage was handed around, but he could not partake.

"Is there a Bible in the house?" said he.

"My dear," replied his wife, apprehensive of the purposed repetition of the act, "did you not burn every Bible that we had, not leaving so much as one?" "Is there any other good book then?" he inquired. His little daughter, thinking that God might be answering her prayer, arose and took him by the hand, and asked him to go with her; and when they had left the room, looking into his face, said, "Father, sure you won't be angry with me. Come with me, and I will get you one." And she brought him and gave him the Bible which, for this very purpose, she had procured. He felt deeply, and trembling, while he handed it back to her, said, "My child, I cannot read this book. Will you read it for me?" She did so. And then taking her in his arms he kissed her, and said, "Tell me, my child, where did you get this book, and how you obtained the knowledge of it?"

She told him all—how she attended the Sunday school, the effect upon herself, and how she became concerned for his salvation. That evening, he accompanied her to the chapel. As they entered, the minister was engaged in prayer. His manner and address made a powerful impression on the father's mind, for he seemed to walk with God. The sermon aided in deepening the impression. It was an interesting sight, when, two or three Sundays afterward, that father appeared in that chapel, with his wife and nine children, and openly renounced his infidelity. That was the Weigh House chapel; the minister, Thomas Binney; and that infidel, reclaimed through the influence of Sunday school instruction on the heart of his child, was the celebrated author of "The Every Day Book."

THE CONVERSION OF MR. COLLINS'S FATHER.

SHORTLY after Mr. Collins removed his family to the West, he became deeply solicitous for the conversion of his father. The old gentleman remained in New Jersey, and was a very respectable member of the Quaker society. This feeling became so strong, that he was led to the determination to visit

New Jersey, for the sole purpose of soliciting this parent to seek religion. He set out on horseback with this view; and during the long journey, he scarcely passed over a mile of the road without lifting up his heart to God in prayer for his venerable parent. He arrived at his former home in safety, and was kindly and affectionately received by his family. He talked much of religion, and prayed with the family. Some days after his return, his father observed to him, "John, we are all glad to see thee; but I don't like thy religion." This was unexpected, and it greatly depressed him. After some reflection, he resolved to spend the whole ensuing night in prayer for his father. Accordingly, after nightfall, he retired to the barn, that he might not be interrupted. Here he was engaged in fervent prayer, until near ten o'clock. Some one knocked at the door; but he made no answer. In a short time, another messenger came, and opening the door, discovered him. This messenger was his sister, who had experienced religion, and who informed him that he had been sought for in his room, at his brother's, near by, and at other places, and that he was supposed to be in the barn. And she told him that their father was suffering the greatest mental agony, and wished to see him.

With a joyful heart, Mr. Collins hurried to the room of his father, and, embracing him, wept and prayed with him. The struggle continued till near daylight, when deliverance came.

His father was filled with peace, with joy, and triumph. This was a glorious answer to his tears and prayers. His joy was inexpressible, and full of glory. The father and son were united more closely than they ever had been. Having fulfilled his mission, and attained its great object, Mr. Collins separated from his friends, and returned to his home in Ohio.—*Life of Collins.*

THE BEGGAR AND THE DIVINE.

The celebrated mystical writer, Taulerus, gives an interesting account of a certain divine, who, being ignorant of true religion, most earnestly besought God, with strong cries and fervent prayers, for the space of eight years, that he would direct him to some one who would point out to him the way to heaven. At length he received an intimation, that if he would go to the church, he would there find one who would satisfy the longing desires of his soul. When he came to the church, he saw no person but a poor, care-worn beggar, clothed in tattered garments. He saluted the beggar thus:—

"God grant that this may be a pleasant morning to thee."

The beggar replied, "Sir, I do not recollect of ever having experienced an unpleasant morning."

"What is this thou sayest?" exclaimed the astonished divine. "I hope that God may confer every favor upon you."

The beggar replied, "Sir, God's favors have always been upon me."

The divine, being much perplexed, and not knowing how to understand the beggar, requested him to explain himself.

"That I will, most cheerfully," answered the beggar. "You first wished me a pleasant morning. I replied that I had never experienced an unpleasant one, and this is actually the case; for, when I am hungry, I praise God; when I am cold, I praise him; when it rains or snows, when it thunders and lightens, no matter what kind of weather it is, I always praise the Lord; and this is the reason why I have never experienced an unpleasant morning. You then wished that God might confer every favor upon me. To this I replied, that God's favors had always been upon me, and this is also true. For I commit myself into the hands of God, and am certain that he does all things for the best. Everything, therefore, that God permits to befall me, whether it be sweet or sour, joyful or sorrowful, fortunate or unfortunate, I look upon as intended for my good, and receive it with gratitude; for all things must work together for the good of them that love the Lord."

At this discourse the divine was astonished, and asked him this question: "What would you do, if God should cast you into hell?"

"Cast me into hell!" exclaimed the beggar; "that God will not do: but if he were to cast me into hell, I have two arms—an arm of faith, and an arm of love: with these I would lay hold on God, and cling to him so firmly, that I would take him with me down to hell. And surely no evil could befall me then; *for I would rather be with God in hell, than to be in heaven without him.*" It is scarcely necessary to say, that the divine found out that the way to heaven is to believe and love.

ANSWER TO PRAYER.

"Have you heard," said a friend whom I met one morning, "of the conversion of —— —— and his wife?" Is it possible! Is it possible! I was well acquainted with Mr. —— —— and his wife. I knew him to be a skeptical Universalist, who had failed in trade, and seemed to be unfriendly towards every thing, but especially towards the religion of Christ. I knew him to be in many respects, "far from righteousness," and to human appearance, very unlikely to become a disciple of Christ.

The circumstances of his conversion, which it was my principal design to relate, were the following. His wife, who was naturally an unassuming and amiable woman, had her attention by some means arrested, and became anxious to attend the public worship of God. On Sabbath morning she stated to her husband her desire, if he had no objection, to attend meeting at the "white meeting-house:" apparently offended, he instantly expressed his unwillingness; but added, that he had no objection to her going to the other house. The only cause doubtless of his preference at that time was, the revival existed almost exclusively among the congregation belonging to the "white house." Being grieved with his refusal, and at the spirit which he exhibited, the woman, when their breakfast was passed, unobserved left the house for a thicket of bushes which stood at a little distance across a field. The husband also left the house and directed his course to the same place, but for very different purposes. The house and most of the farm being concealed by hills and forests from the inspection of all but now and then a traveller, it afforded him an opportunity, which he was too ready to improve, to waste the holy Sabbath in wandering about the fields. At this time, he was furnished with a powerful temptation, by the clusters of berries that grew upon the borders of the field. Here, while busily partaking of these clusters, he heard indistinctly a human voice; he listened—and the first distinct sentence that fell upon his ear, was a prayer in a voice that he instantly recognised, and from a heart that felt beyond the power of description. *It was a prayer for him.* That was the time for the Spirit of God. His heart melted, and he literally fell to the ground. After a short season he arose and returned to his house, and with a pale countenance, and trembling solemnity that can scarcely be conceived, informed his wife (who had returned home before him, not knowing where he had been) that he would accompany her to church, and to the "white meeting-house," if she would assist him in making preparations. With astonishment she heard this, and immediately began to bring forward his clothes. The shock, however, which he had received, was too much for his hardy constitution. He threw himself upon his bed, and began audibly to cry for mercy. His distress of mind continued to increase, till the powers of his body were prostrate, and about the middle of the afternoon service, a messenger was despatched for the minister at the "white meeting-house," the man, who of all others, till then, he had most sincerely hated. At the close of divine service, the minister went immediately to see him, and found him writhing and groaning upon his bed. In this state of mind he continued till near morning, when he became a little composed. It was not, if I correctly remember, more than two or three days, before he was rejoicing in the Lord, apparently a "new man." In process of time, he and his wife both united with the people of God, and, according to the best information I had, they were walking in the "footsteps of his flock."

THE SIXPENCE.

Some time in the latter part of the last century, says Rev. Mr. Grinnell, a missionary from one of the New England Societies was laboring in the interior of the state of New York, where the settlements were very few and far between. This missionary was much devoted to his work, meek and affable, and possessed of a remarkable faculty for introducing the subject of religion to every individual with whom he came in contact. On a hot summer's day, while his horse was drinking from a small brook through which he rode, there came along a poor-dressed, bare-headed, bare-footed boy, about seven years old, and stood looking at the missionary from the bridge just above him.

" My son," said the missionary, " have you any parents ?"

" Yes, sir; they live in that house," pointing to a cabin near by.

" Do your parents pray ?"

" No, sir."

" Why do they not pray ?'

" I do not know, sir."

" Do you pray ?"

" No, sir."

" Why do you not pray ?"

" I do not know how to pray."

" Can you read ?"

"Yes, sir; my mother has taught me to read the New Testament."

"If I will give you this sixpence, will you go home and read the third chapter of John, and read the third verse over three times?" The little boy said he would; and the missionary gave him the sixpence and rode on.

Some twenty years had elapsed, and the same missionary, advanced in years, was laboring in a sparsely peopled region, in another part of the same state. While on his way to a little village one day, late in the afternoon, he called at a small house, and inquired the distance. "Six miles," was the reply. He then stated that himself and horse were very weary, and inquired if he could not stay all night. The woman of the house objected on account of their poverty, but the husband said, "Sir, you shall be welcome to such as we have."

The missionary dismounted and went in. The wife began to prepare his supper, while the husband proceeded to take care of the horse. As he came in, the missionary addressed him: "Do you love the Lord Jesus Christ?" "That," said the man, "is a great question." "True," said the missionary, "but I cannot eat till you tell me." "Sir," said the man, "about twenty years ago, I lived in the interior of this state, and was then about seven years old. While playing in the road one day, a gentleman in black rode into the brook near by me, to water his horse. As I stood on the bridge above looking at him, he began to converse with me about praying, and reading the Bible; and told me he would give me a sixpence if I would read the third chapter of John, and the third verse three times— "And Jesus answered and said unto him, Verily I say unto thee, except a man be born again he cannot see the kingdom of God." I gave him my promise, took the money, and felt wealthy indeed. I went home, and read as I had promised. That verse produced an uneasiness in my mind, which followed me for days and years, and finally I was led by its influence, as I trust, to love Jesus as my Saviour!" "Glory to God!" said the missionary, rising from his seat; "here is one of my spiritual children; the bread cast on the waters is found after many days!"

They took their supper, and talked, and sang, and prayed, and rejoiced together all night long, neither of them having any disposition to sleep. The missionary found him to be poor in this world's goods, but rich in faith, and an heir of the kingdom. Early in the morning they parted, and the missionary went his way, inspired with fresh zeal for the prosecution of his pious labors.

THE CHILD AND THE SHOEMAKER.

When Mr. Whitfield was preaching in America, a certain lady in New England became a subject of grace, and a praying, experienced Christian. But she was alone in her exercises; she could influence none to pray with her but her little daughter, between nine and eleven years of age. This child she took into her closet with her, from day to day, a witness to her cries and tears. It pleased God, after some time, to touch the heart of the child, and after sorrow for sin, to give her the knowledge of salvation through the remission of sin. The child, then about eleven years of age, in a transport which is so peculiar to such a blessed experience, said, "O, mother, if all the world knew this! I wish I could tell everybody! Pray, mother, let me run to some of the neighbors, and tell them, that they may be happy, and love my Saviour too."

"Ah! my dear child," said the mother, "that would be needless; for I suppose if you were to tell your experience, there is not one in many miles but what would laugh at you, and say it was all delusion."

"O, mother," said the child, "I think they would believe me. I must go over to the shoemaker and tell him; he will believe me."

She ran over, and found him at work in his shop. She began by telling him that he must die, and that he was a sinner, and that she was a sinner, but that her blessed Saviour had heard her mother's prayers, and had forgiven all her sins; and that now she was so happy she did not know how to tell it! The shoemaker was struck; his tears flowed down like rain; he threw aside his work, and cried for mercy, by prayer and supplication. That alarmed the neighborhood, and in a few months from that time there were above fifty people brought to the knowledge of Jesus, and experienced his power and grace.

THE EMPEROR ALEXANDER.

The following incident is related in a letter of the Russian Princess, Mestchersky, and published in a volume of observations on Russia, which has just appeared in London, from the pen of Dr. Pinkerton, the well known agent of the British and Foreign Bible Society:—

About the middle of the year 1812, the emperor, about to quit St. Petersburg, and having already taken leave of his august family, had retired into his cabinet, and, quite alone, was employed in arranging some affairs before his departure. All at once he beheld a female enter, whom at first he did not recognise, there being little light in the room. Astonished at this apparition—for never was a woman permitted to enter his cabinet without leave, not even of his own family, and above all at this unseasonable hour—he however arose, went to meet her, and perceived it to be the Countess Tolstoi, who, excusing herself for the liberty she had taken, from a desire to wish him a happy journey, presented him at the same time with a paper. The emperor, at all times condescending, and sensible of the least proof of attachment, thanked her, and bade her adieu. The paper he supposed to contain a petition for something, and therefore put it into his pocket; and when she was gone resumed his former employment. Soon after he took his departure without thinking more about it.

At the first night's quarters, fatigued with cares, and alone, he wished to ease his thoughts by turning them to some specific object. He took out the paper from his pocket, opened it, and saw with surprise that it contained the ninety-first psalm. He read it with pleasure, and its Divine contents calmed his troubled spirit: and his heart said in secret, "O that these words were addressed to me!" As this thought passed through his mind some one entered the room and interrupted him. He again set off, and all was forgotten.

A considerable time after this he found himself in Moscow, in one of the most critical periods of his life (Who can be ignorant of the terrible events of the memorable year 1812?). Alone in his cabinet he was arranging some books on a table, one of which caused a volume of the Bible to fall down (it was De Sacy's version in 4to). In falling it opened, and the emperor on taking it up happened to cast his eye upon the page, and behold again the psalm which had once comforted him!—At this time he recognised the voice which called him, and he replied and said, "Here I am, Lord! speak to thy servant!" He read—he applied what he read—and he found every word suitable to himself; and ever after, until his last breath, he carried this psalm about his person, learned it by heart, and evening and morning recited it at his devotions.

The princess gives the following as the observations of the emperor on his religious progress:—

"I felt myself," said he, "like a child. Experience has taught me my insufficiency. Faith made me commit myself entirely to Him who hath spoken to me in the psalm, and had inspired me with a security and a force altogether new to me. At every fresh difficulty to be overcome, at every decision to be taken, or question to be solved, I went, if I had an opportunity, and threw myself at the feet of my Father who is in heaven, or recollecting myself for a few moments, I cried to him from the bottom of my heart, and all was smoothed, decided, and executed marvellously—all difficulties fled before the Lord, who marched before me. Without ceasing I read his word." These are his own words. She adds:—

And I must say that I have often been astonished—and not only I, but other persons also, even the most instructed and advanced Christians have been compelled to admire his enlightened faith, and his deep knowledge, drawn purely from the sacred Scriptures—his true humility, and how he gave himself up to that simplicity which the Lord requires when he promiseth, "Verily I say unto you, except ye be converted, and become as little children, ye shall not enter into the kingdom of heaven."

GOD MEANT IT FOR GOOD.

A few years since, says a writer in Pastor's Journal, I was engaged in a wholesale mercantile business in the city of New York; but ill health and other circumstances compelled me to close it and remove to the country. My young men were most of them from pious families; some were warm-hearted Christians, and all of them succeeded in finding eligible situations but one. S. was my youngest clerk; his talents were respectable; his conduct, as far as I could judge, was irreproachable; but my best efforts, and those of his friends, could not secure him a situation. After months spent in vain endeavors to find an opening in the business of his choice, and a year occupied on a foreign voyage without success, he returned to the country and engaged reluctantly in a mechanical business, which his father followed, near the place where I had settled. I saw him but seldom; but when I met him as his friend, I was treated with marked coldness. I was at a loss to account for it, and at length demanded an explanation, when I found the whole family considered me culpably to blame in not procuring him a situation in New

York, after I had no longer occasion for his services. It was indeed a mystery even to myself, that the path to manhood chosen by S. and his friends, should be so hedged up as to compel him to walk in another. S. however continued his mechanical pursuits, and, in the providence of God, was directed to the neighborhood of a protracted meeting. He was the child of many prayers, and had more than once lived through an awakening unchanged, though not unaffected. He was now drawn, by an impulse he could not resist, to attend this meeting, feeling that it might be the last strivings of the Spirit. With trembling he took his place on the anxious seat, and, overwhelmed with emotion, he retired from the meeting to a field, where he gave himself away to his Saviour, and the Spirit spake peace to his soul. It was but a few days after this happy event, S. returned to our village (where his parents still reside), and the humble, meek, and gentle air which his manly countenance had assumed, in place of the haughty, discontented form, was apparent to every one. I was confined to my house by indisposition, and was delighted to welcome him who had scarcely entered my dwelling since his return from the city. He modestly gave me an account of the change in his feelings and happiness, in presence of some members of my family, and solicited a private interview. On retiring with him, he said to me, with tears in his eyes: *"My mind has been sorely troubled by the recollection of some things I did*

in your store. I was tempted to take sundry small articles, for my own use, without your knowledge or consent, amounting, I should think, to five dollars, and I cannot rest until I have paid you for them!!"
A crowd of reflections rushed into my mind. I felt overwhelmed for a moment with a sense of the goodness of God, in so counteracting all his plans as to save him from the vortex which was opening before him. He had begun to rob his employer, and, as the progress in vice is rapid downward, had not a kind Providence interposed, S. would, in all probability, have become, ere this, a tenant of the state prison, and brought down the gray hairs of his parents with sorrow to the grave. I pointed out to him, as I trust, faithfully and profitably, the finger of God in his rescue, and encouraged him to persevere unto the end. It is now nearly two years since this interview, and S. has continued to give evidence of the sincerity of the change, and bids fair to become an ornament to society and a pillar in the church of Christ.

SECTION II.

Conversions by the Bible or Unintelligent Agents.

THE INFIDEL AND THE FIRST CHAPTER OF JOHN.

FRANCIS JUNIUS, the younger, was a considerable scholar, but by no means prejudiced in favor of the Scriptures, as appears by his own account, which is as follows:—

My father, who was frequently reading the New Testament, and had long observed with grief the progress I had made in infidelity, had put that book in my way in his library, in order to attract my attention, if it might please God to bless his design, though without giving me the least intimation of it. Here, therefore, I unwittingly opened the New Testament, thus providentially laid before me. At the very first view, as I was deeply engaged in other thoughts, that grand chapter of the evangelist and apostle presented itself to me, "In the beginning was the Word," &c. I read part of the chapter, and was so affected, that I instantly became struck with the divinity of the argument, and the majesty and authority of the composition, as infinitely surpassing the highest flights of human eloquence. My body shuddered; my mind was all in amazement; and I was so agitated the whole day, that I scarce knew who I was. "Thou didst remember me, O Lord my God, according to thy boundless mercy, and didst bring back the lost sheep to thy flock." From that day God wrought so mightily in me by the power of his Spirit, that I began to have less relish for all other studies and pursuits, and bent myself with greater ardor and attention to everything which had a relation to God.

THE PERTINENT TEXT.

ONE Sabbath morning, while the Rev. Dr. Bedell, of Philadelphia, was preaching, a young man passed by, with a number of companions, as gay and thoughtless as himself. One of them proposed to go into the church, saying, "Let us go and hear what this man has to say, that everybody is running after." The young man made this awful answer: "No; I would not go into such a place if Christ himself was preaching." Some weeks after, he was again passing the church, and being alone, and having nothing to do, he thought he would go in without being observed. On opening the door, he was struck with awe at the solemn silence of the place, though it was much crowded. Every eye was fixed on the preacher, who was to begin his discourse. His attention was instantly caught by the text, "I discerned among the youths a young man void of understanding:" Prov. vii. 7. His conscience was smitten by the power of truth. He saw that *he* was the young man described. A view of his profligate life passed before his eyes, and, for the first time, he trembled under the feeling of sin. He remained in the church till the preacher and congregation had passed out; then slowly returned to his home. He had early received infidel principles, but the Holy Spirit who had aroused him in his folly, led him to a constant attendance on the ministry of Dr. B., who had been the instrument of awakening his mind. He cast away his besetting sin, and gave himself to a life of virtue and holiness. He afterwards declared openly his faith in the Lord Jesus Christ, and his desire to devote himself to his service.

THE SPIRITUAL LIFE-BUOY.

SAID a youth to one of the secretaries of the Bethel Companies: "I sailed from London, in a Scotch vessel, for the West Indies, second mate, the most abandoned wretch that ever sailed on salt water, particularly noted for profane swearing. Our captain, though a good seaman, and kind to his ship's company, cared not either for his own soul, or for the souls of his ship's crew. We had been at sea about sixteen days, when one night, during my watch on deck, a sudden puff of wind caused the vessel to give a heavy lurch. Not being prepared to meet it, I was capsized, and came head on against one of the stanchions. Feeling much hurt, I gave vent to my anger by a dreadful oath, cursing the wind, the ship, the sea, and (awful to mention) the Being who made them. Scarce had this horrid oath escaped me when it appeared to roll back upon my mind with so frightful an image, that I ran aft, and for a moment or two thought I saw the sea parting, and the vessel going down. All that night my awful oath was passing before my eyes like a spectre, and its consequences, my certain damnation. For several days I was miserable; ashamed to say the cause. I asked one of the men for a book; he gave me one of Rousseau's novels. I asked him for a Testament, and he sneeringly answered by asking me if I was going to die. He never troubled himself with these things; he left Bibles and prayer-books to the priests. Several days thus passed in the greatest torment, this dreadful oath always before me, and the devil continually harassing me with the dreadful thought, 'I shall be damned, I shall be damned.' I could not pray; indeed, I thought it of no use. On the fifth day I was turning over some things in my chest, when I found some trifles I had purchased for sea-stock wrapped in paper—this piece of paper (putting his hand at the same time into his pocket, and from a small red case taking out a leaf containing nearly the whole of the first chapter of Isaiah). Oh! how my heart throbbed, when I found it a part of the Bible! But, sir," said he, with a tear, "conceive what I felt at these words, 'Though your sins be as scarlet, they shall be white as snow; though they be red like crimson, they shall be as wool!'" He paused to wipe away the tears. Indeed, says the secretary, my eyes needed wiping too. "O, sir," he continued, "like a drowning man I clung to *this life-buoy;* on this I laid my soul, while the billows were going over me. I prayed, and the Lord was graciously pleased to remove in some measure the great guilt from my conscience, though I continued mournful and bowed down until last evening, on board the Mayflower, I stowed away among the Bethel Company. There the Lord spoke my pardon and peace. I am now like poor Legion, going home to my friends, to tell them what great things the Lord has done for me. Farewell, sir." Farewell, my lad; the Lord go with you.

A FAITHFUL PHYSICIAN.

In the year 1826, I was requested by a Universalist to call at his house to see an aged uncle, who had been confined to his room two years, and to his bed eighteen months, with the rheumatism. I called the next day, and on observing a collection of books on the table in the parlor, I inquired of the lady whether they owned a *large family* Bible. She replied, " We never owned a Bible." I was then shown the way up to the small garret where lay the sick man, whose furrowed face and gray hairs seemed to tell me that time with him would soon be no more. He pressed my hand, and said he was glad to see me. I inquired into the history of his life. He said he was about sixty-three years of age; that he had lived a single life; and that he had left him by his friends a farm worth between six and seven thousand dollars. By associating with bad company, he contracted the habit of using liquor to excess. He had been a drunkard many years, and had spent all his property at the intoxicating cup. He had not owned a Bible for thirty years, nor been inside a church for fifteen years. I addressed to him some words of advice suited to his case. He said he was sensible he must die; and if there was a judgment-seat in the *future world*, he could not be saved. The next day I called on him again. I offered to bring him a Bible, on condition that he would read a chapter a day. He declined. I tried twenty verses a day. Finally he agreed to take the Bible, on condition that he should read five verses in a day. The next day I carried him the Bible, and the first night he read the book of Genesis through. The next morning, as I spoke to him of the interests of his soul, he said I was the only person who had conversed with him on the subject of religion for thirty years. A day or two after, I called again, when he burst into tears, and said his soul was in distress, and that he could not sleep; that he felt he was a poor, guilty, helpless sinner; and he had been praying that he might repent, and have his many sins forgiven.

His health improved, and in six weeks he removed from this to another village. I heard nothing from him, but supposed, from his previous habits, and the inveteracy of his disease, that he was dead. One day, about sunset, as I was standing on the step of my door, I observed an old man approaching. He came up to me, and took hold of my arm, and asked me if I was the doctor. I answered yes, and invited him into my office, when he asked me if I knew him. I told him I did not. He burst into tears; and then with great earnestness stated, that he was the old man that I attended in —— a year ago. I immediately recognised him. "I have come," said he, "sixteen miles on purpose to tell you that my health is restored, and that *Bible* you gave me *has saved my soul.* I am a new man. I can earn a comfortable living; and all I care about is to fit my poor soul for the kingdom of heaven. I carry that Bible in my bosom into the field, and into my shop. I go to church regularly on the Sabbath, and have become a professor of religion. I thank God that I have been spared to taste of the bread of life at the eleventh hour." "Is not my word, saith the Lord, like a hammer, that breaketh the rock in pieces?"

THE BULLET AND THE BIBLE.

Dr. John Evans, the author of some excellent sermons on the Christian temper, introduced, on one occasion, a sermon to young people, in the following manner:—

Shall I be allowed to preface this discourse with relating a passage concerning an acquaintance of mine, who has been many years dead, but which I remember to have received, when young, from himself? When he was an apprentice in this city, the civil war began; his inclination led him into the army, where he had a captain's commission. It was fashionable for all the men of that army to carry a Bible along with them; which, therefore, he and many others did, who yet made little use of it, and hardly had any sense of serious religion. At length he was commanded, with his company, to storm a fort, wherein they were, for a short time, exposed to the thickest of the enemy's fire. When he had accomplished his enterprise, and the heat of the action was over, he found that a musket ball had lodged in his Bible, which was in his pocket, upon such a part of his body, that it must necessarily have proved mortal to him, had it not been for this seasonable and well-placed piece of armor. Upon a nearer observation, he found the ball had made its way so far in his Bible, as to rest directly upon that part of the first unbroken leaf, where the words of my text are found. It was Ecclesiastes, xi. 9 :—" Rejoice, O young man, in thy youth; and let thy heart cheer thee in the days of thy youth, and walk in the ways of thine heart, and in the sight of thine eyes; but know thou, that for all these things, God will bring thee into judgment." As the surprising deliverance, you may apprehend, much affected him, so a passage, which his conscience told him was very apposite to his case, and which Providence in so remarkable a way pointed to his observation, made the deepest and best impression on his mind; and, by the grace of God, he from that time attended to religion in earnest, and continued in the practice of it to a good old age; frequently making the remark with pleasure, that his Bible had been the salvation both of his body and his soul.

THE BIBLE IN THE WAY.

An individual in the interior of this state, says the Charleston Observer, gives the following account of the manner in which he was first arrested by the power of divine truth :—

He had been one of those who had paid no regard to the subject of religion. "God was not in all his thoughts," though his awful name was frequently upon his lips in oaths and blasphemies. One morning, as he arose, his eyes fell upon the Bible which lay upon a shelf immediately over his washstand, and it seemed to him a silent reprover of his ways. It had long occupied its present position, without exciting the slightest notice. He took it down, brushed the dust from it, and put it back again. The next morning, the first object that arrested his attention was that very Bible; and it continued there morning after morning to reprove him, till he became so much annoyed by its presence, that he resolved to put it out of the way. Taking it down with this view, he opened it, and the first passage upon which his eye lighted, was descriptive of his own character. He continued to read, and was troubled and affected by the accuracy with which it delineated his own heart and life. He closed it, returned it to its former position, and engaged in the occupations of the day with a heavy heart. At length, while he was reading it one morning, supposing himself to be unobserved, he turned around to see whether his wife, who had not yet risen, was awake or asleep, and found her bathed in a flood of tears. She had long been anxious for his salvation, and she was much affected at seeing him morning after morning stealing a glance at the word of life. When he saw he was discovered, he remarked, "It is of no use to conceal it any longer. I am a poor miserable sinner, and I find there is no redemption but in Christ Jesus. Will you pray for me? and will you go to the house of God? for, from this time forth, I am resolved to prepare for heaven." And from that time forth he did become an altered man—a happy, consistent, humble, and devoted Christian. Thus, the Bible, casually placed in the way of a wicked man, proved instrumental, through the Spirit, in bringing him to Christ, and in hiding a multitude of sins.

SECTION III.

Conversions effected by Mental Impressions, Dreams, &c.

THE CONVERSION OF JOSEPH W——.

IN the year 18— the Rev. E. J. W—— was converted to God. He was the first of his family to become a Methodist, and met with much opposition, particularly from his brother, J. W. This brother continued his persecutions, with little or no intermission, for several months. It happened on a certain occasion, they were both invited to spend an evening with Mr. Powel Clayton, a religious neighbor. At the close of the evening, E. J. W. was requested to read the Scriptures and pray with the company. He opened the Bible, and proceeded to read the fifty-fifth Psalm. As he read the 12th, 13th, and 14th verses—"For it was not an enemy that reproached me; then I could have borne it: neither was it he that hated me that did magnify himself against me; then I would have hid myself from him: But it was thou, a man mine equal, my guide, and mine acquaintance. We took sweet counsel together, and walked unto the house of God in company." The countenance of his brother was seen to fall, and he became very grave. The brothers left and went home in silence; when they had retired to their room, J. W. asked, "Why did you select that chapter to read this evening?" "I made no selection," replied his brother, "I opened the book and read that psalm without any design; if there was any selection the Lord made it." From this time the convictions of his sinfulness never left him until his conversion.

Some weeks after the above incident, he came down to breakfast one morning, and related at the table, in a humorsome way, that he had dreamed in the night, he was in company, and finding it necessary to button his coat he attempted to do so, but found unexpectedly that it was too small, and after an ineffectual effort he gave it up, greatly perplexed and distressed. "That," said a pious friend sitting at the table, is your coat of morality, and at the judgment, you will find it too small for you." This was a "nail in a sure place." So powerful was the impression made on his mind, that he went at once to the throne of grace, and ceased not to struggle until he found peace in Christ.

AN INCIDENT.

It was during mid-winter of '36, a passer-by of the "Sailor's Home," so called, in H——, might one evening have heard sounds of boisterous merriment proceeding from the crowded bar-room, while occasionally a stunning oath fell upon the ear. The room was filled with a motley crowd, such as usually were to be found there—sailors, boatmen, and raftsmen, and all apparently in high uproarious mirth.

On one side of the room was a cheerful fire, around which sat a number of dozing topers, while on the opposite was the bar, with the usual array of well-filled decanters dimly seen through the murky cloud of smoke. In the centre of the crowd, and the object of their undivided attention, stood a man in appearance about fifty years of age. In former years he had been distinguished in political life, and was known as a man of fine talents and acquirements. During his early life he had become a member of the Methodist persuasion, and was still remembered as a prominent and favorite class-leader. His hair was gray, tangled and matted, and fell in spare locks upon his shoulders. His eye was dim and bloodshot; his face bloated and unshaven, and his whole appearance gave evidence of his wretched and miserable condition. A silly smile was playing over his haggard features, as he listened to the rude and profane commendations of the wretches around him, for he had just finished a song.

"Give us another, Jim," said one.

"Give us one more," roared the crowd.

"Well, what shall it be, gentlemen?" said he.

"Methodist," said the first speaker, and a peal of laughter followed.

"Give us a regular Methodist, old fellow."

For a moment he hesitated, and then with a voice shattered, but still noble, he commenced a beautiful Methodist hymn. As he proceeded, it seemed to come home to his heart. For a time his voice faltered, and his face seemed as if a shadow had fallen upon it. Were the turbid fountains of the heart being troubled by an angel? or had that simple melody brought back a tide of recollections of old times—bright, hopeful, happy days long since passed, and which had long assumed the dream? Perchance voices from the spirit land, which had in the dreamy past mingled their earthly song with his, and who in the dew of his youth had passed away radiant with hope from his tearful gaze; perchance, as it were, a soft, thrilling, and ever-lingering echo had stolen upon his degraded heart to find there its fellow. He ended, and the rude and noisy crew loudly applauded, mingling many an oath in their commendations; but his face had lost its smile. Then one called upon him for a prayer to end with, as he expressed himself, and they all gathered still closer around him.

"No, no, I can't pray—I can't pray now," exclaimed the poor wretch, and he seemed to be troubled. But they would have no refusal—he must give them a prayer. Prayer! He used to pray much once, for then it was dear to him, and it seemed to make life brighter, and joy and happiness nestled always in his heart. But that was a long time ago, and many a weary day and even year has passed since then. Sometimes, to be sure, in his utter and degraded misery, as memory reflected a gleam of momentary light from the past; startled in the instant, perhaps, with hand hard pressed on an aching, burning brow, he would cry out, "Oh, God!" but it was of bitter, despairing misery, and not hope; and then, unable to endure such terrible remorseful thoughts, he would hasten away and plunge into mad intoxication, till all reflection was gone. It was not always thus. At times better and kindlier thoughts came to him, and though he was fallen and very low, still he would certainly try to reform and be a better man; and so, as it were, "smiting on his breast," and scarce daring to lift up his eyes, he would rise and go softly on, till a step failed him, or overpowering temptation within and without seized him and flung him back again, as it were, in derision. But now as he stood there, kind thoughts and even tender, called up by that song, had touched his desolate heart and the feelings of hope seemed returning once more to him —perhaps God would hear his prayer. So slowly lifting his old hat from his head, he said, "Let us pray." The peal of laughter was upon the lips of those around, but the unaffected solemnity of his manner awed and suppressed their noisy mirth, and they gazed upon him in perfect silence.

"Our Father who art in heaven, hallowed be thy name." His voice was broken with emotion; but as he proceeded it became clearer. The spirit of other days had seemingly returned upon him, and he prayed as of old, moving as with the Spirit of God the hearts of all who heard him. He prayed with agonized earnestness for pardon, for reconciliation with the Saviour for all men, for strength in the hour and moment of temptation, and light through all of future life to guide and direct in every devious path, and that at last they might attain to eternal life through the crucified Redeemer.

He ceased; but a spell had fallen upon that brow, and not a word was heard. He took up his old hat, and, turning away, left the house. From that hour he became an altered man; and the earnest, self-denying Christian labors of many subsequent years, though in humble sphere, were not, we trust, in vain. HENDER.

A REMARKABLE ANSWER TO PRAYER.

DURING a powerful revival of religion that took place many years ago, in Salem county, N. J., there was a young woman who was induced by her friends to attend the meeting, and becoming deeply affected, was persuaded to approach the altar, where, after much seeking, with bitter repentance, she was happily converted to God. This person became very exemplary in her deportment, and wherever she went, had something to say in favor of the blessed treasure she had so recently found, having been faithful for a number of years. She married a deeply pious man, with whom she lived happily. In a few years he died, and she, being left a widow, and poor, had to struggle hard for the support of herself and children; but at this time, when the consolations of religion were the most needed, she gave way to a murmuring and repining spirit, fell from grace, and became very wicked and unhappy. She remained in this state many long years. Effort after effort was made to reclaim her, but all apparently in vain. One of her sons at this time embraced religion, and consequently became deeply solicitous for his mother's salvation. He prayed and wept, and with many entreaties urged her to return to the Shepherd and Bishop of souls. To all this her answer was, "You need not grieve for me, my son, for my day of grace is gone—the Spirit has not striven with me for over twenty years; my damnation is sure." At this time her health, which had been very good, began to decline; day by day she became weaker and weaker, until it was apparent to all that the fell destroyer had marked her for his prey. The despair that filled her heart, with the afflictions of her body, soon wore her down to almost nothing. Brethren came from all directions (by the importunity of her son), to pray for her, and point her to Christ, the friend of sinners; but in vain. To all their solicitations and entreaties her answer was, "Leave me alone. I am justly lost. You can do me no good. The few moments I have on earth let me spend them in peace. Your prayers only torment me." Her deeply affected boy now resolved to set aside a day to fast and pray for the salvation of his mother; he therefore repaired to a lonely wood, and with none to see his grief or tears but God, he fell on his knees, and with many entreaties besought the Lord Jesus Christ to have mercy upon her soul. After this continuing all day, toward evening, with his face bathed in tears, he fell to the earth struggling and crying, "I will not let thee go until thou answer me." A heavenly calm filled his breast, joy sprang up in his heart, and evidence clear and strong was given, Thy prayer is answered—go in peace.

It was Saturday morning; I was at work on my farm, some fifty miles from the scene I am attempting to describe (knowing nothing of this woman), when I felt a powerful impression on my mind to harness my horse to the carriage, and immediately drive to Brother P.'s, whom I had not seen for several years, and who resided thirty-five miles from my house. I tried to put it off, but my peace of mind was gone, and, to get relief, I started. I arrived in the evening, stayed over the Sabbath, and preached twice, intending to return home next morning; but, being awakened several hours before day, the impression was renewed to go fifteen miles further to see Brother T., also, whom I had not seen for several years. I arose at daybreak, and found it raining. Resolving to go home, I started, but O the horror of mind that seized me! To get relief I turned my horse and drove for the brother's. He was not at home when I arrived, but soon came, and with joy welcomed me. I related to him the circumstances of my coming, and said, "Brother T., in the name of the Lord, is there anything for me to do here?" He solemnly paused, then related to me the case of this woman, who lived only a few rods off, telling me she was only alive apparently, and dying in sin. Now faith sprung up, and, with strong confidence, I went to see her. On entering the room, I approached the bedside, and beheld a pale and emaciated form propped up, coughing almost incessantly, with her son weeping sadly at the foot of the bed. She related to me her doleful condition, begging me not to pray, or mention the name of Christ, as it filled her with indescribable torment. Lifting my heart to God, I sat several minutes in silence, only broken by the sobs of her affectionate son, when I felt it required of me to reason with her on the sin and folly of grieving the

Holy Spirit by despairing of that mercy that was ready to receive her; and surely the Holy Ghost helped me, for, fixing her dying eyes upon me, she appeared to drink in every word, her son and the brother who went with me looking on with great interest. We fell on our knees, and, after Brother T. had prayed, I was drawn out with as much power as I ever experienced in prayer, to urge her case at the throne of grace. Tears of sympathy fell from my eyes, and, laying hold on God, I resolved never to leave the house until salvation appeared. While thus pleading, she sprang up in bed and cried for mercy, in language the most affecting I ever heard, while tears of penitence rolled down her cheeks. Being thus encouraged, we continued pouring out our souls unto Him who had promised to hear us, when, in a moment, while I had my eye fixed upon her, I saw her countenance change; heaven beamed in her eye, joy sprang up in her heart, and Glory, glory, and loud hallelujahs pealed from her tongue; while her son, who had so long looked for her redemption, fell on the floor, and, with rapturous songs, blessed the God of Israel his Saviour. She lived in this heavenly frame of mind three weeks, and died shouting Glory, glory, victory, victory!

COLLINS DIRECTED TO A FUNERAL.

When the country was new and thinly settled, Mr. Collins was riding upon the banks of the Ohio river, some thirty or forty miles above Cincinnati, in company with a friend, when they came to the forks of the road; the left-hand road led more directly to their place of destination, the right was more circuitous; but Mr. Collins, against remonstrance, preferred the latter, from an impression which he did not particularly define. It led to the mouth of Red Oak, where the town of Ripley is now situated.

As they approached this point they saw a funeral procession, which they immediately joined, and followed it to the grave. It was the first funeral in that place. The corpse was the wife of Mr. Benard Jackson, an avowed infidel. After the grave was covered, Mr. Collins made known to the people that he was a preacher of the Gospel, and would then preach a sermon to all who remained. No one went away. He read for his text, "I am the resurrection and the life: he that believeth in me, though he were dead, yet shall he live;" and preached with overwhelming power.

The solemnity of the occasion, and the circumstances which brought him to the place, added, no doubt, to the effect of the discourse. No one could apply circumstances more forcibly than Mr. Collins.

There were many tears and sobs in the congregation. The infidel husband was overwhelmed; and from that day and hour he renounced infidelity, shortly after became a member of the church, lived to adorn the Christian religion, and died in peace. He had one son, who is now a travelling preacher in the state of Indiana.

Mr. Collins believed in a special Providence. The inclination to take the right-hand road, he believed was prompted by it, of which he could entertain no doubt, when he saw the funeral procession, and preached to the mourning crowd. And is this too small a matter for Deity? Peter was called to preach to Cornelius; and his objections were overcome in an extraordinary manner. Philip, being prompted by the Spirit, joined himself to the chariot of the eunuch, and "preached to him Jesus." And who, that believes the Bible, does not believe that the same spirit operates, more or less, upon Christians of the present day? The mode of its action may not seem to be miraculous; but it is spiritually discerned. It is a Divine agency —that spirit, or light, a portion of which is given to every man. It leads to good actions and happy results.—*Life of Collins.*

REAPPEARANCE OF THE DEAD.

At the conference of Wesleyan ministers held in Sheffield in the year 1817, the Rev. Thomas Savage, one of the young preachers who was received into full connection, gave the following account of the appearance of the departed spirit of his brother-in-law. After a very appropriate introduction, in which the reverend gentleman asserted that the "solemn fact" which he was about to relate, "was the first grand means of leading his mind to think seriously of the solemn realities of death, judgment, and eternity," he proceeded as follows:—

"A sister being married to a gentleman in the army, we received intelligence that the regiment to which he belonged had orders for one of the Spanish Isles in the Mediterranean. One night about ten o'clock, sixteen years since, in the town of Doncaster, in Yorkshire, England, as his wife, his child, an elder sister, and myself, were sitting in a back room— the shutters were closed, barred, and bolted, and the yard door locked—suddenly a light shone through the window, and illumined the room in which we were sitting:—we looked—started—and beheld *the spirit of a murdered brother*,—his eye was fixed on his wife and child alternately,—he waved his hand —smiled—continued about half a minute—and then vanished from our sight. The moment before the spirit disappeared, my sister cried, '*He's dead, he's dead,*" and fainted away. Her little boy ran toward the apparition, and wept because it would not stay. A short time after this, we received a letter from the colonel of the regiment, sealed with a black seal— the dark emblem of death—bearing the doleful but expected news that, on such a night, answering to the same on which we saw his spirit, my brother-in-law was found weltering in his blood, having been murdered by the Spaniards when returning from the mess-room: the spark of life was not quite extinct when he was found, and the last wish which he was heard to breathe was that he might see his wife and child once again; which was granted him, in a certain sense, for the very hour he died in the island of Minorca, in that same hour his spirit appeared to his wife, his child, an elder sister, and myself. Before this event, though a boy of nine years only, I was a complete *atheist,* having been taught by my father to disbelieve everything except what I saw; but by this solemn circumstance, I was convinced of the reality of another world's existence; and by the solemn impression that it made upon my mind, I was led to pray for mercy; which mercy I found at the foot of the cross, and now feel the Holy Spirit preparing my soul to enter those eternal and invisible regions—*the world of spirits.* My sister, from the night that she saw the spirit of her husband, and before she received any intelligence of his death, *went into mourning for him;* nor could my father prevent it by any argument. He endeavored to persuade us we were all deluded and deceived, yet he acknowledged that the testimony which the child gave *staggered him;* but when the letter arrived from the colonel of the regiment, with the awful tidings of our brother's death, he was *struck dumb,* so to speak, and had nothing more to say. My two sisters are yet living, and can testify to the truth of this account; beside which at least one hundred persons can prove our mentioning *the hour the spirit appeared,* several weeks before we received the melancholy letter, and that the letter mentioned the night and the hour as the same in which we beheld his spirit.

A REMARKABLE INCIDENT IN THE LIFE OF DR. BOND.

THE following strange occurrence was published in an obituary notice of Dr. Bond, which appeared in the *Christian Advocate* shortly after his death:—

About this time occurred a very extraordinary incident in the life of Dr. Bond, which we narrate with great doubt as to the propriety of the publication. He very rarely mentioned it, and never ventured to designate or explain it. Its truth is, however, beyond question. The circumstances forbid the supposition of optical illusion or temporary hallucination. There are those living who testify to such of the facts as were subject to observation, and the memorials of the transaction are yet distinctly preserved in the religious character of sons and daughters of some who were immediately affected by it.

Being on a visit to his father, he was deeply grieved to find the church, which he had left in a state of prosperous activity, languishing, lukewarm, and weak. His thoughts were much occupied with the subject, and, of course, it was the matter of earnest and frequent prayer. In this state of mind, one morning, he was walking over the fields to a neighboring house, when suddenly he seemed to be in a room where a number of people were assembled, apparently for worship. The room he recognised as an apartment in the house of a neighbor, where a prayer-meeting was to be held on the evening of that day. Had he stood in the midst of it he could not have been more conscious of the scene. There was nothing of the dim, or shadowy, or dreamy about it. He recognised the people, noticed where they sat and stood, remarked his father near the table, at which a preacher was rising to give out a hymn, and near the middle of the congregation he saw a man named C., for whose salvation he felt particular anxiety, standing with his son beside him. While gazing with astonishment upon the scene, he heard the words, "Go and tell C. that he has an offer of salvation for the last time."

Naturally supposing that the too great concentration of mind upon one subject had induced some hallucination of the senses, Dr. Bond fell down on his knees and besought God to preserve his reason. The scene, however, continued; it would not disappear nor change in any of its particulars. In vain he struggled to dispel it; the voice yet repeated with indubitable distinctness, "Go and tell C. that he has an offer of salvation for the last time." Yet how would he dare to deliver so awful a message! For a great length of time he struggled for deliverance from what he still considered an illusion. At length an expedient occurred to him which he adopted. He had never been in the room in which he was apparently present, when it was used for a public religious meeting. He, of course, did not know how it was commonly prepared for such occasions. He therefore noted with great care the particulars of the scene. He saw where the little table for the preacher, the benches and chairs for the people, were placed. He noticed his acquaintances, and where they sat and stood, and when he was satisfied that he had possessed himself perfectly of these details, he said, "I will go to this meeting, and if I see things there to correspond with what I now see, it shall be as a sign from the Lord, and I will deliver the message." Immediately the scene vanished, and he was alone in the green fields.

With a spirit indescribably agitated he returned home, where he found ladies who required him to escort them a long distance, and it was somewhat past the hour fixed for the meeting when he reached the awful place. During the day he had freely indulged the hope that on his entrance into the room his trouble would disappear. He thought he had been the subject of an illusion, the fruit of an excited brain, and that a want of correspondence, immediately to be detected between the real scene and the one presented to his disordered fancy, would at once satisfy him as to the morbid character of his morning vision, and release him from the obligation of delivering the terrible message with which he was conditionally charged. When he opened the door, however, he saw again, in all its minuteness of detail, the morning scene. In vain he searched the room for a variant particular. There sat his father in the designated place. The preacher at the table was rising to give out the hymn. In the midst of the room stood C., with his son beside him. Everything demanded that the message should be delivered.

After the preliminary exercises, he rose and stated the circumstances as we have related them, and then going to C., he laid his hand upon him, and repeated the words he had heard. The effect was indescribable. C. and his son fell down together and called upon God. An awful solemnity rested upon all present. Many cried for mercy, and from that time began a revival of religion which spread far and wide; the fruits of which are yet seen, after many days.

In the midst of this extraordinary scene, the father of Dr. Bond, who was too deaf to hear his words, sat an anxious observer. He was a calm man, whose Quaker education had not lost its influence over his religious character and views. After the meeting he asked Thomas what he had said to produce such an effect. He frankly told him all. The old man mused a while and said, "You did right."

About this incident there will be different opinions. We shall not express any. The principal actor preferred to express none. We only state the facts as related by himself, and confirmed, without inquiry, since his death, by one who was present at the extraordinary meeting. We think, however, with his father, that he "did right." To have done otherwise would at least have been unreasonable, perhaps impious. Philosophy must leave room for God in his own world. Incredulity and superstition are equally dishonorable to the understanding. In all cases right reason determines by evidence.

A SINGULAR PROVIDENCE.

A CURIOUS AND AFFECTING NARRATIVE.

Sir Richard Cradock, a justice of the peace, who was a violent hater and persecutor of the Dissenters, and who exerted himself to enforce all the severe laws then in existence against them, happened to live near Mr. Rogers, to whom he bore a particular enmity, and whom he wanted above all things to have in his power. Hearing that he was to preach at a place some miles distant, he thought it a fair opportunity for accomplishing his base design, and in order thereto hired two men to go as spies, and take down the names of all the hearers whom they knew, that they might appear as witnesses both against them and Mr. Rogers. The plan seemed to succeed to his wishes. These men brought him the names of several persons who were present at the meeting, and he warned such of them as he had a particular spite against, together with Mr. Rogers, to appear before him. Knowing the violence of the man, they came with trembling hearts, expecting to be treated with the utmost severity. While they were waiting in the great hall, expecting to be called upon, a little girl, about six or seven years of age, who was Sir Richard's granddaughter, happened to come into the hall. She looked at Mr. Rogers, and was much taken with his venerable appearance. He being naturally fond of children, took her upon his knee and caressed her, which occasioned her to conceive a great fondness for him. At length Sir Richard sent a servant to inform him and the rest that one of the witnesses being taken ill, was unable to attend, and that therefore they must come again another day.

They accordingly came at the time appointed, and being convicted, the justice ordered their mittimus to be written to send them all to prison. Mr. Rogers, expecting to see the little girl again, brought some sweetmeats with him to give her. As soon as she saw him she came running to him, and appeared fonder of him than before. This child being a great favorite with her grandfather, had got such an ascendency over him that he could deny her nothing, and she possessed such a violent spirit that she could bear no contradiction, so that she was indulged in everything she wanted. At one time, when she had been contradicted, she ran a penknife into her arm, to the great danger of her life. This bad spirit, in the present instance, was overruled for good. While she was sitting on Mr. Rogers's knee, eating the sweetmeats, she looked earnestly at him, and asked, "What are you here for, sir?" He said, "I believe your grandfather is going to send me and my friends to jail." "To jail!" said she. "Why, what have you done?" "Why, I did nothing but preach, and they did nothing but hear me." "He shall not send you to jail!" replied she. "Ay, but my dear," said he, "I believe he is now making out our mittimus to send us all there." Upon this, she ran up to the chamber where Sir Richard was, and knocked with her head and heels till she got in, and said to him, "What are you going to do with my good old gentleman in the hall?" "That's nothing to you," said he, "get you about your business." "But I won't," says she. "He tells me that you are going to send him and his friends to jail; and if you send them, I will drown myself in the pond as soon as they are gone. I will indeed." When he saw the child thus peremptory, it shook his resolution, and induced him to abandon his malicious design. Taking the mittimus in his hand, he went down into the hall, and thus addressed these good men: "I had made out your mittimus to send you all to jail, as you deserve; but at my grandchild's request I drop the prosecution, and set you all at liberty." They all bowed, and thanked his worship; but Mr. Rogers, going to the child, laid his hand upon her head, and lifting up his eyes to heaven, exclaimed, "God bless you, my dear child. May the blessing of that God whose cause you did now plead, though as yet you know him not, be upon you in life, in death, and to all eternity."

The above remarkable story was told by Mr. Timothy Rogers, the son of the ejected minister, who had frequently heard his father relate it with great pleasure; and the celebrated Mr. Thomas

Bradbury once heard it from him when he was dining at the house of Mrs. Tooley, an eminent Christian lady in London, who was distinguished for her religion and for her love to Christ and his people, whose house and table, like Lydia's, were always open to them. What followed is yet more remarkable, as containing a striking proof of Mr. Rogers's prayers for this child, and the blessing which descended upon her who had been such an instrument in the deliverance of the persecuted servants of God. Mrs. Tooley had listened with uncommon attention to Mr. Rogers's story, and when he had ended it, she asked him, "And are you that Mr. Rogers's son?" He told her he was —upon which she said, "Well, as long as I have been acquainted with you, I never knew that before; and now I will tell you something that you do not know: *I am the very girl* your dear father blessed in the manner that you have related, and it made an impression upon me that I never could forget."

Upon this double discovery, Mr. Rogers and Mrs. Tooley found an additional tie of mutual love and affection; and then he and Mr. Bradbury expressed a desire to know how she, who had been brought up in an aversion to dissenters, and to serious religion, now discovered such an attachment to both; upon which she cheerfully gave them the following narrative:—

After her grandfather's death, she became sole

heiress to his estate, which was considerable. Being in the bloom of youth, and having none to control her, she ran into all the fashionable diversions of the age, without any restraint; but she confessed, when the pleasurable scenes were over, she felt a dissatisfaction both with them and herself, that always struck a damp to her heart, which she did not know how to get rid of any other way than by running over the same round again and again. But all was in vain. Having contracted some slight illness, she thought she would go to Bath, hearing that it was a place for pleasure as well as health. When she came thither she was providentially led to consult an apothecary, who was a very worthy and religious man. When he inquired what ailed her, she answered, "Why, doctor, I don't ail much as to my body; but I have an uneasy mind that I cannot get rid of." "Truly, Miss," said he, "I was so too, till I met with a certain book, and that cured me." "Books!" said she; "I get all the books I can lay my hands on—all the plays, novels, and romances I hear of; but after I have read them, my uneasiness is the same." "That may be, Miss," said he, "and I don't wonder at it. But as to this book I speak of, I can say of it what I can say of no other I ever read, that I never tire in reading it, but can read it again and again, as if I had never read it before; and I always see something new in it." "Pray, doctor," says she, "what book is that?" "Nay, Miss," answered he, "that is a secret I don't tell every one." "But could not I get a sight of that book?" says she. "Yes," replied he, "if you speak me fair, I can help you to a sight of it." "Pray, then, get it me, doctor, and I'll give you anything you please." "Yes," said he, "if you will promise me one thing, I'll bring it you, and that is, that you will read it over carefully; and if you should not see much in it at first, that you will give it a second reading." She promised faithfully that she would. After coming two or three times without it, to raise her curiosity, he at last took it out of his pocket and gave it her. This book was the New Testament. When she looked at it, she said, with a flirt, "Poh! I could get it at any time." "Why, Miss," said he, "so you might; but, remember, I have your solemn promise to read it carefully." "Well," said she, "though I never read it before, I'll give it a reading." Accordingly she began to read it, and it soon attracted her attention. She saw something in it, wherein she had a deep concern, but her mind now became ten times more uneasy than ever. Not knowing what to do, she soon returned to London, resolved to try again what the diversions there would do to dissipate her gloom; but nothing of this kind answered her purpose. She lodged at the court end of the town, where she had with her a female companion. On Saturday evening she had a remarkable dream, which was, that she was in a place of worship, where she heard a sermon; but when she awoke, she could remember nothing but the text. This dream made a deep impression upon her mind, and the idea she had of the place, and of the minister's person, was as strong as if she had been long acquainted with both. On the Lord's day morning she told her dream to her companion, and said, that after breakfast she was resolved to go in quest of the place, though she should go from one end of London to the other. They accordingly set out, and went into several churches as they passed along, but none of them answered to what she saw in her dream. About one o'clock they found themselves in the heart of the city, where they dined, and then set out again in search of this place of worship. Being in the Poultry about half after two o'clock, they saw a great number of people going down the Old Jewry, and she determined to see where they went. She mingled with the company, and they conducted her to the meeting-house, where Mr. Shower was the minister, in the Old Jewry. As soon as she entered the door, and surveyed the place, she turned to her companion, and said, with some surprise, "This is the very place I saw in my dream." She had not been long there before she saw Mr. Shower go up into the pulpit, and, looking at him with greater surprise, said, "This is the very man I saw in my dream; and, if every part of it hold true, he will take for his text, Psalm cxvi. 7: 'Return to thy rest, O my soul, for the

Lord hath dealt bountifully with thee.' When he rose up to pray, she was all attention, and every sentence went to her heart. Having finished his prayer he took that very passage for his text, and God was pleased to make the discourse founded upon it the means of her saving conversion; and thus she at last found what she had so long sought elsewhere in vain: "Rest to her soul!" And now she obtained that blessing from God, the fountain of felicity, which pious Mr. Rogers so many years before had so solemnly and fervently implored in her behalf.

INTERESTING STORY.

The following artless and interesting relation is another proof of the advantages of Bible and Tract Societies. It is important that the sinner, through some medium, be warned of his danger. If this be well and faithfully done, the laborer will not always be without his reward.

The W——, a vessel of upwards of 400 tons, was freighted from Liverpool for a trading voyage up the Mediterranean Sea. I was intimately acquainted with the captain's nephew, an accomplished young man, of handsome person, but alas! a willing victim at the shrine of pleasure. He had shipped himself for the voyage as steward. When leaving Liverpool, I put into his hands a small bundle of tracts, and, in proof of his esteem for me, he promised to read them at his leisure, and likewise to distribute some among the ship's company. Not an individual, from the captain to the cabin-boy, had the least sense of religion, nor do I believe they had a Bible or Testament on board. On the return of the vessel, about twelve months afterwards, as soon as my young friend could step on shore, he paid me the first visit. On my saluting him with, "Well, what cheer, my lad?" he answered (at the same time the tears trembling in his eyes), "Through the mercy of God, I am well, and the whole ship's crew." Surprised at hearing a strain of pious gratitude flow from those lips which formerly were seldom opened except to pollute them with profane conversation, I said, "William, what has produced this change in your look, your address, your language? How is it that you acknowledge it is of the Lord's mercies that you are not consumed?" "Sir (said he), I will relate particulars—you recollect on my taking leave of you, you placed in my hand a small parcel of tracts, and I promised to read them : this I have done. On leaving the port we had a favorable wind through the channel; the wind then chopping round direct in our teeth. We had to contend with light, contrary winds, till we entered the Gut of Gibraltar. During this part of our voyage I had little or no opportunity to read the tracts. I did on the first Sabbath turn them over, and put a few in my pocket, and occasionally taking one out, gave it a sneering glance, and then handed it to one of the boys or men, with a smile of ridicule. On passing the Gut, we had a tedious though pleasant voyage to Smyrna.

"Having much time upon my hands, I now and then looked at a tract, to pass away time. One evening (I well remember the evening), about an hour before sunset, scarce a breath of air, we had spread all the canvas we could, which lay flapping idly against the mast; the men on board, some sitting on the forehatch, others lolling over the windlass, now and then whispering a curse instead of a prayer for a breeze; a boy sitting athwart a gun; the captain in the cabin smoking his cigar, with his allowance of grog before him; the wide and beautiful expanse of water, smooth as glass, bounded by a clear and serene sky; the smoke of Mount Vesuvius just visible in the horizon, bearing E. N. E.—every object hushed into silent solitude; not a sound was heard but our own breathings, and the gentle breaking of the sea against the bow of the vessel—I was looking over the ship's side, viewing the calm and peaceful close of another day. This brought to my recollection the scenery and calmness of the evening when I took my last farewell of my friends at home. It was at sunset on a lovely evening in July. Musing thus of home, my mind had acquired a tint of melancholy. I just then put my hand in my jacket pocket, and feeling some paper, took it out, and it proved to be a tract —'The Swearer's Prayer.' I read it aloud, in the hearing of the whole of the crew, and I suppose much of the tincture of my feelings was mixed with my tone of voice. When I had read it, a curious kind of silence ensued; not one of us felt inclined to raise his eyes from what they were fixed upon, fearing to meet the look of another, and knowing that to a man, we were all shockingly guilty of swearing. At length we looked at each other in a sidelong kind of way, and one man said, 'Mr. William, I never heard or thought of this before; this kind of reading has made me feel very strange—I am trembling; I don't think I shall live to swear again; shall you, Jack?' turning short to a seaman alongside of him, who looked him full in the face, and burst into tears. The shedding of tears ran like a contagion through the whole of us, even to the boy across the gun. After weeping in silence, with our faces hid with our hands, one man said, 'Jack, suppose we had up a prayer to God for forgiveness. Mr. William, you have had more learning than we, you can make a prayer.'—Alas! I had never prayed; I could only sigh; I really thought my heart would burst. O, how dreadful did sin appear! One of the men then broke the silence of grief. With his arms across his breast, and the tears of penitential sorrow rolling down his manly countenance, he cried out, 'O God, who made our souls, have mercy, and pardon the miserable and damned crew on this deck.' Not a heart but what responded, 'Lord, hear this prayer and forgive.'

But not to enter too long in detail, the Lord was pleased to work a change in the whole of the ship's company. One circumstance I must not forget to mention. The captain, a drunken, swearing character, thought his men bewitched. On the following morning he came on deck, and, as usual, was giving his orders, mixed with fearful oaths, when one of the men, in a most respectful manner, begged he would not swear at them,—they would obey his orders with more comfort to themselves without it. Indeed, the captain remarked to a person on his return, that he was obliged to refrain from swearing, it began to appear on board so singular."

WONDERFUL SAGACITY IN A DOG.

WILLIAM DREDGE lives about five miles from town, says the California Times, at the base of the mountains which tower north of us. A short time ago, after midnight, he was roused from his slumbers by the howl of a dog. No menace on his part could rid him of the presence of this strange intruder. The dog continued to walk round the cabin, still repeating his dismal moaning and howling, occasionally making efforts to effect an entrance through the closed doorway. Surprised and somewhat alarmed at this singular demonstration, Mr. Dredge at last hastily dressed himself and unbolted the door, when a large mastiff rushed in. The dog at once caught hold of his trowsers, and employed every gentle means to induce the man to accompany him outside. Dredge's first impression was that the animal was mad; and yet so peculiar and earnest were the dumb entreaties, that he finally yielded, and proceeded without the cabin. A joyful yell was the result, and the delighted brute, now capering and wagging his tail before him, and now returning, and gently seizing him by the hand and trowsers, induced Dredge to follow him. Their course was up the precipitous side of the mountain, and soon they were forcing their way through a snowdrift that had settled in one of its numerous fissures.

Here comes the wonder. Upon the snow lay the body of a woman, who had evidently perished from cold and exhaustion. Her limbs were already stiffened in death; but what was the surprise of Mr. Dredge to see that faithful dog ferret out, from a bundle of clothing, that lay by the side of the woman, a young child about two years of age, still warm and living! A little inspection, aided by the starlight and the brightness of the snow, enabled him to discover that the person of the woman was nearly naked. With a mother's affection, she had stripped her own person in order to furnish warmth to her exposed infant. The trusty dog had completed the work of self-sacrifice.

Mr. Dredge immediately conveyed the child to his own cabin, and, arousing some of his neighbors, proceeded again to the mountain, to secure from the attacks of wild beasts the person of the unfortunate woman. Her body was buried the next day. The child and dog have been adopted by this good Samaritan, but as yet he has been unable to obtain light as to the name of the woman, or how she happened to stray on the dismal mountain-side at such an unfortunate hour. The child is doing well, and is truly a handsome boy.

REMARKABLE ESCAPE.

SAMUEL LEWIS, Sen., was the captain of a coasting vessel, and, in the performance of his regular trips from Maine to the Carolinas and the West Indies, was necessarily abroad a great portion of his time. Of course, his influence was much less felt in the formation of his son's character. But those who knew familiarly both father and son, could detect a strong resemblance in the industry, the fearlessness, the devotedness, the stern resolve, which characterized the latter to a remarkable degree. When he was about the age of eleven he accompanied his father on his coasting voyages; and thus his time was partially taken up till the year 1813.

One day, when the vessel was riding at anchor in Vineyard Sound, in sight of the town of Falmouth, the captain and crew left her in charge of the cabin-boy, for this was young Samuel's position on board.

While busily engaged in the performance of his customary duties, he approached the side of the vessel, with his bucket, to draw some water. As he leaned over listlessly, his thoughts wandering away to other scenes, suddenly his feet slipped, his hands failed of their grasp, and he fell into the sea. There was no one in the vessel to aid him in escaping from the water, and he was too far from the land to swim thither, unless he had been an expert; and, up to this time, he had never learned the art of swimming at all. As soon as the first few moments of surprise were over, he looked eagerly around him for some means of escape. No rope, or chain, or other means of ascending to the deck of the ship, was within his reach. The fore-chains hung in their usual place, but some distance above the water. For the first time in his life, he swam, making his way around the vessel as well as he was able, and scanning every part within his reach. Finding no other resource, he struggled back to the fore-chains, and attempted to lay hold of them, leaping upward as far as he could. Failing entirely in the attempt, he soon fell back, so much exhausted as to give over the struggle.

"In a few moments," we have heard him say, "I gave up, and strove to resign myself to die. All the deeds of my short life came across my mind; I tried to pray, and to lie quiet in the hands of my heavenly Father. Soon my mind began to revert to my father's family, and, beyond all others upon earth, to my mother. I thought of her grief and distress when my body should be swept ashore, or all search for it abandoned. I thought of the agony of suspense that would torture her mind, till it was certain that I no longer lived. And as I seemed to see her tears, and to listen to her sighs, I resolved to make still another effort for my life. I swam again to the fore-chains, catching sight in my way of the fields and dwellings of my native town. Armed with additional resolution by such a view, I prayed to God, earnestly as ever I prayed in my life, to aid me in my last trial. As I came up, I observed that the warm sun had softened in a slight degree the pitchy seams in the sides. Into these seams I fastened my nails, and, raising myself as far as possible out of the water, I made one bold leap, caught the chains, and was soon on the deck. But as I turned and looked down upon the water, where I had so lately awaited death, I was horrified at the sight of a monstrous shark, lashing the waves in disappointment as he turned away from the vessel. I fell upon my knees in a moment, and returned thanks to God, who had so wonderfully spared me from a death far more dreadful than the one I had before expected."

A PROVIDENTIAL PROTECTOR.

The following singular story is told by a clergyman who knew the truthfulness of it, concerning an attack made by robbers upon a farm-house, in Canada, several years ago. The farm-house was a solitary one; there was not another within a half-mile of it. On the night of the attack, there was a good deal of money in the house, the proceeds of a large sale of stock made that day. The mother and her three young children, and a maid servant, were the sole inmates. They had retired to rest some time. The wind was howling fearfully, and shook the wooden house at every blast. This kept the poor woman awake, and she thought she heard, in the pauses of the tempest, some strange and unusual noises, seemingly at the back of the house. While eagerly listening to catch the sound again, she was startled by the violent barking of a dog, apparently in a room in the front of the house, immediately beneath the bed-chamber. This alarmed her still more, as they had no dog of their own. She immediately rose, and going to the maid's room, awoke her, and they went down together. They first peeped into the room where they had heard the dog. It was moonlight, at least partially so, for the night was cloudy, still it was light enough to distinguish objects, though but faintly. They saw an immense black dog scratching and gnawing furiously at the door leading into the kitchen, from whence she thought that the noises she first heard had proceeded. She requested the servant to open the door which the dog was attacking so violently. The girl was a determined and resolute creature, devoid of fear, and she did so without hesitation, when the dog rushed out, and the widow saw through the open door two men at the kitchen window, which was open. The men instantly retreated, and the dog leaped through the window after them. A violent scuffle ensued, and it was evident, from the occasional yelping of the noble animal, that he sometimes had the worst of it. The noise of the contest, however, gradually receded, till Mrs. M—— could hear only now and then a faint and distant bark. The robbers, or perhaps murderers, had taken out a pane of glass, which had enabled them to undo the fastenings of the window, when, but for the dog, they would doubtless have accomplished their purpose. The mistress and maid got a light, and secured the window as well as they could. They then dressed themselves, for to think of sleeping any more that night was out of the question. They had not, however, got down stairs the second time before they heard their protector scratching at the outer door for admittance. They immediately opened it, when he came in wagging his bushy tail, and fawning upon each of them in turn, to be patted and praised for his prowess. He then stretched his huge bulk at full length beside the warm stove, and went to sleep. The next morning they gave him a breakfast any dog might have envied; after which nothing could induce him to prolong his visit. He stood whining impatiently at the door till it was opened, when he galloped off, and they never saw him afterwards.

REMARKABLE CONVERSION.

About the 10th of April, 1843, in one of the Middle States, the writer of this article was reading in his room a portion of the thirty-third chapter of Ezekiel, the tenth to sixteenth verses inclusive; he was impressed to mark the verse and chapter, and read them to the next mourner in Zion he met. On the 12th, two days after, early in the morning, while working in his garden, a woman was sent to him, desiring his immediate attendance on a man who seemed to be almost in despair. She stated that she had called on several ministers in the place,—some were engaged, and others promised to come, but with the mourner time was precious, so his wife sent again. The case was this. One of the engineers on the railroad starting from that place was led to see himself a lost sinner. He had been at the altar for prayer, and such had been his mighty struggle for mercy, that the body seemed to partake of the inward conflict, so much so, that it took two or three men to hold him. He received no relief there. He was not quite ready to receive it in the simple way of faith. The afternoon before his conversion, while on the engine, his distress was so great, that it is said that another person had to take his place. He was unable to attend to anything more till his burden was removed. The writer went to his house, and entering the second story, saw the trembling penitent on the bare floor; he had no coat on; he was lying on his back. He was crying earnestly to God to have mercy on him and forgive him all his sins. His wife was sitting on a chest alongside of him, with her dear little children around her; all were weeping.

The brother said to him immediately, "Here is good news for you; be as quiet as you can till you hear it." It was read slowly and seriously, and commented on in a few words. Kneeling before the Lord, faith was explained. He was then shown how God could be just and yet forgive the sinner. How Christ was the end of the law for righteousness to all that believe. He seemed to fix his mind intently on what was said, his countenance brightened, but again it was clouded. The brother said:

"Perhaps you now think that God could not pardon such a sinner as you are, and that the offers of mercy read to you are too good to be true?"

He said, "I was just thinking so."

He was told that that was unbelief; that he must have faith in God, and the work would be done;

that without faith it was impossible to please God. He looked up with a heavenly smile, and claimed the promise, and was filled with the Holy Ghost. There had been no time for prayer. This only occupied about ten minutes; he needed light on the plan of salvation, and "Out of Zion, the perfection of beauty, God shined." He arose to his feet and stood with his arms stretched heavenward for one or two hours, praising God; his face shone with glory beaming forth; being weak, he staggered. He said:—

"Friends, I am not drunk with wine, but with the Spirit."

About twenty of his neighbors had run in, hearing the noise. Among them was one who was the keeper of a tenpin alley, or a billiard saloon; he hung down his head and wept like a child.

Some time after, the converted brother called for advice. He was desired to run the cars on the Sabbath; he was told to "obey God rather than man." He obeyed God and kept the Comforter, but lost his place. He left wife, children, and home, for a distant city, but after a time returned, and received something to do from one who is ever ready to help God's children.

In about two years he was invited to resume his place on the engine, and have the Sabbath to himself. So after he was tried in the furnace, God gave him favor with the people. It is now thirteen years since. He has been a leader a number of years. He is still on the engine; his soul is on the wing for glory; his mouth is filled with the high praises of God; may we meet in heaven.

PART V.

ILLUSTRATIONS OF DIVINE PROVIDENCE IN FAVOR OF THE SABBATH.

"If thou turn away thy foot from the Sabbath, from doing thy pleasure on my holy day, and call the Sabbath a delight, the holy of the Lord, honorable; and shalt honor him, not doing thine own ways, nor finding thine own pleasure, nor speaking thine own words; then shalt thou delight thyself in the Lord, and I will cause thee to ride on the high places of the earth, and feed thee with the heritage of Jacob."—ISAIAH lviii. 13-14.

REPORT IN THE BRITISH HOUSE OF COMMONS.

In the year 1832, the British House of Commons appointed a committee to investigate the effects of laboring seven days in a week, compared with those of laboring only six, and resting one. That committee consisted of Sir Andrew Agnew, Sir Robert Peel, Sir Robert Inglis, Sir Thomas Baring, Sir George Murray, Fowell Buxton, Lord Morpeth, Lord Ashley, Lord Viscount Sandon, and twenty other members of parliament. They examined a great number of witnesses, of various professions and employments. Among them was John Richard Farre, M. D., of London, of whom they speak as "an acute and experienced physician." The following is the testimony:—

"I have practised as a physician between thirty and forty years; and during the early part of my life, as the physician of a public medical institution, I had charge of the poor in one of the most populous districts of London. I have had occasion to observe the effect of the observance and non-observance of the seventh day of rest during this time. I have been in the habit, during a great many years, of considering the *uses* of the Sabbath, and of observing its *abuses*. The abuses are chiefly manifested in labor and dissipation. Its use, medically speaking, is that of a day of rest.

"As a day of rest, I view it as a day of *compensation*, for the inadequate restorative power of the body under *continued* labor and excitement. A physician always has respect to the preservation of the restorative power; because, if once this be lost, his healing office is at an end. A physician is anxious to preserve the balance of circulation, as necessary to the restorative power of the body. The ordinary exertions of man *run down* the circulation every day of his life; and the first general law of nature, by which God prevents man from destroying himself, is the alternating of day and night, that repose may succeed action. But, although the night apparently equalizes the circulation, yet it does not sufficiently restore its balance for the attainment of a long life. Hence, one day in seven, by the bounty of Providence, is thrown in as a day of compensation, to perfect by its repose the animal system.

"I consider, therefore, that, in the bountiful provision of Providence for the preservation of human life, the sabbatical appointment is not, as it has been sometimes theologically viewed, simply a precept, partaking of the nature of a political institution, but that it is to be numbered among the *natural* duties, if the preservation of life be admitted to be a duty, and the premature destruction of it a suicidal act."

At a regular meeting of the New Haven Medical Association, composed of twenty-five physicians, among whom were the professors of the medical college, the following questions were considered:—

1. Is the position taken by Dr. Farre in his testimony before the committee of the British House of Commons, in your view, correct?

2. Will men who labor but six days in a week be more healthy and live longer, other things being equal, than those who labor seven?

3. Will they do more work, and do it in a better manner?

The vote on the above was *unanimously in the affirmative;* signed by Eli Ives, chairman, and Pliny A. Jewett, clerk.

Dr. F. Backus, and seven other respectable physicians of Rochester, New York, have given the following testimony:—

"Having most of us lived on the Erie Canal since its completion, we have uniformly witnessed the same deteriorating effects of seven days' working upon the physical constitution, both of man and beast, as have been so ably depicted by Dr. Farre." They are more sickly than others, bring upon themselves, in great numbers, a premature old age, and sink to an untimely grave.

MATTHEW HALE'S EXAMPLE.

The following declaration of Sir Matthew Hale is an illustration of this truth:—

"Though my hands and my mind have been as full of secular business, both before and after I was judge, as, it may be, any man's in England, yet I never wanted time in six days to ripen and fit myself for the business and employments I had to do, though I borrowed not one minute from the Lord's day to prepare for it, by study or otherwise. But, on the other hand, if I had, at any time, borrowed from this day any time for my secular employment, I found it did further me less than if I had let it alone; and therefore, when some years' experience, upon a most attentive and vigilant observation, had given me this instruction, I grew peremptorily resolved never in this kind to make a breach upon the Lord's day, which I have now strictly observed for more than thirty years."

THE CAPTAIN OF THE WHALESHIP.

Some twenty years ago Rev. Mr. Y——, a godly minister, used to preach alternate Sabbaths in an old meeting-house, some two miles east from New London, Connecticut. One Sabbath, preaching upon the omnipotence of God, he noticed a boy of ten years who appeared unusually attentive. The thought that God's eye was ever upon him, was to the boy strange and new, and it made an impression on his mind that influenced his destiny.

Ten years from that time he had become a sailor, and one of the most wicked men living. If his comrades wished to engage in any reckless, heaven-daring enterprise, he was the leader. Returning from a distant port, he fell into some dispute with others of the crew; and to settle it he appealed to the Bible. He said, with an oath, that his mother had put one into his chest years before, and he would go and look up the —— thing. He went below, and, after searching a while, found and opened it; and the first words that met his eye were, "*Thou God seest me,*" the text that had arrested his attention in the old church, and with it the thought that God had seen all his past wickedness. A sense of guilt overwhelmed him. What could he do? He resolved to pray; but where? There was no place to retire. His companions, wondering at his long absence, had already entered the room. But pray he must; and there before those wicked men, partners in sin, with eyes streaming with tears, he fell on his knees and asked God to be merciful to him a sinner. In a short time he found peace.

Ten years after he was captain of a whaleship. One Sabbath morning, for the first time on the voyage, they fell in with a school of whales. All hands were delighted with the prospect, and were in readiness to man the boats the moment the order was given; but no order came. The mate, impatient of the delay, went to the captain to ascertain the reason. He received answer from Captain M——, "We have not worked on the Sabbath yet, and we shall not begin to-day." The importunity of officers and men could not change the commander's purpose. The ship moved on; in a few hours there was not a whale in sight. When night came the order was given to put about; and the next morning what was their surprise to find the vessel surrounded with many more than they had seen the previous day! The voyage was one of the most prosperous ever made; and there was no more murmuring because God's day was kept holy.

That captain, since his conversion, has been a praying man; has always kept the Sabbath; has had repeated revivals on board his ship; has been perhaps the most successful whaler that ever sailed; has given away large sums of money; and, though yet early in life, has the means of extensive and long-continued usefulness.

Should this meet the eye of that godly preacher, now fast nearing his end, let it assure him that eternity only will unfold the good wrought by that one sermon. And let it satisfy all, that to *obey God* is the only sure path to success, happiness, and heaven.

MANUFACTURERS AND THEIR TEAMS.

A MANUFACTURING company, which had been accustomed to carry their goods to market with their own teams, kept them employed seven days in a week, as that was the time in which they could go to the market and return. But by permitting the teams to rest on the Sabbath, they found that they could drive them the same distance in six days, that they formerly did in seven, and with the same keeping preserve them in better order.

EXPERIMENT WITH CATTLE.

A NUMBER of men started together from Ohio, with droves of cattle for Philadelphia. They had often been before, and had been accustomed to drive on the Sabbath as on other days. One had now changed his views as to the propriety of travelling on that day. On Saturday he inquired for pastures. His associates wondered that so shrewd a man should think of consuming so great a portion of his profits by stopping with such a drove a whole day. He stopped, however, and kept the Sabbath. They, thinking that they could not afford to do so, went on. On Monday he started again. In the course of the week he passed them, arrived first in the market, and sold his cattle to great advantage. So impressed were the others with the benefits of thus keeping the Sabbath, that ever afterwards they followed his example.

THE TEAMSTER AND HIS HORSES.

A GENTLEMAN in Vermont, who was in the habit of driving his horses twelve miles a day, seven days in a week, afterwards changed his practice, and drove them but six days, allowing them to rest one. He then found that, with the same keeping, he could drive them fifteen miles a day, and preserve them in as good order as before. So that a man may rest on the Sabbath, and let his horses rest, yet promote the benefit of both, and be in all respects the gainer.

EXPERIMENT IN A MILL.

THE experiment was tried in a large flouring establishment. For a number of years they worked the mills seven days in a week. The superintendent was then changed. He ordered all the works to be stopped at eleven o'clock on Saturday night, and to start none of them till one o'clock on Monday morning, thus allowing a full Sabbath every week. And the same men, during the year, actually ground thousands of bushels more than had ever been ground, in a single year, in that establishment before. The men, having been permitted to cleanse themselves, put on their best apparel, rest from worldly business, go with their families to the house of God, and devote the Sabbath to its appropriate duties, were more healthy, moral, punctual and diligent. They lost less time in drinking, dissipation, and quarrels. They were more clear-headed and whole-hearted, knew better how to do things, and were more disposed to do them in the right way.

FOUR FISHING VESSELS.

CAPT. BOURNE states that about 1829, he went out from Rhode Island in a brig on a fishing voyage along the coast of Labrador, with a crew of thirteen men. Three other vessels, with larger crews, from the same state, accompanied him. When they arrived upon the ground, Captain B. determined that he and his crew should sacredly regard the Sabbath; but the other crews prosecuted their employment on that day the same as on others. After fishing with them in company for two weeks, and finding it in some respects quite disagreeable, he parted from them, and went farther north, and fished in company with English vessels, who pursued the same course respecting the Sabbath day which he did himself. Trusting in that Providence which favors those who regard the true and right, he was not disappointed. He and his men succeeded in getting a "full voyage," cured their fish and sold it some four weeks sooner than any of the Sabbath-breaking vessels that accompanied them. What was better, Capt. B. and his crew made more profits to a share in less time, than those who profaned the Sabbath and wore themselves out by laboring hard seven days in the week.

SABBATH-BREAKING UNNECESSARY.

At the second annual meeting of the Society for Promoting the due Observance of the Lord's Day, the Rev. H. Stowell stated, that at a large meeting, which was held at Manchester, England, to petition the legislature on the better observance of the Sabbath, a leading spinner came forward, and said, that there was nothing more common than to hear from his brother spinners and master manufacturers this assertion, "If you stop the mill altogether on Sunday, you must frequently stop it on Monday also; because, if the engine gets out of order, or any other necessary repair be required, it must be done on the Sunday, or the mill cannot proceed on the Monday." Now, all this seems mighty plausible, said the good man, but I can prove it to be false; for in my mill I never suffer a stroke to be struck on the Sabbath; and on one occasion, my boiler had suffered a misfortune on a Saturday, and I feared the mill must stop on the Monday, but determined to try what could be done. I sent for a leading engineer, and said to him, "Can you have the mill ready to work on Monday morning?" "Yes, certainly I can." "But then," said I, "you mean to work on Sunday?" "Of course, sir." "But," said I, "you shall not do it in my mill." "But I cannot mend the boiler, if I do not," said he. I said, "I do not care, you shall not work in my mill on Sunday. I would rather that my mill stood the whole of Monday, than that the Sabbath should be violated in it!" The man said, "You are different from all other masters." I said, "My Bible, not the conduct of others, is my rule; and you must do it without working on Sunday, or I will try to get somebody else." This had the desired effect: they set to work, and worked till twelve o'clock on the Saturday night, and began again at twelve o'clock on the Sunday night; and the repairs were finished, and the mill was in full work, at the usual hour on Monday morning.

THE POOR BARBER AND THE SABBATH DAY.

In the city of Bath there lived a barber who made a practice of following his ordinary occupation on the Lord's day. As he was pursuing his morning's employment, he happened to look into some place of worship just as the minister was giving out his text, "Remember the Sabbath day to keep it holy." He listened long enough to be convinced that he was constantly breaking the laws of God and man, by shaving and dressing his customers on the Lord's day. He became uneasy, and went with a heavy heart to his Sabbath task. At length he took courage, and opened his mind to the minister, who advised him to give up Sabbath dressing and worship God. He replied, beggary would be the consequence. He had a flourishing trade, but it would almost be lost. At length, after many a sleepless night, spent in weeping and praying, he was determined to cast all his care upon God, as, the more he reflected, the more his duty became apparent. He discontinued Sabbath dressing, went constantly and early to the public services of religion, and soon enjoyed that satisfaction of mind which is one of the rewards of doing our duty, and that peace of God which the world can neither give nor take away. The consequences he foresaw actually followed. His genteel customers left him, as he was nicknamed a Puritan, or Methodist. He was obliged to give up his fashionable shop, and, in the course of years, became so reduced as to take a cellar under the old market-house and shave the common people.

One Saturday evening, between light and dusk, a stranger from one of the coaches, asking for a barber, was directed by the ostler to the cellar opposite. Coming in hastily, he requested to be shaved quickly, while they changed horses, as he did not like to violate the Sabbath. This was touching the barber on a tender chord. He burst into tears—asked the stranger to lend him a halfpenny to buy a candle, as it was not light enough to shave him with safety. He did so, revolving in his mind the extreme poverty to which the poor man must be reduced. When shaved, he said, "There must be something extraordinary in your history, which I have not now time to hear. Here is half a crown for you. When I return, I will call and investigate your case. What is your name?" "William Reed," said the astonished barber. "William Reed!" echoed the stranger; "William Reed; by your dialect you are from the west." "Yes, sir; from Kingston, near Taunton!" "What was your father's name?" "Thomas." "Had he any brothers?" "Yes, sir; one after whom I was named; but he went to the Indies, and as we never heard from him, we suppose him to be dead." "Come along, follow me," said the stranger; "I am going to see a person who says his name is William Reed, of Kingston, near Taunton. Come and confront him. If you prove to be indeed he who you say you are, I have glorious news for you. Your uncle is dead, and has left an immense fortune, which I will put you in possession of, when all legal doubts are removed."

They went and saw the pretended Mr. Reed, and proved him to be an impostor. The stranger, who was a pious attorney, was soon satisfied of the barber's identity, and told him that he had advertised for him in vain. Providence had now thrown him in his way, in a most extraordinary manner, and he had much pleasure in transferring a great many thousand pounds to a worthy man—the rightful heir of the property. Had the barber possessed a half-penny, or the credit for a candle, he might have long remained unknown; but he trusted in God, who delivered him from trouble.

THE HAND OF GOD IN IT.

A GENTLEMAN of business started with a horse and sulkey from New York. On Saturday night he put up at a distant village. On Sabbath morning, after considerable hesitation, he started again and proceeded till noon, trying all the way to silence the remonstrances of conscience, by the common, but vain plea, that he could serve God and keep the Sabbath as well on the road as in a tavern or a church. At noon he stopped and called for dinner. Whilst it was preparing he took up a magazine, and one of the first articles that caught his eye, was a memoir of his own mother, which he had never before seen. As he read he became deeply affected, and the tears flowed so freely, that he thought it needful to apologize to the landlady for his weakness. He told her that the subject of the memoir which he was reading was his own mother. "Is it possible," said she, "that the son of such a godly mother can be guilty of travelling on the Sabbath?" The man was confounded, and felt as if he wished to hide his head. He attempted to excuse himself; but his tongue faltered, and seemed reluctant to perform so mean an office. The people were assembling for public worship, and he had again a mighty contest with conscience. But pressed with business, and having once overcome its dictates, he prevailed again, and started off, resolving to reach a certain place by tea-time. He pressed onward: but the heavens began to gather blackness, the lightning to flash, and the thunder to break over his head. He put his horse to the utmost speed, and arrived just as the rain began to fall in torrents. He threw up the reins, told the servant to put the horse in a cool place, and ran into the house. The landlord knew him, and soon informed him that the tea was ready, and offered to show him the way. But the thought struck him that he would first just look at his horse (for he was a favorite animal), and see if he stood in a cool place, and was well taken care of. He therefore stepped into the barn, saw that he stood in a good place, and went out without laying his hand on him, as he generally did, when he went to see him. As he left the barn, his limbs seemed to fail him and his senses departed. He, however, came to, and went in; there was great confusion in the house, for they said that a stroke of lightning certainly struck the house or some object near by. Soon a messenger came and told a man that his fine horse was dead. He ran to the stable, but soon came back and said it was not his horse, but the gentleman's from New York. His horse, it seems, had been taken out of that stall, and the gentleman's from New York put in his place, in order to cool off. So that one was saved and the other killed by the same stroke of lightning, that came so near killing also its owner. The man saw, or thought he saw, in this *the hand of God:* and resolved from that time forward never to break the Sabbath. And though we are not authorized by such events to say that such men are sinners above all others, yet we are authorized to say that when men hope to gain, by breaking the known commands of God, the frequency of their disappointment, as well as the remonstrances of conscience and their dependence on God, ought to prevent them from giving way to the temptation, and lead them to be contented with what they can gain by obeying him.

THE HIDE TRADERS.

I WAS in command of a vessel, says Captain S., engaged in the hide trade between N—— and a port in Brazil. It was the custom of the port to load the vessels in turn as they were ready to receive cargo. My turn came to load. The work commenced and continued until Saturday night, when I ordered the hatches closed till Monday morning. The stevedore, wanting to work as usual on the Sabbath, left the ship with his gang muttering curses. Monday came. I made application to the commission merchant, for the completion of my load, but was told that I had lost my turn in loading, and must wait until it came round again, and that the *stevedore* and his *gang* had gone on board another vessel.

To aggravate my disappointment, I found that a hostile feeling had sprung up against me, and was participated in by all around. The merchant was studiously polite and respectful as before, but no longer familiar. Masters of vessels avoided my society. Evil disposed persons busied themselves in doing me secret injuries, cutting my rigging in the night time, and in other ways showing their malice. Our devotional exercises, morning and evening, were interrupted, and our efforts to do good derided and mocked.

Thus things went on, until our turn came round again; when, there being no other vessel ready to load, we were left to do our work in our own way. The loss of time occasioned by the refusal to load on the Sabbath, amounted to several weeks; but, after all, was it in fact a loss? The result will show.

It was now Saturday night again; the lading of

the ship was completed, and we were ready for sea. The Sabbath dawned, and with it came a fresh and fair wind. Shall we improve it, and violate the day, and that, too, after so many sacrifices to promote its sanctification? It was not to be thought of; and, hoisting the Bethel flag, as an invitation for our shipmates to come on board, we spent the day in devotional exercises. It was a happy Sabbath to all on board.

Monday morning early we were under sail for the lower harbor, several miles distant. On our way, we passed two brigs aground with lighters alongside discharging their hides, in order to lighten them and get them off. *They* left the upper harbor on the Sabbath, and here they were, and like to be until the next fair wind had blown itself out. On reaching the lower harbor, we found, to our surprise, lying at anchor, upwards of forty sail of shipping, waiting for a wind. Among them were all the vessels that had cleared for the last month or more, including every vessel that had obtained an advantage over us in respect to loading.

We had now to obtain a pilot and get to sea when the wind came fair and before it had spent itself. These were by no means matters easy to be accomplished. Pilots were few, and vessels many, and here, too, the principle of rotation was rigidly enforced. The winds, meanwhile, when fair, were short-lived and feeble, and the *bar* at the entrance of the harbor, too dangerous to pass without a pilot.

But He who had sustained us through previous trials for his name's sake, did not forsake us now. A pilot who had been on a long visit to the *interior*, returned to the sea-board and resumed his duties on the very day we reached the outer harbor, and presenting himself on board, offered to pilot us to sea.

Tuesday morning found us, with a fair wind, a pilot on board, and under way at daylight. We were the second vessel over the *bar*, and among the first to arrive in the United States.

The getting out of cargo, its exposure and sale, were matters of no little interest. We *then* found that "in keeping the commandments of God there is great reward." Our cargo, owing to the delay in getting it on board, received unusual attention at our hands, and was in perfect shipping order when stowed away, and came out in the same good condition.

The cargoes of the other vessels came out very differently, with a loss in some cases of 20, 30, and even 50 per cent. This loss was occasioned in part by hurrying the hides on board in the first instance without their being thoroughly dried, in order to greater despatch, and in part to the unusual detention of the vessels at the port of lading. From these two causes combined, and the activity of the *weevils* that took possession of the hides, and riddled them through and through, several of those voyages turned out splendid failures.

/ TESTIMONY OF CRIMINALS.

A GENTLEMAN, who was conversant with prisoners for more than thirty years, stated, that he found in all his experience, both with regard to those who had been capitally convicted and those who had not, that they referred to the violation of the Sabbath as the chief cause of their crimes; and that this has been confirmed by all the opportunities he has had of examining prisoners. Not that this has been the only cause of crime; but, like the use of intoxicating liquors, it has greatly increased public and private immorality, and been the means, in a multitude of cases, of premature death.

THE MURDERER'S FIRST STEP IN CRIME.

THERE is at this moment, in the place where I reside, a young man under sentence of death, for murder. He is but little over twenty years of age, and early has he become a most hardened wretch; and the crime for which, in a few days, he is to suffer the penalty, was committed under circumstances of so much coolness and forethought, as to render the murderer an object of peculiar abhorrence.

Since his conviction, he has said to a clergyman,

that if he had been religiously educated in his childhood, he would not now be in a dungeon. But his father and mother were both ungodly, and this, *an only son*, was brought up with no fear of God before his eyes.

He has also said, that *Sabbath-breaking* was the first step in his career of crime. With a companion he went off into the country for a ramble on the Lord's day, and thus dishonored and defied the most high God, and slighted the means of grace, and hardened his heart against the influence of truth.

Of course, he did not go to the Sabbath school, and the restraints that its instruction throws around the young, were never felt by him. He grew up without God, and now, in the morning of his days, and in the midst of his awful sins, he is to be hung, and sent away to the bar of an offended God.

There are two great lessons to be learned from this fact, both having a bearing on the Sabbath school cause, viz., the value of early instruction, and the danger of Sabbath-breaking. How many facts might we gather from the records of our criminal courts, to impress these truths upon the minds of those who may labor for the young! Some years ago, I caused an examination of the State Prison at Sing Sing, New York, to be made, with reference to the influence of Sabbath schools, and out of nearly a thousand prisoners, not one was found who had been a regular attendant; and O, how many confessed that Sabbath-breaking was their first step in crime!

LESSON FOR YOUNG MEN.

SEVEN young men, in a town in Massachusetts, started in the same business nearly at the same time. Six of them had some property or assistance from their friends, and followed their business seven days in a week. The other had less property than either of the six. He had less assistance from others, and worked in his business only six days in a week. He is now (1845) the only man who has property, and has not failed in his business.

DISAPPOINTED HOPES.

A YOUNG man, in Massachusetts, hoped to increase his enjoyment by going into the water for amusement on the Sabbath, instead of going, as all persons should do, to the house of God, to worship him. His friends, however, remonstrated against his profaning that holy day by such amusements, and urged him strongly to attend public worship. He at length consented, but declared he would go into the water after meeting. He did so. But almost immediately after he plunged into the water, information came to his friends that he was drowned. They hastened to the fatal spot. The water was shallow, and he was soon found, but apparently dead. All means were used to restore him, but in vain. The vital spark had fled; and he had gone to render up his account of the deeds done in the body, and all his hopes of an increase of enjoyment by the violation of the Sabbath, *were disappointed.*

THE THREE SHIPOWNERS.

SEVERAL years ago, there lived in one of our sea ports, A., B., and C., all of whom were owners of merchant vessels. Each of these men loaded a ship at the same time, which was to go first to Egypt, and then to the Baltic, to one of the Russian ports. All being loaded, they waited for a favorable wind. On Sabbath morning the wind was fair. The masters of the vessels went to their respective owners for sailing orders. A. and B. immediately had their ships put to sea; but C. told the master he must remain in port till the next day. Before Monday the wind changed, and kept her in port till the next Sunday, when it again became fair. The master again repaired to the house of C. for sailing orders; to his astonishment, C. remarked that his vessel must not leave port on the Sabbath. The captain attempted to reason the point with him, but in vain. He was determined to honor the Lord's day, and trust in Divine Providence. Sometime during the following week the ship sailed. It arrived in Egypt just as the ships of A. and B. were about to sail for the Baltic. In the mean time, information had circulated through the country that American vessels were in port, wishing to sell their cargoes, and purchase rice. By the time C.'s ship arrived, the market was glutted; in consequence, his cargo sold at a better price, and his ship was loaded at a much better rate than the others. C.'s vessel then proceeded to the Baltic. Providence operated here as in the Mediterranean. All these ships reached America about the same time; C.'s having cleared by the voyage as much as both the others. Thus C. found by experience that "in keeping God's commandments there is great reward," even in this life.

PART VI.

ILLUSTRATIONS OF FAITH IN DIVINE PROVIDENCE.

"Are not two sparrows sold for a farthing? and one of them shall not fall on the ground without your Father. But the very hairs of your head are all numbered. Fear ye not, therefore, ye are of more value than many sparrows." MATTHEW x. 29–31.

Faith in Divine Providence.

THE TRAVELLER'S GIFT.

About the year 1797, Mr. M. was travelling from a town on the eastern border of Vermont, to another town on the western side of the same state. As he passed over the mountainous part of the country, a heavy shower of rain was seen to be fast approaching. The traveller was then in a forest; no place of shelter appeared, and he hastened on until he arrived at a small cottage on its border. The rain had just then begun to rush down with great violence. He sprang from his horse, and without ceremony went into the house. Surprised to see no family, but a female with an infant child, he began to apologize for his sudden appearance; and hoped she would not be alarmed, but permit him to tarry till the rain abated. She replied, that she was glad he happened to come in, for she was always much terrified by thunder. "But why, madam," asked he, "should you be afraid of thunder? It is the voice of God, and will do no harm to those who love and commit themselves to his care."

After conversing with her awhile on this topic, he inquired if she had any neighbors who were religious. She told him she had neighbors about two miles off; but whether they were religious or not she did not know; only she had heard that some man was in the habit of coming there to preach once in a fortnight. Her husband went once, but she had never been to their meetings. In regard to everything of a religious kind, she appeared to be profoundly ignorant.

The rain had now passed over, and the face of nature smiled once more. The pious traveller, about to depart, expressed to the woman his thanks for her hospitality, and his earnest desire for the salvation of her soul. He earnestly besought her to read her Bible daily, and to give good heed to it, as to "a light shining in a dark place." She, with tears in her eyes, confessed that she had no Bible. They had never been able to buy one. "Could you read one, if you had it?" "Yes, sir, and would be glad to do so." "Poor woman," said he, "I do heartily pity you; farewell." He was preparing to pursue his journey. But he reflected: "This woman is in very great need of a Bible. Oh, that I had one to give her! But I have not. As for money to buy one, I have none to spare; I have no more than will be absolutely necessary for my expenses. I must go: but if I leave this woman without the means to procure the word of God, she may perish for lack of knowledge. What shall I do?" He recollected the Scriptures, "He that hath pity on the poor, lendeth to the Lord." "Cast thy bread upon the waters, for thou shalt find it after many days." His heart responded, "I will trust the Lord." He took a dollar from his purse, went back, and desired the woman to take it, and as soon as possible procure for herself a Bible. She promised to do so, saying, that she knew where one could be obtained. He took his leave, and set off. As there were then but few taverns on the road, he asked for a lodging at a private house, near which he found himself when night overtook him. He had yet a few pieces of change in his pocket; but as a journey of two more days was before him, he purposed to make his supper on a cold morsel which he had with him. But when the family came round their table to take their evening repast, the master of the house very urgently invited the stranger to join with them—not only so, but to crave God's blessing on their meal. He now began to feel himself among friends, and at liberty to speak freely on Divine things. The family appeared gratified in listening to his discourse till a late hour: it was a season of refreshing to their thirsty souls. In the morning, the traveller was urged to tarry till breakfast, but declined, the distance he had to travel requiring him to set off early. His host would take no compensation, and he departed, giving him many thanks. He travelled on till late in the morning, when, finding no public-house, he stopped again at a private one for refreshment. While waiting, he lost no time to recommend Christ and him crucified, to the family. When ready to depart, he offered to pay the mistress of the house, who had waited upon him very kindly, for his repast, and the oats for his horse; but she would receive nothing. Thus he went on, asking for refreshment as often as he needed it, and recommending religion wherever he called; and always offering, as another traveller would do, to pay his expenses; but no one would accept his money, although it was not known that his stock was so low, for he told them not, and his appearance was respectable : at home he was a man of wealth. "What," thought he, "does this mean? I was never treated in this manner on a journey before." The dollar given to the destitute woman recurred to his mind; and conscience replied, "I have been well paid. It is, indeed, safe lending to the Lord." On the second day after he left the cottage in the wilderness he arrived safely at home; and still had money for the poor, having been at no cost whatever.

About a year and a half after this, a stranger called at the house of Mr. M. for some refreshment. In the course of conversation, he observed that he lived on the other side of the mountain, near Connecticut river. Mr. M. inquired whether the people in that vicinity paid much attention to religion. The traveller replied, "Not much; but in a town twenty or thirty miles beyond the river, with which

I am acquainted, there has been a powerful revival. The commencement of it was very extraordinary. The first person that was awakened and brought to repentance, was a poor woman, who lived in a very retired place. She told her friends and neighbors that a stranger was driven into her house by a thunderstorm, and talked to her so seriously, that she began, while listening to his discourse, to feel concerned about her soul. The gentleman was much affected when he found that she had no Bible; and, after he had left the house to go on his journey, returned again, and gave her a dollar to buy one; and charged her to get it soon, and read it diligently. She did so; and it had been the means, as she believed, of bringing her from darkness into light; from a state of stupidity and sin, to delight in the truth and ways of God. The name of this pious man, or the place of his residence, she knew not. But she believed it was the Lord that sent him. At this relation, and the great change which was obvious in the woman, her neighbors wondered much. They were induced to meditate on the goodness, wisdom, and power of God, displayed in this singular event of his providence. They were led to think of the importance of attending more to the Bible themselves; and were finally awakened to a deep concern for the salvation of their souls. As many as thirty or forty are already hopefully converted, and rejoicing in God their Saviour." Mr. M., who had listened to this relation with a heart swelling more and more with wonder, gratitude, and joy, could refrain no longer; but, with hands and eyes upraised to heaven, exclaimed, "My God, thou hast paid me again!"

THE WIDOW'S SON AND HIS BIBLE.

There was a pious widow living in the northern part of England, on whom devolved the sole care of a large family, consisting of seven daughters and one son. It was her chief anxiety to train up her children in those virtuous and religious habits, which promote the present happiness and the immortal welfare of man. Her efforts were crowned with the best success, so far as the female branches of her family were concerned. But, alas! her boy proved ungrateful for her care, and became her scourge and her cross. He loved worldly company and pleasure; till, having impoverished his circumstances, it became necessary that he should go to sea. When his mother took her leave of him, she gave him a New Testament, inscribed with his name and her own, solemnly and tenderly entreating that he would keep the book, and read it for her sake. He was borne far away upon the bosom of the trackless deep, and year after year elapsed, without tidings of her boy. She occasionally visited parts of the island remote from her own residence, and particularly the metropolis; and, in whatever company she was cast, she made it a point to inquire for the ship in which her son sailed, if perchance she might hear any tidings of the beloved object who was always uppermost in her thoughts. On one occasion, she accidentally met, in a party in London, a sea captain, of whom she made her accustomed inquiries. He informed her that he knew the vessel, and that she had been wrecked; that he also knew a youth of the name of Charles ——; and added, that he was so depraved and profligate a lad, that it were a good thing if he, and all like him, were at the bottom of the sea. Pierced to her inmost soul, this unhappy mother withdrew from the house, and resolved in future upon strict retirement, in which she might at once indulge and hide her hopeless grief. "I shall go down to the grave," was her language, "mourning for my son." She fixed her residence at one of the sea-ports on the northern coast. After the lapse of some years, a half-naked sailor knocked at her door, to ask relief. The sight of a sailor was always interesting to her, and never failed to awaken recollections and emotions, better imagined than described. She heard his tale. He had seen great perils in the deep, had been several times wrecked, but said he had never been so dreadfully destitute as he was some years back, when himself and a fine young gentleman were the only individuals, of a whole ship's crew, that were saved. " We were cast upon a desert island, where, after seven days and nights, I closed his eyes. Poor fellow, I shall never forget it." And here the tears stole down his weather-beaten cheeks. "He read day and night in a little book, which he said his mother gave him, and which was the only thing he saved. It was his companion every moment; he wept for his sins, he prayed, he kissed the book; he talked of nothing but this book and his mother; and at the last he gave it to me, with many thanks for my poor services. 'There, Jack,' said he, 'take this book, and keep it, and read it, and may God bless you—it's all I've got.' And then he clasped my hand, and died in peace." "Is all this true?" said the trembling, astonished mother. "Yes, madam, every word of it." And then, drawing from his ragged jacket a little book, much battered and time-worn, he held it up, exclaiming, "And here's the very book, too." She seized the Testament, descried her own handwriting, and beheld the name of her son, coupled with her own, on the cover. She gazed, she read, she wept, she rejoiced. She seemed to hear a voice, which said, "Behold, thy son liveth." Amidst her conflicting emotions, she was ready to exclaim, "Now, Lord, lettest thou thy servant depart in peace, for mine eyes have seen thy salvation." "Will you part with that book, my honest fellow?" said the mother, anxious now to possess the precious relic. "No, madam," was the answer, "not for any money,—not for all the world. He gave it me with his dying hand.

I have more than once lost my all since I got it, without losing this treasure, the value of which, I hope, I have learned for myself; and I will never part with it till I part with the breath out of my body."

THE UNNATURAL MOTHER.

The Rev. James Churchill relates, in his "Analecta," that a widowed mother lived to see her youngest son, who was a babe at her husband's death, grow up to manhood in the esteem of all but herself. His temper was mild, and his manners affable; yet it is said that when he had attained the age of twenty, he had never known what the affection of a mother was towards him; nay, nor had ever received a single kind word from her. Blessed, however, by Providence, he flourished greatly in conducting his late father's business, employing a number of men. He took his mother under his own roof, settled upon her a liberal annuity, and studied to make her happy. It was all in vain. She murmured, reproached him, and, on one occasion, rushed into the manufactory and abused him violently before all the men. The people were shocked at her conduct; and the son withdrew, overwhelmed with grief. But worse events were yet in reserve for him. She immediately commenced legal proceedings against him for an assault! The men offered readily to appear on their master's behalf. Their master thanked them, but chose rather to be accounted guilty, and suffer judgment to go by default, than to appear against his own mother; and, though he had a fine to pay, this made no alteration in his conduct towards her. About three months after this, she was found dead in her bed, with marks of violence about her body. The coroner's verdict was, wilful murder, against her son. The poor youth was confined some months in prison, among the vilest of characters, to await his trial. His mind was at times distressed to a very great degree; reflecting that his character was ruined, his business nearly lost, and his prospect that of ending his days at a gallows: but what harrowed his heart most was, that all this was brought about by his own mother! Still his confidence in that Providence which watches over all, did not entirely fail him. He could exercise hope; and that hope was sustained not in vain. For as the time for his trial drew near, two of the men who had worked in his manufactory were taken up, on the charge of having committed some petty depredations; and, feeling the torments of a conscience burdened with guilt, these wretched creatures voluntarily confessed to a magistrate, that they could no longer endure the thought that so innocent and so worthy a master should lie under the vile imputation; that they were the murderers of Mrs. ———; and that the idea of getting her money and jewels had induced them to strangle her one night while in her sleep! The prison doors were soon thrown open to the suffering young man; joy was diffused through the town; his character shone out with a greater lustre; God prospered his reviving business; his family increased; and his children and grandchildren treated him with the respect and tenderness which he always manifested to his mother.

DELIVERANCE FROM STARVATION.

A CLERGYMAN of the state of New York (says the *Religious Museum*), through a misapprehension of a leading member, was precipitately deprived of his pulpit, which involved a large family in necessity. At supper, the good man had the pain of beholding the last morsel of bread placed upon the table, without the least means or prospect of a supply for his children's breakfast. His wife, full of grief, with her children, retired to her bed. The minister chose to sit up and employ his dark hours in prayer, and reading the promises of God. Some secret hope of supply pervaded his breast; but when, whence, or by whom, he knew not. He retired to rest, and in the morning appeared with his family, and performed the duty of prayer. It being the depth of winter, and a little fire upon the hearth, he desired his wife to hang on the kettle, and spread the cloth upon the table. The kettle boiled—the children cried for bread—the afflicted father, standing before the fire, felt those emotions of heart unknown to those whose tables are replenished with affluence.

While in this painful state, some one knocked at the door, entered, and delivered a letter into the minister's hand. When the gentleman was gone, the letter was opened, and to the minister's astonishment, it contained a few bank bills with a desire of acceptance. So manifest an interposition of Divine goodness could not but be received with gratitude and joy; and should be a lesson to others to trust in that Saviour who hath said, "Verily thou shalt be fed;" Psalm xxxvii. 3. "I never will leave thee nor forsake thee;" Heb. xiii. 5.

This remarkable occurrence being communicated to the editor, who having an intimacy with the gentleman said to be the hand that offered the seasonable relief, was determined the next time he made him a visit to introduce the subject, and if possible, to know the reason that induced the generous action. The story being told, the gentleman discovered a modest blush, which evinced the tenderness of his heart. On interrogation, he said, "he had frequently heard that minister; on a certain morning he was disposed for a walk; thought in the severity of the winter season a trifle might be of service, as fuel was high; felt a kind of necessity to enclose the money in a letter, went to the house, found the family adjusted as was described;

delivered the paper and retired; but knew not the extreme necessity of the minister and his family until this moment.

GOD BETTER THAN HIS WORD.

IN a large and populous village, in one of the hundreds, or wapentakes, of Yorkshire, England, lived a poor, but honest and pious man, whose name was Jonathan. He was an afflicted man, and much paralyzed by disease. He had a wife and two or three children, whose chief dependence in life was upon his small earnings. Jonathan was patient, industrious, and persevering in his efforts to provide for himself and for his household, all of whom were content with homely fare. At the time the writer of this account knew him, he might be from forty to fifty years of age. Amongst other occurrences of his life, he says, I distinctly recollect the following, which he related to me:—

During the time of harvest, while employed in gathering the fruits of the earth, he accidentally slipped from the top of a barley mow, and sprained one or both of his ankles; in consequence of which he was confined to his room and bed for some weeks. It is unnecessary to state, that, in the mean time, his family must have felt the loss of his weekly labor and income. His wife, on one occasion, went up stairs into his room weeping. " What is the matter?" said Jonathan; "what is distressing thee?" "Why, the children are crying for something to eat, and I have nothing to give them," was the affecting reply. "Hast thou faith in God?" asked Jonathan. "Dost thou believe in his providence, and in his word? Has he not said, 'Bread shall be given thee, and thy water shall be sure?' Isaiah, xxxiii. 16. Kneel down," he continued, "at the bedside, and pray to God. Tell him how thy children are circumstanced; that they have no bread; that thou hast nothing wherewith to buy them any; and I will also pray. Who can tell what God may do? He heareth prayer."

Jonathan and his wife prayed earnestly together; they pleaded the promises of God, and waited the result. Soon after, a person came to the door with a loaf of bread. She came from a house in the immediate neighborhood of Jonathan, the occupier of which was one of several branches of a family who were proprietors of very extensive iron works, carried on in the village where Jonathan lived. No sooner did the good woman receive the loaf of bread, than she ran to Jonathan to tell him how God had answered their prayer. "Now," said Jonathan, "before anything else be done, kneel down at the bedside, and return thanks to God for having heard our prayer." She did so: they praised his name together; and then ate their food with gladness and singleness of heart. Not many hours elapsed before another kind interposition of Providence presented itself. A second visitor brought them a joint of meat. When this was told Jonathan, he replied to his wife, "Ay! See! God is even better than his word! He promised bread, and he sends flesh in addition. Kneel down, and thank him again."

THE PIOUS FARMER PROTECTED.

Soon after the surrender of Copenhagen to the English, in the year 1807, detachments of soldiers were, for a time, stationed in the surrounding villages. It happened one day that three soldiers, belonging to a Highland regiment, were sent to forage among the neighboring farm-houses. They went to several, but found them stripped and deserted. At length they came to a large garden, or orchard, full of apple trees, bending under the weight of fruit. They entered by a gate, and followed a path which brought them to a neat farm-house. Everything without bespoke quietness and security; but as they entered by the front door, the mistress of the house and her children ran screaming out by the back. The interior of the house presented an appearance of order and comfort superior to what might be expected from people in that station, and from the habits of the country. A watch hung by the side of the fireplace, and a neat book-case, well filled, attracted the attention of the elder soldier.

He took down a book: it was written in a language unknown to him, but the name of Jesus Christ was legible on every page. At this moment, the master of the house entered by the door through which his wife and children had just fled.

One of the soldiers, by threatening signs, demanded provisions: the man stood firm and undaunted, but shook his head. The soldier who held the book approached him, and pointing to the name of Jesus Christ, laid his hand upon his heart, and looked up to heaven. Instantly the farmer grasped his hand, shook it vehemently, and then ran out of the room. He soon returned with his wife and children laden with milk, eggs, bacon, &c., which were freely tendered; and when money was offered in return, it was at first refused. But as two of the soldiers were pious men, they, much to the chagrin of their companion, insisted upon paying for all they received. When taking leave, the pious soldiers intimated to the farmer that it would be well for him to secrete his watch: but, by the most significant signs, he gave them to understand that he feared no evil, for his trust was in God; and that though his neighbors, on the right hand and on the left, had fled from their habitations, and by foraging parties had lost what they could not remove, not a hair of his head had been injured, nor had he even lost an apple from his trees.

"The angel of the Lord encampeth round about them that fear him, and delivereth them."

A MINISTER'S FAITH IN PROVIDENCE.

About the year 1839, says Rev. W. H. Spencer, I attended the Bridgewater Association in Pennsylvania, and was called upon to preach a discourse on Foreign Missions. I felt deeply, and the sympathies of the audience became so enlisted in behalf of the object that an unusually large contribution was taken up.

In the afternoon a warm and excellent discourse was preached by another minister on Home Missions. During his sermon the intrinsic importance of the subject forced itself upon my mind, and led me to agitate the question how much it would be possible to give to the cause myself. I was indeed in a great strait between charity and necessity. I felt desirous to contribute; but then I was on a journey, and I had given so much in the morning, that I really feared I had no more money than would bear my expenses. But when, at the conclusion of the discourse, the speaker said he could hardly expect a large collection after the amount they had given in the morning, my mind was decided; and I arose and stated my convictions of the importance of Home Missions, and for the sake of example, I informed the assembly what were my circumstances, but that I had made up my mind to give a dollar and trust in God to provide. And the result was, that as large a contribution was obtained as in the morning. At the close of the Association I proceeded on my journey; and the next day called on a friend and paid him some forty dollars, which I had collected for him. I was now about 140 miles from home, with scarce a dollar in my pocket; and how my expenses would be met, I could not imagine. But judge my surprise, when on presenting the money to my friend he took a hundred dollars, and adding it to the forty, placed the whole amount in my hand, saying, *he would make me a present of it!* I had, to be sure, rendered him some small services of a similar nature before, but I considered him under no obligations, and was expecting nothing of the kind! Gratitude and joy swelled my bosom; my mind at once recurred to my contribution the day previous, and I felt convinced that I had seen a literal fulfilment of the promise, "Give, and it shall be given unto you; good measure pressed down and running over, shall men give into your bosom."

THE POOR REMEMBERED.

A VENERABLE clergyman in the west of England, of the name of Thompson, had annually for many years made it his custom to distribute the overplus of his farm among the poor of his parish, after having supplied the wants of his own household.

One year, however, he was compelled to depart

from this plan. His benevolence had led him to engage to give thirty pounds towards the erection of a chapel, in a town whose inhabitants needed more church room. He was compelled, instead of giving his corn to the poor, to sell as much of it as would raise the sum promised. He regretted the circumstance, but it was unavoidable.

Having thus procured the money, he left his home to be the bearer of his own benefaction. On the road he overtook a young lady, mounted on a single horse like himself, whom he accosted with frankness and kindness. They travelled together over a down, and found they were going to the same place. His conversation and manner won much on the respect of the young lady, who listened with attention to his serious and holy conversation. She learned his name, and his residence, and, when they were about to part, was invited by the old clergyman to call upon him at his friend's house in the town.

In the course of the evening, the young lady related with great pleasure, at her friend's where she was on a visit, the very gratifying journey she had travelled, with a clergyman of the name of Thompson.

"Thompson!" exclaimed the lady of the house; "I wish it was the Mr. Thompson for whom we have for many years been inquiring in vain. I have money, tied up in a bag by my late husband, due to a person of that name, who desired to leave it till called for. But I suppose he is dead, and his executor, whoever he be, knows nothing of it." It was proposed that the old clergyman should be asked if this were any relation of his. He was sent for, came, and it soon appeared, that the Mr. Thompson, to whom the money was so long due, was his own brother, who had been dead several years, and to whose effects he was executor and residuary legatee. The money was paid him; he fell on his knees, blessed God, who had thus interposed on behalf of his poor people, hastened to his friend to tell him the joyful news, and as he entered his house exclaimed, "Praise God, tell it in Gath, publish it in Askelon, that our God is a faithful God."

THE WIDOW'S TRUST IN PROVIDENCE.

"One evening," said a pious widow lady, "we were eating our supper—we had nothing but bread, and of that not sufficient to satisfy our hunger. 'Mother,' said little John, when he was finishing his last morsel, 'what shall we do to-morrow morning? there is no bread in the house; we shall have no breakfast.' I answered him, 'Do not fear, John: God has not forsaken us; let us pray to him, and be assured he will remember us.' I made him kneel down by my side, and prayed to God that he would, in his goodness, have pity upon us, and give us bread for the morrow. I then put my child to bed, telling him to go to sleep quietly, and to depend upon his God, who never forgot those who put their trust in him. I myself went to bed, firmly believing that God had heard my prayer, and, commending myself to the protection of our Lord Jesus Christ, I slept comfortably till four in the morning, when John woke me; 'Mother,' said he, 'is the bread come?' Poor little fellow! he had but a scanty supper, and was very hungry. 'No,' I answered, 'it is not yet come, but be quiet and go to sleep again; it will come.' We both went to sleep; I was awakened a little before six in the morning, by some one rapping at my window. 'Dame Bartlet,' said a woman, 'you must get up immediately; Mrs. Martin's dairymaid is taken very ill, and you must come and milk her cows.' Here then was bread for us.

"I went to Mrs. Martin's, and milked her cows, and afterward sat down in the kitchen to breakfast; but I thought of my child, and could not eat. Mrs. Martin observing me, said, 'You do not eat your breakfast, Dame Bartlet.' I thanked her, and told her I had left a little boy at home in bed, very hungry; if she would permit me, I should prefer carrying my breakfast home to him. 'Eat your breakfast now,' was the kind reply; 'and you may carry some home to your little boy besides.' Mrs. Martin then gave me a basket of provisions, sufficient for myself and child for several days. As I returned home, I could not but thank my God, and feel grateful to him, and my kind benefactress. I rejoiced my little boy's heart by the sight of his breakfast. He got up directly, eager to partake of Mrs. Martin's kindness; after a good breakfast, I made him kneel down again by my side, whilst I returned thanks to our gracious God, who had heard our prayers the evening before, and who had given us a kind benefactress. When we rose, I took him in my lap, and said to him, 'Now, John, I hope what has happened to us will be remembered through your whole life. Last evening we had eaten all our bread; we had none left for this morning; but we prayed to God that, through his mercy, and for the sake of Jesus Christ, he would give us our daily bread. God has heard us, and has given us bread; may this teach you through life to put your trust in your Heavenly Father. I most earnestly pray God that you may never forget it.'" "And, madam," continued the good woman, "I have never wanted bread since. I am blessed in my son, who is now a man. He is dutiful and good to me, and has never forgotten the exhortation I then gave him to trust in God."

And who will dare say that this poor, humble woman, and the interests of her little household, were objects too insignificant for the care and attention of Almighty God? Is there a child of His, or any circumstance which bears in the smallest degree upon the well-being of His children, too insignificant for His attention? "Cast thy care upon the Lord for He careth for thee." Do such promises as this belong to the kings and princes and great ones only of the earth? Nay, verily, God has pledged the honor of His name, and the sanctity of His character, to comfort, sustain, and save every one, high or low, rich or poor, that trusteth in Him.

TWO WOMEN PRAYING.

In the county of A. there lived, remote from a village, two pious females, who had been recently united with husbands opposed to the gospel of Christ. These young women beheld, with the keenest sensation, the dear partners of their lives pursuing a path which must soon end in everlasting death. Each had often carried her troubles and sorrows to the throne of grace, and laid them before One who knew the anxiety of her heart, and each had often shed the silent tear. As a great intimacy had existed between those young females, they jointly agreed to spend one hour daily in praying for their husbands. They continued this prayer for seven years without any visible effect. At length, with hearts full of anguish, they met to mingle together their sorrows. Their inquiry was, shall we no longer pray for our dear partners— must they, Oh, must they be for ever miserable? They concluded that although their prayers had not been answered, yet they would persevere even unto the end of life, in the course they had adopted; and if their husbands would go down to destruction, they should go loaded with their prayers. They moreover resolved to renew their strength, and to pray more earnestly than ever. Thus they continued for three years longer. About this time one of them was awakened in the night by the mental distress of her husband. Sleep had departed from his eyes; distress and anguish had seized his soul, for the prayers of these females had come up in remembrance before the throne of God; and the man who could once ridicule the tender anxieties of a distressed wife, was now upon his knees in the greatest agony. Now, with earnestness, he entreated her to pray for him; for, said he, the day of grace is almost over, and the door of mercy is ready to be closed against me for ever. His distress, and the hope of the wife, continued to increase. As soon the day dawned she went with an overflowing heart to tell her praying companion, that God was about to answer their petitions. But great was her surprise, to meet her friend coming on the same errand, to tell her what God was doing for her own husband.

Thus, after ten years' perseverance in calling mightily upon God, these Christian females had the unspeakable satisfaction of seeing both their husbands brought on the same day to realize their undone condition, and about the same time to accept, as it is hoped, the offers of mercy.

RETURN OF THE PRODIGAL.

F—— was the son of a devoted New England minister, and the child of many prayers. His mind was carefully stored with religious knowledge, and disciplined in the best schools of his native city. Evil companionships, however, early led him astray from the paths of virtue. A vicious habit of novel-reading alienated him from the open fountains of wisdom, and drew him away from parental influence and restraint.

At length his restless and adventurous spirit sought a sphere of unchecked indulgence, and he went to the Pacific coast. There he found his associates among the thoughtless sons of fortune, and gave himself up to the life of a homeless adventurer. Prosperity and adversity served alike to harden his heart. Early convictions were stifled; the house of God neglected.

But there were bands in his wickedness stronger than those of Satan. The anxious and aching hearts of his parents were turned to God. Unceasing, believing prayer ascended in his behalf. His father, especially, cherished the unwavering conviction that his wayward son, after running the prodigal's career of vice and folly, would trace the prodigal's steps of penitence and salvation. Year after year he clung to the divine promises, and pleaded them earnestly at the mercy seat. He felt that he could not be denied.

A few days ago the hearts of father, mother, and friends were gladdened by the intelligence that the lost was found—that the prodigal had returned. He had visited a remote South American port, and on his return voyage he was the only cabin passenger. The captain had depended on him to furnish a supply of cards, novels, and other sources of time-killing, soul-destroying amusements; and he, in turn, knowing the disposition of the captain, had looked to him for an adequate supply. The few means of diversion were soon exhausted, and after being ten days at sea the young man found nothing to do but think. His past life came up in review before him, and conscience revived. Early teachings whispered around him. An injured father's persevering faith, and a weeping mother's counsels, haunted his solitary berth. The emptiness of worldly pleasures and the vanity of earthly plans led him to reflect on the surer joys and riches of the Christian. He turned to the word of God and read his condemnation. His guilt rose mountain-high, as the Holy Spirit unfolded the immaculate law. He fell upon his knees and cried for pardon.

By one of those providences which call forth the adoration of the devout, there were in the cabin of this ship copies of Nelson's Cause and Cure of Infidelity, Baxter's Call to the Unconverted, James's Anxious Inquirer, and Abbott's Young Christian—

the first to dispel his sceptical doubts, the second to fasten the arrow of conviction in his heart, the third to instruct his inquiring soul, and the last to present encouragements and allurements to the Christian life. He read them all prayerfully. Before the vessel landed at San Francisco, the great question was settled, we hope, for ever. He found peace in believing, and entered at once on the new life of Christian discipleship. He made his way immediately to the sanctuary, engaged in Sabbath school instruction, sought the company of ministers and godly men—abandoning his former companions in sin, or visiting them only to labor for their salvation; and his letters to his parents breathed the spirit of penitence and consecration, coupled with the most touching expressions of gratitude and affection. The "fatted calf" would be a small testimony of the joy that fills the house long saddened by the wandering prodigal, but now gladdened by his return.

Christian parents, and especially those whose sons are far away from home and from God, will find encouragement to their faith in this narrative. There are few cases apparently more hopeless of reformation and conversion than the one before us. Pride kept him from coming home; an evil conscience restrained him from places and companionships likely to benefit him: only a vigorous faith could anticipate the possibility of a change. Yet grace triumphed; God's truth is vindicated; everlasting promises have their fulfilment; the prodigal returns. Trust that grace; cling to those promises: *your* prodigal son may yet be saved.

KNOLLYS' DELIVERANCE.

The Rev. Hanserd Knollys suffered much persecution for his conscientious attachment to the truth. In the early part of his ministry, he emigrated from England to America, the common asylum at that time, for all who wished to enjoy liberty of conscience. There he sojourned four years, but returned in 1641, at the earnest request of an aged father. On his arrival in England he was reduced to great straits, but experienced the goodness of Providence in a peculiar manner. The following particulars are extracted from his own account: "I was still poor and sojourned in a lodging till I had but sixpence left, and knew not how to provide for my wife and child. Having prayed to God and encouraged my wife to trust in him, and to remember former experiences, and especially that word of promise, 'I will never leave thee nor forsake thee,' I paid for my lodging and went out, not knowing whither God's good hand would lead me to receive something towards my present subsistence. About seven or eight doors from my lodgings, a woman met me in the street, and told me she came to seek me, and her husband had sent her to tell me that there was a lodging provided and prepared in his house by some Christian friends for me and my wife. I told her my present condition, and went along with her to the house. There she gave me twenty shillings which Dr. Bastock, a late sufferer, had given her for me, and some linen for my wife, which I received, and told her husband I would fetch my wife and child and lodge there. I returned with great joy, and my wife was greatly affected with this seasonable and suitable supply. After we had returned praises to God, we went to our new lodgings, where we found all things necessary provided for us, and all charges paid for fifteen weeks." When the time was expired, he undertook a school, and by the blessing of God was successful in bringing up a large family creditably, and though several times imprisoned for religion, continued the laborious and esteemed pastor of a poor church, for fifty years, till he went to his reward, September 19, 1691, aged ninety-two years.

ERSKINE'S DELIVERANCES.

The Rev. Henry Erskine was often in great straits and difficulties. Once when he and his family had supped at night, there remained neither bread, meal, flesh, nor money, in the house. In the morning the young children cried for their breakfast, and their father endeavored to divert them, and did what he could at the same time to encourage himself and wife to depend upon that Providence that hears the young ravens when they cry. While thus engaged, a countryman knocked hard at the door, and called for some one to help him off with his load. Being asked whence he came, and what he would have, he told them he came from Lady Reburn with some provisions for Mr. Erskine. They told him he must be mistaken, and that it was more likely to be for another Mr. Erskine in the same town. He replied, no, he knew what he said, he was sent to Mr. Henry Erskine, and cried, "Come, help me off with my load, or else I will throw it down at the door." Whereupon they took the sack from him, and on opening it, found it well stored with fish and meat.

At another time, being at Edinburgh, he was so reduced that he had but three half-pence in his pocket. When he was walking about the streets, not knowing what course to steer, one came to him in a countryman's habit, presented him with a letter in which were enclosed several Scotch ducatoons, with these words written, "Sir, receive this from a sympathizing friend. Farewell." Mr. Erskine could never find out whence the money came.

THE AGED CHRISTIAN'S ADVICE TO A YOUNG MINISTER.

I WELL remember, said an eminent minister in North Wales, that when the Spirit of God first convinced me of my sin and danger, and of the many difficulties and enemies I must encounter, if ever I intended reaching heaven, I was often to the last degree in fear; the prospect of the many strong temptations and allurements, to which my youthful years would unavoidably expose me, greatly discouraged me. I often used to tell an aged soldier of Christ, the first and only Christian friend I had any acquaintance with for several years, that I wished I had borne the burden and heat of the day like him. His usual reply was, that so long as I *feared*, and was humbly *dependent upon God*, I should never fall, but certainly prevail. I have *found* it so. O, blessed be the Lord, that I can now raise up my Ebenezer, and say, " Hitherto hath the Lord helped me."

STILLING'S TRUST IN PROVIDENCE.

IN youth, Stilling was extremely poor, destitute of the common comforts and necessaries of life. After a long season of anxiety and prayer, he felt satisfied that it was the will of God that he should go to a university, and prepare himself for the medical profession. He did not at first make choice of a university, but waited for an intimation from his Heavenly Father; for as he intended to study simply from faith, he would not allow his own will in anything. Three weeks after he had come to this determination, a friend asked him whither he intended to go. He replied, he did not know. "O," said she, "our neighbor, Mr. T., is going to Strasburg, to spend the winter there;—go with him."

This touched Stilling's heart; he felt that this was the intimation he had waited for. Meanwhile, Mr. T. entered the room, and was heartily pleased with the proposition. The whole of his welfare now depended on his becoming a physician; and for this a thousand dollars at least were requisite, of which he could not tell in the whole world where to raise a hundred. He nevertheless fixed his confidence firmly on God, and reasoned as follows:—

"God begins nothing without terminating it gloriously. Now, it is most certainly true, that he alone has ordered my present circumstances, entirely without my co-operation. Consequently, it is also most certainly true, that he will accomplish everything regarding me in a manner worthy of himself."

He smilingly said to his friends, who were as poor as himself, "I wonder from what quarter my Heavenly Father will provide me with money?" When they expressed anxiety, he said, "Believe assuredly that he who was able to feed a thousand people with a little bread lives still, and to him I commend myself. He will certainly find out means. Do not be anxious, the Lord will provide."

Forty-six dollars was all that he could raise for his journey. He met unavoidable delay on the way; and while at Frankfort, three days' ride from Strasburg, he had but a single dollar left. He said nothing of it to any one, but waited for the assistance of his Heavenly Father. As he was walking the streets, and praying inwardly to God, he met Mr. L., a merchant from the place of his residence, who says to him, "Stilling, what brought you here?"

"I am going to Strasburg, to study medicine."

"Where do you get your money to study with?"

"I have a rich Father in heaven."

Mr. L. looked steadily at him, and inquired, "How much money have you on hand?"

"One dollar," said Stilling.

"So," said Mr. L. "Well, I'm one of your Father's stewards;" and handed him thirty-three dollars.

Stilling felt warm tears in his eyes; says he, "I am now rich enough; I want no more."

This first trial made him so courageous, that he no longer doubted that God would help him through everything.

He had been but a short time in Strasburg, when his thirty-three dollars had again been reduced to one, on which account he began again to pray very earnestly. Just at this time, one morning, his roommate, Mr. T., says to him, "Stilling, I believe you did not bring much money with you;" and offered him thirty dollars in gold, which he gladly accepted, as an answer to his prayers.

In a few months after this, the time arrived when he must pay the lecturer's fee, or have his name struck from the list of students. The money was to be paid by six o'clock on Thursday evening. Thursday morning came, and he had no money, and no means of getting any. The day was spent in prayer. Five o'clock came, and yet there was no money. His faith began to waver; he broke out into a perspiration; his face was wet with tears. Some one knocked at the door. "Come in," said he It was Mr. R., the gentleman of whom he had rented the room.

"I called," said Mr. R., "to see how you liked your room?"

"Thank you," said Stilling, "I like it very much."

Says Mr. R., "I thought I would ask you another question; have you brought any money with you?"

Stilling says he now felt like Habakkuk when the angel took him by the hair of the head to carry him to Bayblon. He answered, "No; I have no money."

Mr. R. looked at him with surprise, and at length

said, "I see how it is; God has sent me to help you."

He immediately left the room and soon returned with forty dollars in gold. Stilling says he then felt like Daniel in the lion's den when Habakkuk brought him food. He threw himself on the floor and thanked God with tears. He then went to the college, and paid his fee as well as the best.

THE POOR PHYSICIAN.

A YEAR last November, says a missionary agent, I preached a missionary sermon in the town of ——, and took a subscription. A physician subscribed and paid five dollars. A gentleman standing by told me that the five dollars was all he had, or was worth: that he had lost his property and paid up his debts and moved into town to commence practice, with no other resources than that five dollar bill. He and his wife were obliged to board out, as he was not able to keep house.

I resolved at once that I would keep watch of that man, and see what the Lord would do with him.

About a year after this interview, I visited the place again, and put up with this physician. I found him keeping house in good style. In conversation with him, I brought up the duty of

Christian benevolence, and spoke of God's faithfulness to fulfil his promises to the liberal.

He told me he knew a physician, who, the last year, gave away the last five dollars he had in the world, resolving to trust the Lord for the future. During the next summer, while the cholera raged in the country, by a series of events guided, as he believed, by the providence of God, most of the practice was thrown into the hands of this physician, and he had taken more than $2500.

I told him I knew him to be the man referred to, and that I had been keeping watch to see what the Lord would do with him.

Oh, sir, if we would, all of us, only trust in the Lord, and more abundantly give of our substance to aid in spreading the gospel, and throw open our eyes to read the providence, as well as word of God, we might not only speedily supply the whole world with Bibles, but our hearts would overflow with constant gratitude in view of the evident interpositions of Providence in our behalf.

THE BROKEN VOW.

Some years ago, a poor lad came to London, in search of a situation as errand-boy; he made many unsuccessful applications, and was on the eve of returning to his parents, when a gentleman, being prepossessed by his appearance, took him into his employment, and after a few months, bound him apprentice. He so conducted himself during his apprenticeship, as to gain the esteem of every one who knew him; and after he had served his time, his master advanced a capital for him to commence business. He retired to his closet with a heart glowing with gratitude to his Maker for his goodness, and there solemnly vowed that he would devote a tenth part of his annual income to the service of God. The first year his donation amounted to ten pounds, which he gave cheerfully, and continued to do so till it amounted to £500. He then thought that was a great deal of money to give, and that he need not be so particular as to the exact amount: that year he lost a ship and cargo, to the value of £15,000, by a storm! This caused him to repent, and he again commenced his contributions with a resolution never to retract; he was more successful every year, and at length retired. He then devoted a tenth part of his annual income for several years, till he became acquainted with a party of worldly men, who by degrees drew him aside from God: he discontinued his donations, made large speculations, lost everything, and became almost as poor as when he first arrived in London as an errand-boy. "There is," saith Solomon, "that scattereth, and yet increaseth; and there is that withholdeth more than is meet, but it tendeth to poverty."

"WILL YOU TRUST MY FATHER?"

An aged Christian, who had long been an invalid, and was dependent on Christian charity for her support, on sending for a new physician who had just come into the place, and united with the same church of which she was a member, said to him, "Doctor, I wish to put myself under your care, but I cannot do it unless you will *trust my Father.*" "Well, ma'am," replied the physician, "I believe your Father is rich; *I may safely trust Him.*"

THE WIDOW PROSNI.

During the siege of the Protestant city of Rochelle, under Louis XIII. and Cardinal Richelieu, the inhabitants endured great miseries before they yielded to an honorable capitulation, the terms of which were, however, far from being kept by their enemies. One of the many touching incidents of the siege is recorded by Merivault. "He gives the names of the parties chiefly concerned," says Smedley; "and the narrative is marked by an air of truth, which renders its authenticity undoubted. During the height of calamity among the Rochellois, some charitable individuals, who had previously formed secret magazines, relieved their starving brethren without blazoning their good deed. The relict of a merchant, named Prosni, who was left in charge of four orphan children, had liberally distributed her stores, while anything remained, among her less fortunate neighbors; and, whenever she was reproached with profusion and want of foresight by a rich sister-in-law of less benevolent temper, she was in the habit of replying, 'The Lord will provide for us.' At length, when her stock of food was utterly exhausted, and she was spurned with taunts from the door of her relative, she returned home destitute, broken-hearted, and prepared to die, together with her children. But it seemed as if the mercies once displayed at Zarephath were again to be manifested; and that there was still a barrel and a cruse in reserve for the widow, who, humbly confident in the bounty of heaven, had shared her last morsel with the supplicant in affliction. Her little ones met her at the threshold with cries of joy. During her short absence, a stranger, visiting the house, had deposited in it a sack of flour; and the single bushel which it contained was so husbanded as to preserve their lives till the close of the siege. Their unknown benefactor was never revealed; but the pious mother was able to reply to her unbelieving kinswoman, 'The Lord hath provided for us.'"

THE SABBATH-KEEPING ESQUIMAUX.

In December, says Mr. Barsoe, the missionary, a pleasing circumstance occurred; it showed the reverence of our Esquimaux for the Lord's day. Owing to the state of the weather during the preceding month, but few seals had been taken; and Saturday, the second of December, was the first day on which the state of the ice permitted our people to go out on the seal-hunt. Considering the great uncertainty which ever attends this occupation, the inducement to pursue it on the following day, in the hope of securing a better provision for their families, was anything but slight. We were, therefore, not a little pleased to learn that a meeting of fathers of families had been convened on the Saturday evening, and that it had been resolved that they would none of them go out on the ensuing day of the Lord, but would spend it in a manner becoming the disciples of Christ, who were invited thankfully to commemorate his coming into the world to save sinners. They expressed their belief that their Heavenly Father was able to grant them on Monday, a sufficiency for the supply of their wants. The meeting they closed with the singing of some verses, during which they felt the presence and peace of their Lord and Saviour. Their confidence in God was not put to shame. On Monday, the weather proved so favorable, that they captured no fewer than one hundred seals; but in the course of the following night the frost became so intense as to close all the bays and inlets, and to preclude any further seal-catching.

THE HAPPY MEETING.

Some years ago, a pious widow in America, who was reduced to great poverty, had just placed the last smoked herring on her table, to supply her hunger and that of her children, when a rap was heard at the door, and a stranger solicited a lodging and a morsel of food, saying, that he had not tasted bread for twenty-four hours. The widow did not hesitate, but offered a share to the stranger, saying, "We shall not be forsaken, or suffer deeper for an act of charity."

The traveller drew near to the table; but when he saw the scanty fare, filled with astonishment he said, "And is this all your store? And do you offer a share to one you do not know? Then I never saw charity before! But, madam, do you not wrong your children, by giving a part of your last morsel to a stranger?" "Ah!" said the widow, weeping, "I have a boy, a darling son, somewhere on the face of the wide world, unless Heaven has taken him away; and I only act towards you as I would that others should act towards him. God, who sent manna from heaven, can provide for us as he did for Israel; and how should I this night offend him, if my son should be a wanderer, destitute as you, and he should have provided for him a home, even as poor as this, were I to turn you unrelieved away!"

The widow stopped, and the stranger, springing from his seat, clasped her in his arms: "God, indeed, has provided just such a home for your wandering son, and has given him wealth to reward the goodness of his benefactress. My mother! O, my mother!"

It was, indeed, her long-lost son, returned from India. He had chosen this way to surprise his family, and certainly not very wisely; but never was surprise more complete, or more joyful. He was able to make the family comfortable, which he immediately did: the mother living for some years longer, in the enjoyment of plenty.

THE WIDOW'S COMFORT.

The writer would beg leave to present the following brief statement of facts, which exhibit, in a striking manner, the effects which the lively reception of the glorious and all-important truths of religion produce in the soul.

A Sunday school teacher who esteems it not only

her duty but her happiness, to visit frequently the scholars committed to her care, was led to the dwelling of a poor widow, the mother of four children, with whose appearance she became much interested. She was still young, and was possessed of that peculiar softness and propriety of demeanor which never fails to command attention, while the narrative of her desolate and affecting situation, and the supports with which she was sustained and comforted, filled the mind of her young visitor with the mingled emotions of sympathy and congratulation. The widow, Mrs. C., had been married early in life, and lived in independence and comfort for several years. She was attached to her husband, devoted to her children, and employed her time in a diligent attention to her domestic avocations, except that occasionally when the weather was fine, she took a walk to the church, which was not far distant.

About four years ago, her husband's business led him to the West India islands, where he was soon seized with a contagious fever, and died in a few days, leaving his affairs in a confused and unsettled state. When they were arranged, and all his engagements met, there was nothing left for the support of the widow, who saw herself cast penniless on the wide world, surrounded by her children, with nothing to relieve the darkness and gloom which settled thick upon her. Agitation and grief produced a lingering sickness, which confined her to her bed for many weeks, during which time those articles of furniture which had been spared to her were one by one disposed of, to procure the necessary provisions for the family.

"It was now (to adopt Mrs. C.'s own words) that I was made to see the transitory and fleeting nature of all earthly possessions and enjoyments. Those which I had relied upon, to which I had clung as my *sole* dependence, were fled for ever. The world was to me a barren wilderness, a desolate waste, with nought to console or relieve me. I turned my eye upward, but thence I could derive no comfort. The words of God himself were repeated to me: 'Leave thy fatherless children, I will preserve them alive—and let thy widows trust in me.' But I could not *trust* in God; I did not *know* him. I had lived without God in the world, and was ignorant of the way in which to seek him. I began to view myself in the character of a sinner, exposed to the wrath of a provoked and neglected God; and was convinced if I continued in that state, I could never hope for peace, either here or in the world to come. My earnest inquiry now was, 'What shall I do to be saved?' Gradually the Gospel plan of salvation through faith in a crucified Redeemer, was disclosed; and as one guilty and perishing I came unto Jesus, and besought that his free mercy might be extended to me, and his Spirit sent to purify and renew my depraved and sinful heart. That mercy *has*, I trust, been extended; I receive my pardon as the purchase of the cross—and I am now enabled to look up to God, and to trust in him, as a reconciled Father in Jesus Christ." She further added, "I bless and praise the Lord for his chastening hand; for if my path had been smooth and prosperous, I should probably have continued a stranger to God, and should have brought up my children to live for this world only."

It was astonishing to witness the great change wrought in her feelings and conduct by the adoption of these new views and sentiments. She was no longer oppressed with that weight of care and anxiety which before had bowed her to the earth—but was enabled, with filial confidence, to cast herself and her children on the protecting care of him who is emphatically "the Father of the fatherless, and the widow's friend;" and her declaration to the young lady, who was now for the first time sitting with her, was, "I have found all his promises sure—I have been provided for from day to day, in a remarkable manner; for often, when my stock has been quite exhausted, and I had no resource left, I have gone to God, and having made my wants known to him, he has not only given me peace of mind, and strong faith in him, but has always raised up some friend whom he has sent as his messenger to supply my need. So that although our fare is of the simplest kind, and we have sometimes had no breakfast, sometimes no dinner, yet we have never passed a *whole day* without seeing the hand of God stretched out to provide for us."

In the course of a conversation which I afterwards had with her, I was much delighted, and I trust not a little profited, by some remarks of Mrs. C., to the following effect:—" I know by experience that happiness is not confined to the splendid circles of the great, nor to the profusely covered tables of the rich; for when God wisely withholds this world's goods, he bestows those dispositions of mind, and those inward comforts, which abundantly compensate for them. I remember that one day I had nothing in the house but a little meal, which I put over the fire to boil for our dinner; then I looked about for some salt, but there was none to be found. In a moment of despondency I sat down, and thought my lot uncommonly severe—not to have a little salt to season our meal with, and no means to obtain any! I took up my Bible, which has been a source of unspeakable comfort in many a trying hour, when these words caught my attention,—'Jesus went with his disciples through the corn fields, and his disciples plucked the ears of corn, and did eat, rubbing them in their hands.' When I reflected on the privations and hardships which my blessed Lord cheerfully endured for my sake, my discontented and repining thoughts fled in an instant. Gratitude, love, and joy, took possession of my breast. I gathered my children together, and we partook with thankfulness of that plain repast, for, receiving it as the gift of God, and knowing it to be better than I deserved, it was to me sweeter, and yielded more satisfaction, than the most costly dainties which wealth can purchase."

It was the sense of the favor of God, a lively perception of his excellence and perfection, his love shed abroad through her heart, his Spirit rectifying and elevating her nature, which had transformed this woman from a depressed and unhappy, to a thankful and joyful being, even in this life; and caused her to look to scenes beyond, with a "hope full of immortality;" and thus constrained her to adopt, with much feeling, the poet's words:—

"Give what thou wilt, without *Thee* we are poor;
And with Thee rich, take what thou wilt away."

THE FRENCH PASTOR.

THE above anecdotes remind us of the case of a living French pastor, eminent as an author in his own country, and well known to a large portion of the religious world in ours. He had no income but the scanty stipend of a pastor, and upon this had to maintain eleven children. His poverty was deep, his difficulties constant; but his heart was ever full of cheerful gratitude, and his hand ever open to those who were poorer than himself. His friends say that on more than one occasion he has been left without a single *sous*, or a morsel of bread for his children. Meal-time coming, his wife told him they could have no dinner. He replied, "Yes, we shall dine as usual: lay the cloth." It was objected, that to lay a cloth was very useless, when there was nothing to place upon it.

"Lay it," he insisted, "lay it, just as usual: the Lord will provide." The cloth was laid, and seemed for a while to mock faith by its bareness; but a knock was heard, and the family soon surrounded a board which they all felt the Lord himself had spread.

REMARKABLE ANSWER TO PRAYER.

BEFORE the birth of her third child, August 17th, 1815, Mrs. Mather, daughter of the late Rev. Joseph Benson, became so reduced that her friends entertained many fears for her safety. She gave birth, however, to a fine boy, and gradually recovered her strength. But a lameness, with which she had long been afflicted, continued unrelieved. Mr. Benson was, as might be expected, much concerned to witness his daughter's infirmity from year to year, and ceased not to present her case before the Lord, endeavoring to encourage her to rely on the Divine promises, as being all yea and amen in Christ Jesus. On the Sunday previous to Mrs. Mather's confinement, his mind was much comforted in hearing the late Rev. Samuel Lear, whom he denominated "an excellent young preacher," deliver a "very instructive" sermon on our Lord's words, "Verily, verily I say unto you, whatsoever ye shall ask the Father in my name, he will give it you:" and his "faith had been increased with regard to Ann." That his hope was not in vain, nor his faith unheeded, as to her unhappy lameness, an extract from his journal will fully manifest. I wish to remark, says Mr. Samuel Benson, that I was myself present on the occasion, and will bear witness to the correctness of the statement in every part. The Rev. James Macdonald, who was also present, observes in his life of Mr. Benson, "All believed that the power to walk, which she received in an instant, was communicated by an immediate act of Omnipotence."

"Oct. 4th.—This evening the Lord has shown us an extraordinary instance of his love and power. My dear Ann, though safely delivered of a fine and healthy child, and restored in a great measure with respect to her appetite and digestion, yet remained without any use of either of her feet, and indeed without the least feeling of them, or ability to walk a step, or lay the least weight upon them, nor had she had any use of them for upward of twelve months. I was very much afraid that the sinews would be contracted, and that she would lose the use of them for ever. We prayed, however, incessantly that this might not be the case; but that it would please the Lord, for the sake especially of her three little children, to restore her. This day being appointed for the baptizing of the child, a part of my family and some pious friends went to drink tea with her, and Mr. Mather her husband; Mr. Mather bringing her down in his arms into the dining-room. After tea I spoke a little on the certainty of God's hearing the prayers of his faithful people, and repeated many of his declarations and promises to that purpose. I also enlarged on Christ's being the same yesterday, to-day, and for ever, and still both able and willing to give relief to his distressed and healing to his afflicted people; that though he had doubtless done many of his miracles of healing chiefly to prove himself to be the Messiah, yet that he did not do them for that end only; but also to grant relief to human misery, out of his great compassion for suffering mankind; and that not a few of his other miracles of mercy he had wrought principally or only for this latter purpose; and that he was still full of compassion for the miserable. I then said, 'Ann, before we go to prayer, we will sing the hymn which was so consolatory to your mother;' and I gave out—

> 'Thy arm, Lord, is not shortened now,
>   It wants not now the power to save;
>   Still present with thy people, thou
>   Bearest them through life's disparted wave.
>
> By death and hell pursued in vain,
>   To thee the ransomed seed shall come;
> Shouting, their heavenly Sion gain,
>   And pass through death triumphant home.

The pain of life shall there be o'er,
　The anguish and distracting care;
There sighing grief shall weep no more,
　And sin shall never enter there.

Where pure essential joy is found,
　The Lord's redeemed their heads shall raise,
With everlasting gladness crowned,
　And filled with love, and lost in praise.'

We then kneeled down to pray; and Ann took the child to give it the breast, that it might not disturb us with crying, while we were engaged in prayer. I prayed first, and then Mr. Macdonald; all present joining sincerely and fervently in our supplications. We pleaded in prayer the Lord's promises, and especially that he had said, that whatever two or three of his people should agree to ask, it should be done for them: Matt. xviii. 19. Immediately on our rising from our knees, Ann beckoned to the nurse to take the child, and then instantly rose up, and said, 'I can walk, I feel I can;' and proceeded half over the room; when her husband, afraid she should fall, stepped to her, saying, 'My dear Ann, what are you about?' She put him off with her hands, saying, 'I don't need you; I can walk alone;' and then walked three times over the floor: after which, going to a corner, she kneeled down (not having been able to kneel for more than twelve months), and said, 'O, let us give God thanks!' We kneeled down, and gave thanks; Ann continuing on her knees all the time, at least twenty minutes. She then came to me, and with a flood of tears threw her arms about my neck; and then did the same first to one of her sisters, and then to the other, and afterwards to Mrs. Dickinson, &c.; every one in the room shedding tears of gratitude and joy. She then desired her husband's brother to come up stairs; and when he entered the room, she cried out, 'Adam, I can walk!' and, to show him that she could, immediately walked over the floor and back again. It was indeed the most affecting season I ever witnessed in my life. May the Lord confirm the wonder he has done, and restore her strength more and more! She afterward, without any help, walked up stairs into her lodging-room, and with her husband kneeling down, joined in prayer and praise. I afterward learned from her the following particulars:—That when she was brought down into the dining-room, a little stool was put under her feet, but which she felt no more than if her feet had been dead. While we were singing the hymn, she conceived faith that the Lord would heal her; began to feel the stool, and pushed it away; set her feet on the floor, and felt that. While we prayed she felt a persuasion she could walk, and was half inclined to rise up with the child in her arms; but thinking to do that would be thought rash, she delayed till we had done praying; and then immediately rose up, as above related. Blessed be the Lord for his goodness! O that we may praise him, and live to his glory!"

A CLERGYMAN'S WIDOW.

THERE lived in the east of Scotland a pious clergyman, who had presided for a number of years over a small but respectable congregation. In the midst of his active career of usefulness he was suddenly removed by death, leaving behind him a wife and a number of helpless children. The small stipend allowed him by his congregation had been barely sufficient to meet the current expenses of his family, and at his death no visible means were left for their support. The death of her husband preyed deeply on the heart of the poor afflicted widow, while the dark prospect which the future presented filled her mind with the most gloomy apprehensions. By her lonely fireside she sat the morning after her sad bereavement, lamenting her forlorn and destitute condition, when her little son, a boy of five years of age, entered the room. Seeing the deep distress of his mother, he stole softly to her side, and placing his little hand in hers, looked wistfully into her face, and said, "Mother, mother, is God dead?" Soft as the gentle whisper of an angel did the simple accent of the dear boy fall upon the ear of the disconsolate and almost heart-broken mother. A gleam of heavenly radiance lighted up, for a moment, her pale features. Then snatching up her little boy, and pressing him fondly to her bosom, she exclaimed, "No, no, my son, God is not dead! He lives, and has promised to be a father to the fatherless, a husband to the widow. His promises are sure and steadfast, and upon them I will firmly and implicitly rely." Her tears were dried, and her murmurings for ever hushed. The event proved that her confidence was not misplaced. The congregation over whom her husband worthily presided generously settled upon her a handsome annuity, by which she was enabled to support her family, not only comfortably, but even genteelly. The talents of her sons, as they advanced in years, soon brought them into notice, and finally procured them high and honorable stations in society.

A SPECIAL PROVIDENCE.

For the purpose of attending the Genesee Annual Conference at Lundy's Lane, U. C., some years since, I set out in company with the Rev. Charles Northrop, and took a passage in the Ontario steamboat at Ogdensburgh, destined for Lewiston, Niagara county, the distance of three hundred miles, in which we had a very pleasant and interesting passage. We returned in one of the common vessels of the lake, in company with the Rev. William Case, and Rev. Truman Dixon.

For two days we were moored in front of Little York, having no wind but a few land breezes. But on the third evening an unexpected gale filled our sails, and the breeze increasing to a mighty wind, we sailed down the lake with great velocity. But in the great commotion of the waters we anticipated no disastrous event. The commotion of the waters, however, under the quick succeeding gales, and the struggles of the hurried vessel, together with the novelty of the scene, which was heightened by the gradual approach of darkness, forbade my retreat to the cabin to join my companions in the slumbers of the night, consequently I remained on deck indulging myself in serious meditation until nearly midnight, when my attention was called to a distant light, nearly in front of us. I immediately inquired of the captain if we were not approaching some vessel. He said he thought it must be the great Canadian steamboat, which he called the King of the Lake, which, in our late struggle with England, was a ship of war, mounting seventy-four guns; but, since its close, had been converted into a steamboat, and was now freighting up and down the lake. He said he would direct our vessel so as to give us a fair prospect of King George as he passed by. I asked what distance he thought it was from us; he said eight or ten miles. I suppose the deception was owing to the peculiar state of the atmosphere, for, to our unutterable surprise, the next surge rolled us furiously against the unyielding monster; why it did not at once bury us in the waters beneath, none but an Almighty Providence can tell; the first complaint was a blow and a word; by which he broke off our boom, stove in the bow, tore away our anchors, and stripped every sail from the masts, which left nothing but a trembling wreck. It, however, fastened itself by some means to the great anchor chains of the steamboat, so that it remained beating itself against the side of its unfeeling conqueror.

In the mean time the screams in the cabin, together with those in the forecastle, mingling with the rattling of the breaking crockery and glass, and the mighty cracking of the vessel, keeping pace with the horrid oaths and blasphemies from those on the steamboat, rendered it a scene horrible beyond description. I however found myself on the deck of the steamboat, which was the first of my recollection after the collision, which I have ever deemed little short of a miracle, it being from ten to fifteen feet from the deck of our vessel up to the railing of the steamboat. Every soul on the wreck were making their escape as fast as possible; and although the Canadian captain, like an unfeeling tyrant, was wishing them at the bottom of the lake, &c., he was at the same time giving direction for assistance to those below. The reverend gentlemen were hurrying to secure their baggage, and handing it to me, as I had suspended myself for that purpose, as well as to aid their persons in escaping the wreck.

All having made a safe retreat to the steamboat,

excepting the captain and Brother Case, who were detained a little, I began to hope that all would be well, when at this dreadful moment the wreck broke loose from the steamboat, and the troubled waters appeared to be furiously engaged to separate the two vessels. The unfortunate individuals, beholding their critical situation, called aloud for assistance, but the forbidding waters rendered it impracticable. I stood for a few minutes with my spirits paralyzed, catching the last appearance of the departing wreck, containing one of the worthies of the nineteenth century, and conveying its contents, as I supposed, to a watery grave. Repeated calls from the wreck, which seemed to penetrate the very heavens, were to me like the last agonies of despairing hope. I retired a little to resolve on the last alternative, which was to try to save them by means of one of the small boats; and feeling an uncommon witness of the Divine approbation, I resolved to make an appeal to the humanity of the captain for one of his small boats, in which to find the wreck and aid those unfortunate men. But upon the proposition he poured upon me a volley of oaths and anathemas too horrid to relate. I told him I had a friend on that wreck, whose life was too useful to the world to be lost. But, said he, would you risk your own to save his? I told him I would. He said he wished he could persuade himself to believe he had such a friend. I said, Perhaps you are a stranger to that principle which unites the missionaries of the cross of Jesus. Ah! said he, I have always understood that these Methodists like each other better than all the world besides. But, said he, my small boat cannot live on this sea a minute, therefore you had better make yourself contented. I told him nothing but an absolute refusal would silence my intercession; consequently he consented; and the arrangement being made, I said to Brother Dixon, All will be well. Yes, said he, if we stay where we are; and, to my utter astonishment, not one of the whole crew or of the passengers would join me, except a colored man and one other, who did not seem to care whether he lived or died.

Under these embarrassments they let us down into the boat, and we shoved off. Knowing that much depended on every blow of the oar and paddle, I took the stern, and put the colored man to the oars, and the other on the bottom of the boat. At first my faith well nigh failed me. The lake boiled like a cauldron, and our little craft trembled to its centre. These, together with the darkness of the night, and the howlings of many waters, rendered it a scene not easily to be forgotten. To return to the steamboat was impossible, and the uncertainty attending the wreck called up some reflections to which I had hitherto been a stranger: the steamboat had now just collected its steam, and was leaving us.

We were now on the broad lake, in a common

skiff, in a dark night, fifty miles at least from any port. We continued our direct course for half an hour or more, when I thought I discovered a small light, and supposing it to be upon the wreck, we pursued it with all diligence until we arrived within call of the vessel, and gave them a salute which was returned with joy.

With some difficulty we reached the deck, and made our small boat fast to the stern. I inquired, "What is the prospect?" "Uncertain," was the reply. My next inquiry was, what had been their feelings since they left the steamboat; they said they had entertained some hope that relief would be afforded by some means from the boat; but when they raised their steam and went on, the last remnant of hope vanished, and the only alternative was to do all they could to preserve the wreck; and though human probability was against them, yet, said Brother Case, I have not entertained a doubt but God would provide means for our escape, consequently my mind has been as calm as though I had been in the sanctuary of the Lord. He said he had an impression for a day or two past that he should be called to some uncommon trial of his faith, but by the overruling providence and grace of God he should come out as gold tried in the fire. Upon which he put his arms around me, and said, "Brother, be of good cheer, we shall get safe to land." We then went to work at the pumps, and to clearing the deck as fast as possible; and in the space of two hours we were able to raise the main sail about half way up the mast, which gave such an impetus to the vessel as to take us on at the rate of eight or ten miles an hour.

We still considered ourselves in great danger; for we knew if the vessel outlived the sea we must pass a certain chain of islands called the Ducks; and how near we had approached them was mere conjecture; consequently, the fear of dashing against some one of them, or unfortunately striking the wrong channel, was, through the remainder of the night, a source of constant anxiety. But when the long-wished-for morning dawned, we found we had not yet arrived in sight of the much dreaded islands. A moment's reflection on what we had passed the preceding night, together with our present prospects, humbled us in the dust before our great Benefactor. We retired to the cabin, and poured out our souls in thanksgiving to that Being who had sustained us even in the seventh trouble.

The majesty of this morning transcended anything I had ever witnessed. I thought I could fully comprehend the saying of the inspired psalmist, "If I take the wings of the morning and dwell in the uttermost part of the sea, even there shall thy hand lead me, and thy right hand shall hold me." The lake presented vast columns of moving mountains and heaving valleys, over which we were passing, without any variety of change or prospect. The wind had ceased its roaring, and with a strong and steady breeze cleared away the fogs and vapors of the morning. We now had but little to fear, except the lulling of the wind into a calm, or its changing to an opposite direction; but realizing no farther disaster, we happily came to anchor at Cape Vincent, where the good people received us courteously. Yours, in much love,

TIMOTHY GOODWIN.

THE POWER OF PRAYER.

IN his "Rural Life of England," Howitt cites the following instance of heroism and calm presence of mind, inspired by Christian faith, which is a striking illustration of the power of prayer to sustain the courage of the weakest believer in the most trying circumstances:—

In one of the thinly-peopled dales of the Peak of Derbyshire stood a lone house, far from neighbors, inhabited by a farmer and his wife. Such is, or at least was wont to be, the primitive simplicity of this district, that it was usual for persons to go to bed without taking any precautions to bolt or bar the doors, in the event of any of the inmates not having come home at the usual hour of retiring to rest. This was frequently the practice with the family in question, especially on market days, when the farmers, having occasion to go to the nearest town, often did not return until late.

One evening, when the husband was absent, the wife, being up stairs, heard some one open the door and enter the house. Supposing it to be her husband, she lay awake, expecting him to come up stairs. As the usual time elapsed and he did not come, she rose and went down, when, to her terror and astonishment, she saw a sturdy fellow searching the house for plunder.

At first view of him, as she afterward said, she felt ready to drop; but being naturally courageous, and of a deeply religious disposition, she soon recovered sufficient self-possession to suppress the cry which was rising to her lips, to walk with apparent firmness to a chair which stood on one side of the fireplace, and seat herself in it. The marauder immediately seated himself in another chair, which stood opposite, and fixed his eyes upon her with a most savage expression.

Her courage was almost spent; but, recollecing herself, she put up a prayer to the Almighty for protection, and threw herself upon his providence, for "vain was the help of man." She immediately felt her courage revive, and looked steadfastly at the ruffian, who now drew a large clasp-knife from his pocket, opened it, and, with a murderous expression in his eyes, appeared ready to spring upon her.

She, however, showed no visible emotion, but continued to pray earnestly, and to look upon the man with calm seriousness. He arose, glanced first at her, then at the knife; again he seemed to hesitate, and wiped his weapon upon his hand; then once more glanced at her, she all the while continuing to sit calmly, calling earnestly upon God.

Suddenly a panic appeared to seize him; he blenched beneath her still fixed gaze, closed his knife, and went out. At a single spring she reached the door, shot the bolt with convulsive rapidity, and fell senseless on the floor. When she recovered, she recognised her husband's well-known step at the door, and heard him calling out in surprise at finding it fastened. Rising, she admitted him, and, in tones tremulous with agitation and gratitude, told him of her danger and deliverance.

PART VII.

MISCELLANEOUS ILLUSTRATIONS OF DIVINE PROVIDENCE.

"The Lord is good to all: and His tender mercies are over all His works."
SALM cxlv. 9.

Miscellaneous.

REMARKABLE DREAM.

IN my eighteenth year, says the Rev. E. J. Way, I dreamed that in riding through a crossroads near my father's residence, my horse threw me, by which I was severely injured. The dream was very distinct, and made a deep impression upon my mind at the time. Several days after that, I was sent, in company with my brother, for some oats. We were both on horseback; I was riding a young colt. As we neared the crossroads, we started our horses for a race, when the colt, by a sudden movement, threw me off in the very spot and in the very manner that I had previously dreamed.

THE DRUNKARD'S DREAM.

THE Rev. Mr. Tennent, of Freehold, N. J., had a neighbor, a carpenter by trade, who was a habitual drunkard, and spent much time, particularly evenings, and Sabbath days, in company with people of like habits, and never went to church or religious meetings. This man dreamed one night that he had a fit of sickness and died; and as he had always expected, after death, he went to hell. Hell was not to him what he expected to find it; but was a very large tavern, with a bar-room full of benches, well lighted up, all the benches filled with people, all silent, each with a hat on his head, and each covered with a black cloak reaching to his feet. The man went up to the landlord and said: "I expected to find hell full of fire and a place of torment, as it was always represented to me while living; but I find it very agreeable." Upon this, every one of the persons stood up, and each one slowly and silently opened wide his cloak; and holding it open, displayed his body a solid mass of fire. The man was so struck by the sight that he begged the landlord to allow him to return to earth again—who, after many entreaties, consented that he should return if he would make a solemn promise to return there again at the end of a year. This the man promised, and awoke. The dream filled his mind with great horror, and in the morning he went to Mr. Tennent and related it. Mr. Tennent advised him to reform, and lead a new life; it seemed a special warning, which if he neglected, it would enhance his future punishment, &c. The man did reform, and for six months avoided his old companions; at the expiration of that time, he was returning from work one evening, and was met by several of them near a tavern, and they began to ridicule him for becoming religious, and dared him to go in and take one drink with them. The man felt strong in his new resolutions, and said he would go in and take one drink to show it would not hurt him. He took one drink, and another, till he was much intoxicated; from that time he returned to his old habits, and grew worse and worse. His family lived in the second story of a house to which there was a staircase on the outside; and one night on which he had drank more than usual, he made shift to get upstairs and to bed—but in the morning when he went out the door to go to work, he was still drunk, and pitched off the stairs to the ground and broke his neck. The news was carried to Mr. Tennent, who, instantly recollecting the man's dream, on looking at a memorandum he had made when the man told him the dream, found it was a year that day since the man told it to him.

AN INFIDEL STRANGELY CONVERTED.

A NATIVE of Sweden, residing in the south of France, had occasion to go from one port to another in the Baltic Sea. When he came to the place whence he expected to sail, the vessel was gone. On inquiring, he found a fishing-boat going the same way, in which he embarked. After being for some time out at sea, the men observed that he had several trunks and chests on board, concluded he must be very rich, and therefore agreed among themselves to throw him overboard. This he heard them express, which gave him great uneasiness. However, he took occasion to open one of his trunks, which contained some books. Observing this, they remarked among themselves that it was not worth while to throw him into the sea, as they did not want any books, which they supposed was all the trunks contained. They asked him if he were a priest. Hardly knowing what reply to make, he told them he was; at which they seemed much pleased, and said they would have a sermon on the next day, as it was the Sabbath.

This increased the anxiety and distress of his mind, for he knew himself to be as incapable of such an undertaking, as it was possible for any one to be, as he knew very little of the Scriptures; neither did he believe in the inspiration of the Bible.

At length they came to a small rocky island, perhaps a quarter of a mile in circumference, where was a company of pirates, who had chosen this little sequestered spot to deposit their treasures. He was taken to a cave, and introduced to an old woman, to whom they remarked that they were to have a sermon preached the next day. She said she was very glad of it, for she had not heard the word of God for a great while. His was a trying case, for preach he must; still he knew nothing about preaching. If he refused, or undertook to preach and did not please, he expected it would be his death. With these thoughts he passed a sleepless night. In the morning his mind was not settled upon anything. To call upon God, whom he believed to be inaccessible, was altogether vain. He could devise no way whereby he might be saved. He walked to and fro, still shut up in darkness, striving to collect something to say to them, but could not think of even a single sentence.

When the appointed time for the meeting arrived, he entered the cave, where he found the men assembled. There was a seat prepared for him, and a table with a Bible on it. They sat for the space of half an hour in profound silence; and even then, the anguish of his soul was as great as human nature was capable of enduring. At length these words came to his mind, " Verily, there is a reward for the righteous : verily, there is a God that judgeth in the earth." He arose and delivered them : then other words presented themselves, and so on till his understanding became opened—his heart enlarged in a manner astonishing to himself. He spoke upon subjects suited to their condition; the rewards of the righteous—the judgments of the wicked—the necessity of repentance, and the importance of a change of life. The matchless love of God to the children of men, had such a powerful effect upon the minds of these wretched beings, that they were melted into tears. Nor was he less astonished at the unbounded goodness of Almighty God, in thus interposing to save his spiritual as well as his natural life, and well might he exclaim,—" This is the Lord's doings, and marvellous in our eyes." Under a deep sense of God's goodness, his heart became filled with such thankfulness, that it was out of his power to express. What marvellous change was thus suddenly brought about by Divine interposition! He who a little before disbelieved in God, was now humbled before him. And they who were meditating his death were moved to affection.

The next morning they put him in one of their vessels and conveyed him where he desired. From that time he was a changed man. From an infidel he became a believer in the Lord Jesus Christ.

COLLINS'S REMARKABLE DREAM.

WHILE the Rev. John Collins was attending one of his appointments in the West, he dreamed that he received at the post office a letter bearing a black seal, and containing intelligence of the death of his father then in New Jersey. It made so deep an impression on his mind that he made a record of it.

Two weeks afterward, on returning home, he received just such a letter as he had seen in his dream, sealed with black; and the date of his father's death agreed with the record in his diary.

A REMARKABLE CASE.

DEAR DR. BOND:—I send you the following particulars of an extraordinary experience, which, in this region of the country, is occasioning considerable excitement.

The subject of the experience is a man about forty years old, and has been a member of the M. E. Church about fifteen years. His name is John Waltdemire. He resides where he was raised from childhood, in the town of Ghent, Columbia county, New York, where he has always been known as a conscientious and exemplary person. He is a man of considerable property, and for a number of years has been one of the most efficient stewards of the circuit in which he lives. I was his pastor during the two years of my labor in the Kinderhook charge, and am well acquainted with him. For nearly three years he has been an invalid, suffering great pain, and was once brought very low; but, through his whole affliction, has been of sound mind. The particulars of this remarkable case I have taken from his own lips, and give them, mostly, in his own words.

The occurrence took place on Sabbath evening, January 27, 1856. Soon after he retired for the night he was seized with a spasmodic affection of the respiratory organs, and suffered extremely for a few minutes, being entirely conscious. He then sunk away, and became silent and motionless, and, after a short time, revived again for a little while, and spoke a few words; then, much in the same way as before, he sunk into a death-resembling state, and, so far as those present could decide, ceased to breathe, and became as one dead. The family physician, Dr. S., a reputable and scientific doctor of the old school, of some fifteen years' practice, was sent for, with all practicable haste. The neighbors were called in; none of them could perceive any sign of life; the body lay as a corpse.

This strange phenomenon came over him, at short intervals, four times during the night; but the second was characterized by the most remarkable mental and spiritual experiences. At this time it was nearly three hours before he revived, and, when he did, lifting his hands and clapping them together, to the great surprise of all present, he said, with a voice so clear and strong that it could be heard several rods from the house, "Bless the Lord for the glorious resurrection." These were his first words. He then shouted, "Glory to God!" though he was never in the habit of shouting. He said many things very remarkable, of which the family and friends retain but an indistinct remembrance. The Scriptures, in particular, seemed to be perfectly familiar to him, and, with wonderful aptness, he repeated passage after passage, interspersing them with praises to God.

It appeared to him, during the time of his bodily insensibility, that he had been for a moment unconscious, and then the faculties of his mind became clear and strong. While he lay there, and they supposed he was dead, he was perfectly conscious of all that passed around him. He thought himself separated from the body, but near it, and expected never to return. The excellent glory, in part, broke upon his view. He had a glimpse of what seemed the throne of God. In his vision there was an innumerable company, clothed in the resurrection body, moving with eagerness on toward the immediate divine presence. They appeared to be ascending a vast even slope, and as far as the eye could reach, the company was unbroken, and all indescribably happy.

During this time of suspended animation there was a clearness and brilliancy of his mind beyond everything he had ever imagined. It was, he says, not faith, but sight—a blessed reality. For a little time after reviving his mind was clear, and his ecstasies unbounded, but, as his strength increased, his body acted as a clog and shade to his mind. He compared it to coming out of the open air to a darkened room. His apparent return to earth seemed to be determined by the Lord himself alone; but at about the same moment he heard and distinctly remembers hearing his wife pray, as she was kneeling by his side, "Spare him, O Lord, spare him." At about the time of this prayer signs of returning life appeared.

Mr. W. is still in feeble health, but is able to ride out, and is everywhere respected among his neighbors as an intelligent and orthodox Christian. This case, in its principal features, so closely resembles the trance of the celebrated William Tennent that I forward it to you, hoping you may give us your views of it, and of the subject in general.

J. N. SHAFFER.

Chatham Four Corners, March 11, 1856.

SINGULAR COINCIDENCE.

THE Rev. Dr. Bedell relates that while Bishop Chase, of Ohio, was at the house of Mr. Beek, in Philadelphia, he received a package from Dr. Ward, Bishop of Sodor and Man, making inquiries relating to certain property in America, of which some old person of his diocese was the heir. The letter had gone to Ohio, followed him to Washington, then to Philadelphia, and found him at Mr. Beek's. When he read it to Mr. B., the latter was in amazement, and said: "Bishop Chase, I am the only man in the world who can give you information. I have the deeds in my possession, and have had them forty-three years, not knowing what to do with them, or where any heirs were to be found." How wonderful that the application should be made to Bishop Chase, and he not in Ohio, but a guest in the house of the only man who possessed any information on the subject!

THE SOLDIER'S SHIELD.

SAMUEL PROCTOR was trained up in the use of religious ordinances, and in early life felt some religious impressions. He afterwards enlisted as a soldier in the first regiment of foot guards, and was made a grenadier. Notwithstanding this, the impressions made upon his mind continued; and the fear of the Lord, as a guardian angel, attended him through the changing scenes of life. There were a few in the regiment who met for pious and devotional exercises; he cast in his lot among them, and always carried a small pocket Bible in one pocket, and his hymn book in the other. He took part in the struggle on the plains of Waterloo in 1815. In the evening of June 16th, in the tremendous conflict on that day, his regiment was ordered to dislodge the French from a wood, of which they had taken possession, and from which they annoyed the allied army. While thus engaged, he was thrown a distance of four or five yards by a force on his hip, for which he could not account at the time; but, when he came to examine his Bible, he saw, with overwhelming gratitude to the Preserver of his life, what it was that had thus driven him. A musket-ball had struck his hip where his Bible rested in his pocket, and penetrated nearly half through that sacred book. All who saw the ball, said that it would undoubtedly have killed him, had it not been for the Bible, which served as a shield. The Bible was kept as a sacred treasure, and laid up in his house, like an heirloom.

THE INHUMAN FATHER DEFEATED.

During a series of religious meetings, held in the school-house of a small village, a very little girl became much interested for the salvation of her soul. Her father, a hater of holiness, who lived next door to the place of meeting, finding that his little daughter was much interested in the meetings, and had been forward to be prayed for, strictly forbade her again entering the "house of prayer." The poor little girl was much oppressed, and knew not what to do, but obeyed her father until the next meeting was nearly half through, then slipping out without his knowledge, and getting through a hole in the back yard fence, she hastily ran to the meeting. It was some time before her father missed her, but when he found her gone, he went immediately to the meeting, where she was on her knees, with others whom the people of God were praying for. So enraged was he, that he went directly forward, and took her in his arms, to carry her from the place. As he raised her from her knees, she looked up with a heavenly smile, and said, " It is too late now, pa; I have given my heart to the Saviour." This was too much for the hardened sinner: he too sunk on his knees, while he was prayed for; and very soon he found that Saviour he had in vain attempted to shut out from his daughter's heart.

TRACT ANECDOTE.

In the district of A——, one Sabbath morning, as some Sunday school children were going to their school, having with them a little bundle of tracts, they passed by the field of a man who had long neglected the sanctuary and ordinary means of grace. One of them passed over the fence, and fastened to the plough-beam the tract called the Swearer's Prayer, and continued on to school.

On Monday morning, when the man came to his plough, he found the tract, but was unable to tell how it came there; and, surprised at the singular circumstance, took it home, and read it carefully again and again. Conviction fastened upon his conscience—he began to attend places of public worship. His anxiety after truth continued, until (as he trusts) he found peace in a Saviour's blood, and has since connected himself with a Christian church.

Another man in the neighborhood, who could not read, hearing of the effect produced upon the mind of the other by the reading of a tract, went to a house where they had a number of these silent preachers, and expressed great anxiety to hear some of those tracts read.

"In the morning sow thy seed, and in the evening withhold not thy hand, for thou knowest not whether shall prosper, either this or that, or whether they both shall be alike good."

PROVIDENCE INTERPRETED BY AN OLD COLORED WOMAN.

The following is a letter which was published some time since in the Western Christian Advocate :—

Messrs. Editors,—A few days since, an aged colored man, belonging to the Methodist Episcopal Church, called to see me. Having listened with interest to some facts which he related in class meetings and love-feasts, I felt desirous to hear his history from himself. Accordingly I made the request, and he, becoming interested in his own story, related it with the feeling and effect peculiar to the simplicity of the "child of nature." The narration contains allusions and reflections which, on account of their originality and pertinency, cannot fail to be useful. While he was talking, I was (unknown to him) writing down the substance of his remarks. I have written it in his own language, believing that it would rob it of half its interest to your readers were it rendered to them strictly correct by "nicest rules of art."

"In de fall of —— I leas part of Judge ——'s farm, up on de river. Move up dar vid my family, an work hard for sevrel year. Judge mity good to me, 'low me many liberties, an I make money dar. But I thought I mout do better down in de Indiana country. So I starts down dar splorin de country, an found a mity good place, as I thought, an tuck a leas for five year. Den I cum up an fotch my family down dar; and I hab hosses, an cows, an five calfs, an ninety-five head of hog. Well, I put up my cabin, an hire hans, an clare out fifteen acres for to put it in kawn. Dar war mity good parster out in de woods, an pea-vine, O man! Well, I didn't know nothin bout de country, an tuck an turn out my hosses an cows to feed. Well, two or three day arter dat, dey cum bout de house, an walk roun, an walk roun an trimble, an one arter de udder fall down an die—hosses too. De caus for dat war, dey bin etin trimblin weed; but I didn't know nothin bout it. Dat same day de young man what lib wid me die; an de next day a young man what I hire he die wid de trimbles too. Dey didn't *eat de trimble weed do*—only dey drink de milk what de cows give what die. My wife war sick wid it too, but troo marcy she war spared. One day dat week, in de mornin, I was sittin on a fence rail, by de kawn field—felt very bad an gloomy. Jes den mammy cum by. She stop an say, 'Sam, what de marter wid you?' I tole her I feel very bad—don't know what I shall do. She say, 'O Sam, all dis is for de best. You bin careless bout your soul, an God now shoin you de folly of de worl, an it may be de casion of your gettin ligun; and den you will say yoursef dat it war de best thing as eber happen to you.' So she pass on to de spring. She war mity good woman, rale Christian, carry de witness in her breast. O yes, mammy war good woman, ebery body 'low dat. Well, as I was sayin, I war sittin on de fence rail, an jes before me dar war rite smart hill rise up, an swell off to de left; and it war covered wid oak trees; an my hogs war dar. Dey hadn't eat no trimblin weed; an *I notice dat de hogs go from tree to tree, an eat akawn, and neber look up once to see whar dey cum from.* Thinks I, dat jes de way wid me. I zactly like hog. God bin smilin on me from my yout up, and porein down blessins on me; an I, jes like de hog, *neber look up to tink whar dey cum from, or to tank God for dem.* Dis tought run troo my heart like dagger, an I jump down, an went an pray. Bout dis time I opened de sugar camp, an tap bout one hundred trees, and I pray at ebery tree I tap. As I turn de auger I pray almost ebery turn. So on I went day arter day—eat little or nottin. Mammy say, 'Sam, why don't you eat nottin?' I say I don't want nottin, I has form resolushun neber to stop till I git ligun. Some time arter dis I hear dar war gwyin to be praar metin tree miles off—Metodis. So Sunday mornin I starts for metin. From whar I den live dar war high hill to climb, mity steep. I start up it. Dat morn had bin snow storm. Snow war shoe-mouth deep. I climb, I climb. I hear once dat Moses went up in mountin, an God meet him an talk to him dar. So I went on, an when I got up to de top I bresht away de snow, an pray, and tole God dat I form resolushun neber to go back to my house till he convert my soul. Feel somewhat couraged dar, and went on to praar metin, which war held at de class-leader's house. Hear dar war gwyin to be prechin at de metin house by de *itirean precher*. At de class-leader's house war de *class-leader an de old professors talkin bout thar farms, an craps, an hosses, an cows, an oder critters—an Sundy, too, an not a word drapt bout ligun*. Thinks I, dis no place for me; so I starts on to de metin house. Jes as I bow my head to enter de house, pearantly somethin struck me. Howasever, I takes my seat way back. Metin begin, dey sing, dey pray, de tears run down my cheek in streams, an I hang my head down away one side so nobody shant see me. An when dey neel down den I gives way, an cry an pray; an jes before de praar closed I wipe my eyes dry so nobody shant know it. Arter while I feel so bad dat I couldn't stand up no longer, an fell down on my face in de floor, and cry to God for marcy. Den de wanderings of my mine kep cumin in, cumin in, cumin in, cumin in, jes like nats, from dis way an dat, cumin in, cumin in. I felt dat I war wortty to be dam'd for my sins, an felt dat if I war saved it would be troo great marcy. *I den felt dat I war jes able to do nottin;* an I tell de blessed Jesus, *dat if anyting war done in my case he would have to do it hisself.* Jes den somethin rise up in me, an swell, an swell, and cum up in my throat. I couldn't speak a word, no nor whisper neither. All at once, *pearantly,* it broke, an I felt such liberty, an peace, an joy, dat I holla out, 'Glory to God!' an arter praisin him wid de people for some time, I went on my way home rejoicin. Arter dat, *I felt as if I were cut loose from my toes to my head; for whar de Spirit of de Lord is, dar is liberty.* O de sweet joy an peace dar is in believin! an *I am still on de way;* an mine I tell you, *whoever gets to heaven, or whoever don't, Sam is on de road.* Glory to God!"

In reviewing the above, I think but one sentiment will prevail, viz., "How true to nature, and how true to grace!" Yours, &c., M.

THE TWO MINERS.

At a meeting of the Wesleyan Missionary Society, the Rev. R. Young, of Truro, mentioned a very remarkable fact that had taken place in Cornwall, England:—

"Two men were working together in a mine, and having prepared to blast the rock, and laid the train, the latter became by accident ignited. In a few moments a tremendous explosion they knew was inevitable, and the rock must be rent in a thousand pieces. On perceiving their danger, they both leaped into the bucket, and called to the man on the surface to draw them up. He endeavored to do so, but his arm was found too feeble to raise the bucket while both the men were in it. What was to be done? The burning fuse, which could not be extinguished, was now within a few feet of the powder; a moment or two, and the explosion must take place. At this awful crisis, one of the men, addressing the other, said: 'You shall live and I will die; for you are an impenitent sinner, and if you now die your soul will be lost; but if I die, I know that, by the grace of the Lord Jesus Christ, I shall be taken to himself.' And so saying, without waiting for a reply, he leaped out of the bucket, and prayerfully waited the result. On the other reaching the surface, he bent over the shaft to ascertain the fate of his companion. At that moment a terrific explosion was heard; a portion of the rock was thrown up and smote him on the forehead, leaving an indelible mark to remind him of his danger and deliverance. But the man of God, when they came to search for him, was found arched over by the fragments of broken rock in the mine, uninjured, and rejoicing in the Lord. This magnanimous miner exhibited in this act an amount of disinterested love and charity which has seldom been equalled, and is never found but in connection with the love of Christ. Here is none of that unholy daring, of which we have instances among the heroes of Greece and Rome, who, actuated solely by a love of notoriety, inflicted upon themselves tortures and even death; but that pure Christian character, which, at all hazards, even at the sacrifice of life itself, seeks to save the immortal soul of man. This is the kind of charity we have met this day to elicit, to strengthen, and to direct, and without which it is impossible that the great object of missionary enterprise can ever be accomplished."

A WONDERFUL RELATION.

The facts hereinafter narrated, occurred in the year 1813, and were fully confirmed to John F. Watson, our annalist of Philadelphia, by the commodore himself, in 1824, through the medium of Joseph Nurse, Esq., Register of the Treasury. After the occurrence, such was the impressiveness of the facts on the mind of the commodore, that he became a religious professor. He stated to Mr. Watson that the surgeon of the ship should some day thereafter give a published account of the whole transaction. This seems to have been fulfilled in the "*Itinerant*" about the year 1824. At all events, the following, as republished in the *Norristown Herald* of 8th July, 1829, gives the same as from the *Itinerant*. Although the name of the surgeon is not given, it is ascertained that R. L. Thorn was surgeon, and William Turk, mate, for the year 1813.

The "*Itinerant*" had prefaced the relation by saying, " It has come to us with evidence sufficient to warrant confidence, as much as any fact in history; and to doubt it would argue an affected scrupulosity foreign from our convictions," to wit :—

" And he that was dead, sat up, and began to speak."

MIRACLE OF MERCY.—Although the events now for the first time recorded, occurred ten years ago, they are still fresh in my recollection, and have made so strong an impression upon my mind, that time can never obliterate them. They partake so much of the marvellous, that I would not dare to commit them to paper were there not so many living witnesses to the truth of the facts narrated; some of them of the greatest respectability, and even sanctioned by Commodore Rodgers. The story is considered by all who have heard it, too interesting to be lost. I therefore proceed to the task, while those are in existence who can confirm it.

Living in an enlightened age and country, where

bigotry and superstition have nearly lost their influence over the minds of men, particularly among the citizens of this republic, where knowledge is so universally diffused, I have often been deterred from relating a circumstance so wonderful as to stagger the belief of the most credulous; but facts are stubborn things, and the weight of testimony in this case cannot be resisted. Unable, for the want of time or room, to enter into any particulars as I could wish, I will give, to the best of my recollection, the most prominent and striking occurrences in the order in which they took place, without comment or embellishment.

Some time in the latter part of December, 1813, a man by the name of William Kemble, aged about twenty-three years, a seaman on board of the United States frigate President, commanded by Commodore Rodgers, on a cruise then near the Western Islands, was brought to me from one of the tops, in which he had been stationed, having bursted a vessel in his lungs. Being at that time in great danger of instant death, the blood gushing with great violence from his mouth and nostrils, it was with much difficulty that I succeeded in stopping the discharge. He was immediately put on the use of remedies suited to his case. I visited him often, and had the best opportunity of becoming acquainted with his temper, habits, and intellectual attainments, and under all circumstances, during his illness, found his language and behavior such as stamped him the rough, profane, and illiterate sailor. It is my belief, though I cannot positively assert it, that he could neither read nor write. It is certain that his conversation never differed in the least from that of the most ignorant and abandoned of his associates—constantly mixed with oaths, and the lowest vulgarity. Had he possessed talents or learning, he must have betrayed it to me during his long confinement.

In the early part of January, a vessel bore down upon us, with every appearance of being an English frigate. All hands were called to quarters; and, after a short and animated address by the Commodore to the crew, all prepared to do their duty. Before I descended to the cockpit, well knowing Kemble's spirit, and how anxious he would be to partake in the glory of the victory (defeat never entering our thoughts), I thought it better to visit him. After stating to him the peculiar situation he was in, and the great danger he would be exposed to, by the least motion, I entreated him and ordered him not to stir during the action, which he promised to observe. We were soon after obliged to fire. At the sound of the first gun, he could restrain himself no longer—regardless of my admonition, and of his own danger, he rushed upon the deck, and flew to his gun, laying hold to help to run her out. A fresh and tremendous discharge from his lungs was the consequence, and he was brought down to me again in a most deplorable state. I apprehended immediate death, but, by the application of the proper remedies, I succeeded, once more, in stopping the hemorrhage, by which he was reduced to a state of extreme debility. Being near the equator, and suffering much from the heat, his hammock was hung upon the gun deck, between the ports, as affording the best circulation of air. He continued some time free from hemorrhage, but was under the constant use of medicines, and was confined to a particular diet. This made him fretful, and he would frequently charge my mates with starving him, and, at the same time damning them in the true sailor style. After some time, being again called to quarters at night, he was necessarily removed below to the sick berth (commonly called bay); this was followed by another discharge of blood from his lungs, which was renewed, at intervals, until his death.

On the 17th of January, in the afternoon, Dr. ———, my first mate, came to me on deck, and reported Kemble to be dead. I directed him to see that his messmates did what was usual on such occasions, preparatory to committing his remains to the deep. About two hours after this, Dr. ——— again called upon me, and said that Kemble had come to life, and was holding forth to the sailors in a strange way. I directly went down, when I witnessed one of the most remarkable and unaccountable transactions, that, perhaps, has ever fallen to the lot of man to behold. Kemble had awakened, as it were, from sleep, raised himself up, called for his messmates in particular, and those men who were not on duty, to attend to his words. He then told them he had experienced death, but was allowed a short space of time to return, to give them, as well as the officers, some direction for their future conduct in life. In this situation I found him, surrounded by the crew, all mute with astonishment, and paying the most serious attention to every word that escaped from his lips. The oldest men in tears—not a dry eye was to be seen, or a whisper to be heard—all was as solemn and as silent as the grave. His whole body was as cold as death could make it. There was no pulsation in the wrists, the temples, or the chest, perceptible. His voice was clear and powerful; his eyes uncommonly brilliant and animated. After a short and pertinent address to the medical gentlemen, he told me in a peremptory manner, to bring Commodore Rodgers to him, as he had something to say to him before he finally left us. The Commodore consented to go with me, when a scene was presented truly novel and indescribable, and calculated to fill with awe the stoutest heart. The sick bay (or berth), in which he lay, is entirely set apart to the use of those who are confined to their beds by illness. Supported by the surgeons, surrounded by his weeping and astonished comrades, a crowd of spectators looking through the lattice work which enclosed the room, a common japanned lamp, throwing out a sickly light, and a candle held opposite his face by an attendant, was the situation of things when the worthy Commodore made his appearance. And well does he remember the effect produced by so uncommon a spectacle, especially when followed by the utterance of these words from the mouth of one long supposed to have been dead:—

"Commodore Rodgers, I have sent for you, sir, being commissioned by a higher power, to address you for a short time, and to deliver the message intrusted to me, when I was permitted to revisit the earth. Once I trembled in your presence, and was eager to obey your commands; but now I am your superior, being no longer an inhabitant of this earth. I have seen the glories of the world of spirits. I am not permitted to make known what I have beheld. Indeed, were I not forbidden, language would be inadequate to the task. 'Tis enough for you and the crew to know, that I have been sent back to the earth, to reanimate, for a few hours, my lifeless body, commissioned by God, to perform the work I am now engaged in." He then, in language as chaste and appropriate as would not have disgraced the lips or the pen of a divine, took a hasty view of all the moral and religious duties incumbent upon the commander of a ship of war; he reviewed the vices prevalent on board a ship; pointed out the relative duties of officers and men, and concluded by urging the necessity of reformation and repentance. He did not, as was feared by our brave Commodore, attempt to prove the sinfulness of fighting and wars; but, on the contrary, warmly recommended to the men the performance of their duty to their country with courage and fidelity. His speeches occupied about three-quarters of an hour; and, if the whole could have been taken down at the time, they would have made a considerable pamphlet, which would, no doubt, have been in great demand. Dr. ——, now at Boston, heard all the addresses; I only the last. When he had finished with the Commodore, his head dropped upon his breast, his eyes closed, and he appeared to pass through a second death; no pulsation, nor the least degree of warmth could be perceived during the time he was speaking. I ordered him to be laid aside, and left him.

I was soon called into the cabin, where the Commodore required from me an explanation of the case on rational and philosophical principles. This I endeavored to give. I but in part succeeded. It would swell this narrative too much to repeat all I said in endeavoring to elucidate the subject; at least it proved a lame attempt. For, when asked how this man, without education or reading, or mixing with other society than that of common sailors, should acquire the command of the purest language, properly arranged, and delivered clearly, distinctly, with much animation and great effect, I gave no reply; and it was, and ever will remain, inexplicable without admitting supernatural agency.

The days of miracles are passed, and I know I shall be laughed at by many for dwelling upon or repeating this story. But never since I arrived at the years of discretion has anything taken a stronger hold upon my mind; and that man must have been made of strange materials, who could have been an indifferent spectator. Was he divinely illuminated? Was he inspired? or was the whole the effect of natural causes? These are questions which have arisen in the minds of many, and must be left for the learned of two professions to answer. I returned to bed deeply reflecting upon the past, unable to sleep, when about nine o'clock, P.M., many hours after Kemble had been laid by, I was called out of bed to visit a man taken suddenly ill in his hammock, hanging near Kemble's apartment. It was an hour when all, but the watch upon deck, had turned in; general silence reigned, and all the lights below put out, with the exception of a single lamp in the sick man's apartment, where lay the remains of Kemble. I had bled the sick man— he was relieved. I entered the sick-room before I retired, to replace something; and was turning round to leave it, being alone, when I was almost petrified upon beholding Kemble sitting up in his berth, with his eyes (which had regained their former brilliancy and intelligence) fixed intently upon mine. I became, for a moment, speechless and motionless. Thinks I to myself, What have I done, or left undone in this man's case, that should cause him thus to stare at me at this late hour?—and alone I waited a long time in painful suspense, dreading some horrible disclosure, when I was relieved by his commanding me to fetch him some water. With what alacrity I obeyed, can easily be imagined. I gave him a tin mug containing water, which he put to his mouth, drank the contents, and returned it to me; then laid himself quietly down for the last time. His situation was precisely the same, in every respect, as before described. The time had now expired which he had said was given to remain in the body.

The next day by noon, all hands attended, as usual, to hear the funeral service read, and see his remains consigned to a watery grave. It was an unusually solemn period. Seamen are naturally superstitious, and on this occasion their minds had been wrought upon in a singular manner. Decorum is always observed by sailors at such times; but now they were all affected to tears. And when the body was slid from the plank into the sea, every one rushed instinctively to the ship's side to take a last look. The usual weights had been attached to the feet; yet, as if in compliment to their anxiety to see more of him, the body rose, perpendicularly from the water, breast high, two or three times. This incident added greatly to the astonishment already created in the minds of the men. I beg leave to remark that it was not thought proper to keep the body longer in the warm latitude we were in. I have now given a short and very imperfect sketch of the important events attending the last illness and death of William Kemble.

The change produced upon the crew, was for a time very remarkable. It appeared as if they would never smile or swear again; but the effect wore off by degrees, except when the subject was renewed.

REMARKABLE DISCOVERY OF FRATRICIDE.

In the beginning of 1815, a circumstance took place that excited much interest in Paris. A surgeon in the army, named Dautun, was arrested at a gambling-house, in the Palais Royal, on the testimony of a scar on his wrist. Some time before, the officers of the night had found, while passing their rounds in the different parts of the city, four parcels tied up. One contained the head, another the trunk, a third the thighs, and a fourth the legs and arms of a man. In the teeth, tightly compressed, was a piece of human flesh, apparently torn out in the dying struggle. The parts were collected, and put together in their regular order, and exhibited for a number of days at the Morgue. The mystery which enveloped this dark transaction excited considerable interest, and numbers went to view the corpse. The general conviction was, that the deceased must have been murdered; but for a number of weeks no light was thrown upon the circumstance. When the body could not be kept any longer, a cast in plaster was taken, fully representing the murdered victim, which remained for some time exposed to the public. Dautun happened to be engaged in gambling at the Palais Royal—he played high and lost; calling for liquor, and being angry because the waiter was somewhat tardy, Dautun emptied the glass and threw it at him. It was shivered into a thousand pieces, one of which entered into Dautun's wrist under the cuff of his coat. The spectators gathered round, and learning the accident, wished to see the gash; he drew down his sleeve, and firmly pressed it round his wrist; they insisted on seeing it, he obstinately refused. By this course the bystanders were led to suppose that something mysterious was involved in this conduct, and they determined at all events to see his wrist. By force they pushed up his sleeve, and a scar recently healed, as if made by tearing out of flesh, appeared. The landlord had been at the Morgue, had seen the murdered man with the flesh between the teeth, and it struck him in a moment that the flesh was torn from this man's wrist. Charging them to keep him safe, he hastened to call in the legal authorities, and arrested him. Dautun afterwards confessed, that being quartered at Sedan, and without money, he came to Paris to try some adventure. Knowing that his brother had a large sum by him, directly on his arrival he went to his lodgings, in a retired part of the city, about eight o'clock in the evening. He entered the house, unnoticed by the porter, and passing to his apartment, found his brother asleep. He immediately commenced his work of death; his brother waking up, defended himself, but being in a feeble state of health, he was speedily overpowered. In the struggle he tore out the flesh. Being killed, Dautun cut up the body, tied it up in four parcels as before mentioned, secured the money, and retired.

He also confessed, that eleven months before this he had murdered an aunt, who was living with a second husband, to obtain money. Her husband was arrested, and imprisoned for a number of months; but as nothing appeared to criminate him, he had been discharged.

THE MURDERER'S REMORSE.

ONE Sunday evening, says the Fredericktown, Md., *Expositor*, of 1831, a man who called himself Daniel Shafer, voluntarily came before Michael Baltsell, a magistrate of this city, and requested to be committed to prison, alleging that he had committed a murder during the last winter, in Marietta, Pa.; and that the reproaches of his conscience had become so severe, that he was unable any longer to endure them. His narrative being perfectly coherent, and he himself appearing entirely sane, the magistrate complied with his request and committed him. Since that time, under his direction, communication has been made with the proper authorities in Marietta, and such intelligence received as confirms the horrid tale. His story is, that during the deep snow of last winter, while in a state of intoxication, he entered the house of a widow named Bowers, then living in Marietta, and after violating her person, put her to death by strangling her. The fact of such a person being found dead in her house, about the time stated, is fully substantiated by the accounts received from Marietta; and the whole demeanor of the prisoner since his confinement, as well as his positive declarations, has induced a general belief in the truth of his singular confession.

The poor wretch was returned to Lancaster county, Pa., tried, convicted, and suffered the extreme penalty of the law.

AN AWFUL WARNING.

THE *Imperial Magazine* contains an account of a remarkable dream related by Rev. R. Bowden, of Darwen, in England, who committed it to writing from the lips of the clergyman to whom it happened. The dream suggests a most solemn and affecting admonition.

A minister of evangelical principles, whose name,

from the circumstances that occurred, it will be necessary to conceal, being much fatigued at the conclusion of the afternoon service, retired to his apartment in order to take a little rest. He had not long reclined upon his couch before he fell asleep and began to dream. He dreamed that on walking into his garden, he entered a bower that had been erected in it, where he sat down to read and meditate. While thus employed he thought he heard some one enter the garden; and leaving his bower, he immediately hastened toward the spot whence the sound seemed to come, in order to discover who it was that had entered. He had not proceeded far before he observed a particular friend of his, a clergyman of considerable talents, who had rendered himself very popular by his zealous and unwearied exertions in the cause of Christ. On approaching his friend, he was surprised to find that his countenance was covered with a gloom which it had not been accustomed to wear, and that it strongly indicated a violent agitation of mind apparently arising from conscious remorse. After the usual salutations had passed, his friend asked the relator the time of the day; to which he replied, "Twenty-five minutes after four." On hearing this, the stranger said, "It is only one hour since I died, and now I am damned." "Damned! for what?" inquired the minister. "It is not," said he, "because I have not preached the gospel, neither is it because I have not been rendered useful, for I have many souls as seals to my ministry, who can bear testimony to the truth as it is in Jesus, which they have received from my lips; but it is because I have been seeking the applause of men more than the honor which cometh from above, and verily, I have my reward!" Having uttered these expressions he hastily disappeared, and was seen no more.

The minister awaking shortly afterward, with the dream deeply graven on his memory, proceeded, overwhelmed with serious reflections, towards his chapel, in order to conduct his evening service. On his way thither he was accosted by a friend, who inquired whether he had heard of the severe loss the church had sustained in the death of their able minister. He replied, "No;" but being much affected at this singular intelligence, he inquired of him the day and the time of the day when his departure took place. To this his friend replied, "This afternoon, at twenty-five minutes after three o'clock."

THE BURNING OF THE RICHMOND THEATRE.

"I was but a boy, and lived in the city of Richmond, Virginia, when the theatre was destroyed by fire in December, 1811, and seventy-five persons perished. I had a brother older than myself, who resided there at the same time. During the day which preceded the fire he approached me, handing me a dollar, and saying he supposed I wanted to attend the theatre in the evening. On my leaving home to reside in the city, my mother had charged me not to go to the theatre; this I told him, adding, I can't disobey my mother. Upon this, he took back the dollar he had given me, expressing much contempt for my course. I was willing, indeed, and even anxious to retain the dollar, but not as the means of violating my mother's command.

"Night came, and my brother attended the theatre, accompanied by a young lady of the city to whom he was shortly to be married. I retired to bed at an early hour, and knew nothing of the fire until after sunrise. Then I learned that my brother, in his efforts to save her, had narrowly escaped death. This bereavement was to him a source of overwhelming grief, and he kept his room closely for nearly a month afterwards. He never subsequently said aught to me in reference to the theatre, or as to my course in refusing to attend."

The above was related to me by Dr. F——, now an esteemed minister of the gospel in North Carolina. Notice, 1. The theatre was new to him, and he might have made this a plea for going. 2. It would have cost him nothing, the price of admission being proffered him as a gift. 3. The example of an older brother was before him, and presented a strong inducement to go. 4. His mother was at some distance from the place, and it was very likely that she would never have heard of her son's disobedience. But the noble boy firmly adhered to his resolution, "I can't disobey my mother." The voice of God seems to have blended with the mother's charge, thus restraining the footsteps of her son, and in all probability saving his soul as well as body from death.

A PROVIDENTIAL REVIVAL.

IN the township of R., in the western part of New York, says a writer in the *Christian Watchman*, without any special or known cause, numbers of individuals were suddenly aroused to anxious inquiry and trembling respecting their souls. Some, in different parts of the town, without any knowledge of the affections of others, were alarmed by the consideration of their sins. Two men, from different directions, came to a clergyman in the morning, asking, What shall we do? About nine o'clock in the same morning, one of the members of the church called upon the same clergyman to go and visit several anxious individuals in his neighborhood; and before night it was ascertained that almost the whole population of a considerable district were solemnly, and with weeping, asking the prayers and instructions of the people of God.

Accompanied by the pastor, on that and the subsequent day, we visited from house to house; but wherever we went the Spirit had preceded us. The whole region was a Bochim. A solemn awe pervaded our souls, and we could not but feel that "God is in very deed in our midst."

Revivals, thus commencing, are, indeed, *rare;* but where they *do* occur, they show very clearly the agency of the Holy Spirit.

MRS. ERSKINE'S RECOVERY FROM DEATH.

There is a remarkable circumstance connected with the history of Ralph Erskine, which is well authenticated in that part of Scotland where he lived. His mother was supposed to have died, and was buried, some years before he was born. She wore on her finger, at the time of her death, a rich gold ring, which, from some domestic cause, was highly valued by the family. After the body was laid in the coffin, an attempt was made to remove it, but the hand and finger were so much swollen that it was found impossible to do so without mutilating the body, which the husband would not consent to. She was therefore buried with the ring on her finger.

The sexton, who was aware of this fact, formed a resolution to possess the ring. Accordingly, on the same night, he opened the grave and coffin. After some ineffectual attempts to remove the ring from the finger, he drew his knife for the purpose of cutting it off. He lifted the stiff arm,—made an incision at the joint of the finger,—the blood flowed,—the body shuddered and lifted itself upright in the coffin. The grave-digger fled with affright. The lady crawled from the grave, and with difficulty, from her weakness, made her way to her dwelling. Her husband, who was a minister, sat in his study conversing with a friend, when she knocked at the door. He started, exclaiming, " If my wife was not in her grave, I should say that was her knock." He rose, opened the door, and stood transfixed with astonishment. There stood his wife in her grave clothes, covered with blood. " My husband!" she exclaimed, as she flung herself into his arms. As soon as fright and surprise allowed, she was borne into the house and laid upon a bed. It was some time before she fully recovered, but she became a healthy woman, and lived several years after this.

QUINCEY MAYNARD.

BY GEORGE C. M. ROBERTS.

THE mere announcement of this name will call up recollections of the most hallowed and touching nature in the minds of scores of God's children, in whose hearts' warmest affections this saint of God has a permanent lodgment.

His name is of *very precious memory*, not alone

to those who were allied to him by the tender ties of consanguinity, but to those also who were his fellow-laborers in the Lord's field, and with whom he used to "*take sweet counsel as they walked together to the house of God in company,*" there to mingle their prayers and praises in the temple of the "Most High." "*And their name was legion.*" Many of them have long since, with Maynard, finished their course in peace and triumph, and gone to join a band, the rapture of whose song an angel's mind can scarce imagine. Some before, and some since, he was called to "*sleep in Jesus.*"

His end was tragical—in a moment, unexpected, and among those who comparatively were strangers to him and to his great spiritual worth. His sacred dust sleeps in undisturbed silence and repose upon the banks of the Susquehanna, near the spot where, in dreadful pain but holy triumph, he met and conquered death. His death was occasioned by his being scalded from the bursting of a boiler of the first steamer employed upon that part of the river, and that, too, on her first experimental trip.

Reluctantly he had consented to leave his family and his business in this city for the purpose of acting as her engineer, for which he was eminently qualified. At the earnest and repeated solicitation of those who knew and appreciated his capacity in this department, he, however, yielded. From some cause, unknown and unforeseen, one of her boilers gave way, and Maynard was so badly scalded as to cause death. By this visitation his large and helpless family was deprived of its earthly stay, and the church of God of one of her brightest lights. The church triumphant, however, realized an addition to its enraptured throng by the entrance of his freed spirit into the joys of heaven. There were tears of sorrow on earth upon the part of those who were left to linger a little longer on this side of Jordan, waiting the summons of their Lord to arise and meet him in the upper sanctuary. There were shouts of praise amid the heavenly host engaged in conveying him to his home *"not made with hands, eternal in the heavens."*

No thought can reach, and no tongue declare the ecstasy which since that period to the present has thrilled the bosoms of MAYNARD and GARY, DIXON and RUSSELL, and scores of others, with whom on earth they so often commingled in labor, and faith, and praise.

I must, however, turn away from this train of thought, pleasant as it is, not being immediately germain to the primary object in preparing this article, viz., to *"illustrate the providence of God,"* by the recital of a few facts by which that providence was most manifestly signal, in seasons of great trial and want in the history of his servant. Maynard, though a star of the first magnitude in the moral heavens, was nevertheless poor; and being called through this path to follow his

God, was not unfrequently exposed to very straitened circumstances.

The facts I am about to relate are of unquestionable authenticity, and derived by myself and others from his own lips. On one occasion, in the depth of winter, himself and family were found with their small stock of wood, laid up for their comfort, almost wholly exhausted; scarce enough wood, for the support and comfort of his tried ones; under similar circumstances, his prayer was upon the altar, and left with his Father in heaven. He retired to bed at night, not knowing *how*, but confident of the fact, that God's immutable and eternal word of truth *would be fulfilled.*

Ere the morning light had entirely dispelled the darkness of night, a load of wood was dropped at his door, through the direction of some kind but unknown friend. "*How* mysterious are the ways of God; past finding out!"

On another occasion, being exceedingly pressed in his circumstances, and needing funds to meet his immediate necessities, his mind became so much exercised that he felt himself for the time wholly disqualified for the work in which he was engaged. Laying aside the tool in his hand (he was a machinist), he walked to the door of his shop. After being there a few minutes, he was accosted by an old and feeble colored man, who inquired of him, whether he knew him. Maynard replied, that he did not remember having ever seen him before.

The colored man made such statements as caused him very soon to recollect him. The sequel proved that several years before this interview, he had done some work for the old man, for which he had never been paid. He assured him that he had not met the claim, because it had been out of his power. His family had been called to pass through a series of protracted afflictions. His wife had died; and, subsequently, he had been ill, and because of his necessitous condition, was compelled to seek an asylum in the almshouse. Since his recovery and dismissal he had been diligently engaged in labor, and by great economy, had succeeded in saving enough to liquidate the debt; for which purpose he had called.

Once more.

At a season of great depression, a gentleman who knew him favorably and esteemed him highly, loaned him a sum of money. This he was unable to return, although considerable time had elapsed since the reception of the favor. His mind became painfully exercised lest the gentleman should lose confidence in him. One morning, after partaking of a scanty meal, and unable to perceive any opening by which more could be obtained to meet the pressing wants of his family, he left his humble dwelling for his shop. On his way thitherward he was necessarily obliged to pass the store of his friend. Before reaching it, he saw him standing in his doorway. Fearing lest he should be asked for what was justly due, and thus be placed under the painful necessity of soliciting further indulgence, he crossed the street to avoid him. On coming to a point opposite where the gentleman was standing, he was called by him. He obeyed the summons, persuaded that he was about to realize the fulfilment of his worst fears.

As he approached him his friend extended his hand toward him in the most friendly manner, and kindly inquired as to the state of his health, and that of his family. He then said, "*Mr. Maynard, I called you because I have this morning been strangely and strongly impressed that you were at this time in actual need. Here are ten dollars, which you will do me the personal favor to receive, and appropriate to your own benefit in such way as you may deem most proper.*"

As might be expected, an interposition of Divine Providence, so clear and decided as this, caused his heart to leap within him with joy and gratitude, and he "*went on his way rejoicing.*"

"An interposition of Divine Providence so clear and decided!" Can any be so sceptical as to doubt it? Can any for a moment suppose, that the impressions upon the mind of that gentleman were the result of chance?

It is alike contrary to *reason*, sound *philosophy*, *common sense*, and *divine revelation*, to attempt to account for it on any other principle than this great truth, based upon numerous declarations of God's word, viz.: God saw the necessity of his faithful child, and used that gentleman as his own special instrument, in providing for him in this hour of his extremity.

R̲e̲a̲d̲e̲r̲, are you in trouble? Let not your heart faint within you. "Have faith in God."

Are you passing through the most severe trials either of a temporal or spiritual character, or both conjoined? If your heart be sincere, *fear not,*— "Have faith in God!" Are you even in the most abject want? Destitute of the common necessaries of life? Unable to perceive one single ray of light in the path before you? Do the companion of your sorrows and the mutual pledges of your love —your children—look up to you in vain for food and raiment? Murmur not. "*Be careful* (*i. e.*, full of care) *for nothing.*" An eye unseen by yours, watches over you. A heart never closed against human woe, feels for you. A hand never withdrawn or closed against any, under any and all the adversities of this life, is now stretched out towards you.

A voice, in strains sweeter than angels use, now whispers in your ear and heart, "Be still; it is I." "Stand still, and see the salvation of God."— Then, "Have faith in God."

A STORY OF A JACK-KNIFE.

THERE is a moral in the following story, taken from the *Boston Ledger*. How rarely does it happen (does it ever happen?) that any amount of wealth a man may have acquired might not be measured by the amount of virtuous effort that he expended in acquiring it! Was a sudden fortune ever a good fortune?

"In 1786 a youth, then residing in Maine, owned a jack-knife, which he, being of a somewhat trading disposition, sold for a gallon of West India rum. This he retailed, and with the proceeds purchased two gallons, and eventually a barrel, which was followed in due time with a large stock. In a word, he got rich, and became the squire of the district, through the possession and sale of the jack-knife, and an indomitable trading industry. He died leaving property, in real estate and money value, worth $80,000. This was divided by testament among four children, three boys and a girl. Luck, which seemed the guardian angel of the father, deserted the children; for every folly and extravagance they could engage in seemed to occupy their exclusive attention and cultivation. The daughter married unfortunately, and her patrimony was soon thrown away by her spendthrift of a husband. The sons were no more fortunate, and two of them died of dissipation, and in poverty. The daughter also died. The last of the family, for many years past, has lived on the kindness of those who knew him in the days of prosperity, as pride would not allow him to go to the poor-farm. A few days ago he died, suddenly and unattended, in a barn, where he had laid himself down to take a drunken sleep. On his pockets being examined, all that was found in them was a small piece of string *and a jack-knife!* So the fortune that began with the implement of that kind left its simple duplicate. We leave the moral to be drawn in whatever fashion it may suggest itself to the reader, simply stating that the story is a true one, and all the facts well known to many whom this relation will doubtless reach."

THE STOLEN WATCH RECOVERED.

THE following is an extract from a letter received not long since from a friend. We insert it for the interest of the event which it narrates.

"On one occasion a man came into my store, and after looking around, selected a gold watch, chain, and other articles, amounting in all to $180, and requested me to send them to his boarding-house, when he would pay for them. They were sent by a clerk, who, after a little while, came back saying, the man had got off with the articles. I immediately went to the boarding-house myself, but nobody knew him there. As it was about time for the Baltimore train to start, I hastened to the depot. The train had started, and a man answering his description had been seen to get out of a carriage just at the moment of leaving. I then went to the mayor's office and telegraphed to Baltimore; and offered a reward of twenty-five dollars for the recovery of my property.

"Feeling greatly distressed, for I could not afford to lose the articles, I lifted my heart to God for deliverance, vowing to give twenty-five dollars to the missionary cause if I recovered my goods. Shortly after this, I felt impressed to go to the depot of the New York line at Kensington. I did so; arriving there just before the train started. I passed through the cars, and in the last one found the thief; had him secured and taken to the mayor's office, where I recovered my goods. Perhaps I need not say, I have paid my vow unto the Lord."

STRANGE FULFILMENT OF A DREAM.

WE have the following from a near relative. Though personally acquainted with the facts at the time of their occurrence, we prefer giving them as related by her.

"In 18— I removed with my husband and family to W——, N. J. My husband was employed as a fireman on the C—— R. R., and was much from home. Far from my parents and friends, among strangers, my children small, I passed many lonesome and unhappy hours. One night I dreamed I was with my husband in a large and crowded market; in the midst of the crowd and bustle, he became separated from me. To add to my distress, I dropped my money, consisting of small change. While endeavoring to gather it up from the feet of the busy crowd, an old Quaker gentleman came to my assistance, and, after collecting my money, offered to take me to my husband. He led me to another gentleman, dressed in a long overcoat, who took me in a carriage drawn by a white horse to my husband.

"I awoke next morning very much depressed; an awful and unaccountable weight seemed to be crushing me. Sometime in the earlier part of the day, I started out to the store; I had not proceeded far, when I met an old Quaker gentleman, living in the village, in company with a stranger wearing a long overcoat. I at once recognised them as the persons of my dream, and grew faint and sick with apprehension. They led me to the house, and informed me my husband had met with an accident. Mr. V., the stranger, an engineer on the railroad, brought a carriage, drawn by a white horse, and took me to the cars, and thence to A——, where my husband was lying, having lost a limb by falling under the locomotive."

REMARKABLE SPECIAL PROVIDENCES.

IT is an authentic fact, that during the terrible massacre in Paris, in which many eminent Christians were cruelly killed, the celebrated preacher, Peter Moulin, was preserved for further usefulness to the cause of the gospel, in a most remarkable manner. He crept into a brick oven to conceal himself, but had little hope of remaining undiscovered in the ferreting search for slaughter that was carried on. In the kind providence of God, a spider immediately crawled to the opening of the good man's retreat, and wove a web across it. The dust blew upon the airy screen and made it dingy; so that the place appeared long unfrequented. The enemies of the Christians soon passed by, and one of them carelessly remarked, "No one could have been in that oven for several days!"

What a touching idea does this incident give of our Father's protecting love for his children!

AN anecdote, similar in character, is related of Mr. Churchill, a native of England, who had taken up his abode in India, about two miles from Vizagapatam. Soon after sunset, on one occason, while he was sitting in his dwelling, of which the outer door was thrown open, meditating with deep sorrow upon the recent loss of his wife, and the helplessness of his little children, who were lying asleep near him, he was suddenly thrilled with terror to see a monstrous tiger cross the threshold of his house, and enter the room, with glaring eyes and a ferocious howl. But the animal caught sight of his full-sized image reflected in a large mirror opposite the door, and rushing at it with all his fury, breaking it into a thousand fragments, he suddenly turned and fled from the spot. Thus providentially did God preserve two little children and their father from the jaws of a wild beast!

Less thrilling, but not less remarkable, is the incident related in the following epitaph, which is copied from a tomb near Port-Royal, in the isle of Jamaica:—

"Here lieth the body of Louis Calda, a native of Montpelier, in France, which country he left on account of the Revocation. He was swallowed up by the earthquake which occurred in this place in 1692, but, by the great providence of God, was, by a second shock, flung into the sea, where he continued swimming till rescued by a boat, and lived forty years afterward."

In the Bartholomew massacre, which we have already mentioned, at the order of the King of France, the Admiral de Coligny was put to death in his own house. His chaplain, the pious Merlin, fled from the murderers, who designed also to take his life, and hid himself in a loft of hay. After the days of blood were over, and the Protestants were suffered to keep their lives and their religion, a synod was convened, of which he was the moderator. In this assembly, when it was stated that many who had taken refuge in similar retreats, perished from starvation, he was asked how he contrived to keep himself alive? He replied—giving thanks to God while he said it—that a hen laid an egg every day during his concealment, in a nest so near to him that he could reach it with his hand!

The celebrated Dr. Calamy, in his "Life and Times," related that he knew a sea captain named Stevens, of Harwich, England, who was once, by a wonderful providence, preserved from drowning, together with all his crew. While on a homeward passage from Holland, the vessel sprung a leak, and the water gained in the hold so rapidly that, in spite of the pumps, which were worked with the energy of despair, all on board soon gave themselves up for lost. Suddenly, however, and to the surprise of all, the water ceased to gain in depth, and the pumps being again plied, the ship safely reached her harbor. After her arrival, it was discovered on examination, that the body of a fish had become so firmly wedged in the leak that it could with difficulty be taken out whole! It is but of little consequence, though it is an established fact, that the fish was preserved in alcohol, and kept as a curiosity in the family of Captain Stevens.

In view of these striking instances of Divine Providence, how can we think of our Father in heaven, and not be touched with the thought of that tender love which leads him to take such wonderful care of his children? Truly, we may "cast all our care upon him, for he careth for us."

A MERCHANT SAVED FROM BANKRUPTCY.

WE have received from a friend the following striking illustration of the ways of Providence in the affairs of men. It occurred during the severe monetary pressure of 1858; and should encourage all hearts to commit to God their temporal interests. We give the substance of his letter. "The heaviest and most important engagements of my business life were maturing in the month of July. I had made them the subject of earnest prayer to God, and felt myself to be in His hands, and at the disposal of his goodness. I laid, in due time, before the Board of Directors of our bank, for discounting, real negotiable paper, in amount 50 per cent. more than my payments about coming due. This resource had never before failed me, but, owing to some peculiar circumstances surrounding the bank at that time, no paper was discounted. I then became not a little distressed in mind, but continued to carry the matter before the Lord regularly in all my private devotions. Bankruptcy and ruin stared me in the face.

"What apparently added much to my difficulties, I was compelled to leave home and attend court in an adjoining county only a few days prior to the maturity of two of the heaviest notes.

"I went, trusting in God for deliverance; all other hope had fled. I remained from Monday morning until Thursday afternoon. On Friday the two notes above referred to must be paid or be protested. I returned home, pledging myself to be back in time to answer the call of my name next morning at 9 o'clock. On reaching home, after speaking a few minutes with my wife and children, I shut myself up in my room and poured out the agony of my mind before the Lord. I then repaired to my place of business, but learned my receipts were even less than usual for the same space of time. I returned home for supper, and at the family altar had liberty in prayer. Immediately after tea I repaired to my closet; the Lord was with me, my soul was made happy, and I felt perfectly resigned to the will of God, be my fate what it might. I still felt it to be my duty to use every possible effort to secure the money. I set out on the endeavor, confidently believing that relief would come, though I knew not how. Up till 9 o'clock in the evening every effort had been unavailing. I was passing along the street on my return from the last place at which I had hoped to secure some money, when a gentleman touched me on the shoulder, and, familiarly calling my name, said he wished to speak to me. We stepped aside, and he said, 'I stopped you to say that if you are in want of some money I can accommodate you.' Here was the deliverance I had looked for; my heart was too full to say more than 'I thank you, Sir.' All necessary arrangements were made for the payment of my notes, and I went home with a heart overflowing with gratitude to God."

A remarkable feature in the above case is, that no application had been made to the person who proffered this relief, but, as he expressed it, he felt himself moved to make the offer.

THE END.

www.ingramcontent.com/pod-product-compliance
Lightning Source LLC
Chambersburg PA
CBHW020546300426
44111CB00008B/807